Music
as an Art

BOOKS BY HERBERT WEINSTOCK

Chopin: The Man and His Music

Handel

Tchaikovsky

—WITH WALLACE BROCKWAY

Men of Music: Their Lives, Times, and Achievements

The Opera: A History of Its Creation and Performance: 1600-1941

Music as an Art

BY HERBERT WEINSTOCK

HARCOURT, BRACE AND COMPANY

NEW YORK

78015
W43m

The music quoted on pages 287 and 288 is from TROIS MOUVEMENTS DE PÉTROUCHKA by Igor Stravinsky. Copyright 1922 by Edition Russe de Musique for all countries. Copyright assigned 1947 to Boosey and Hawkes Inc., New York. Used by permission.

The music quoted on pages 290-291 is from LE SACRE DU PRINTEMPS by Igor Stravinsky. Copyright 1921 by Edition Russe de Musique for all countries. Printed by arrangement Boosey and Hawkes Inc., New York. Used by permission.

The music quoted on page 306 is from WIND QUINTET, Opus 26, by Arnold Schönberg. Copyright 1925 by Universal Edition, A. G., Vienna; renewed 1952 by Gertrud Schönberg; by permission of Associated Music Publishers, Inc., New York.

Library of Congress Catalog Card Number: 53-9223

PRINTED IN THE UNITED STATES OF AMERICA

ACKNOWLEDGMENT

It would be impossible for me here to express my thanks to every-one who has been helpful to me in the writing of this book. I therefore limit myself to thanking a few individuals who con-sciously exerted themselves to be of real assistance. Ben Meisel-man read—or listened while I read—many sections of the manu-script, never failing to make happy suggestions in the direction of simplification and greater clarity. The title *Music as an Art* was given me by Jacques Barzun, whose expert editorial hand also materially improved the Introduction as it first appeared in the third issue of *Perspectives USA*. Sam Morgenstern willingly and helpfully answered many theoretical and technical questions. Joseph Kerman, besides granting me permission to quote from one of his essays and from a personal letter, directly influenced ideas expressed in the Introduction. Miss Gladys Chamberlain, Director of the 58th Street Music Library of New York City, and Miss Mary Lee Daniels of that Library were, as I have always known them to be, cheerfully helpful and generous with good ideas. To all these people, and to many not here named, I am genuinely grateful.

H. W.

PREFACE

Manners of listening to music must be as numerous as ways of composing and of performing it. Varieties of musical composition shade from the "lightest," most inconsequential "popular" tunes of a patently ephemeral sort to the "heaviest," most serious, and most ambitiously laid out works of large and complex organization, created as though for eternity. Performance ranges from whistling, strumming at a piano, and amateur readings to the massive smoothness of a concert presentation of Beethoven's Ninth Symphony, with great orchestra, chorus, and vocal soloists. And the intensity of attention paid by listeners varies just as widely. Music may be heard when it is not listened to: it may go on as the persistent background of murmuring (or even crashing) sound at a public event without a single person present concentrating on it sufficiently to recognize what music it is. At the other extreme of these gradations of attention, the dedicated music-lover often prepares himself in advance to react to every element of pleasure and significance in a performance which he is equipped to absorb— and then concentrates so as to exclude from his attention for the duration of a given composition all elements of consciousness but those required for listening to it.

When it is realized fully that what we commonly call "music" comes into full existence only in the best possible collaboration of creator, performer, and attentive listener, the extreme importance of the third member of this trio becomes clear. I have every sympathy for those wrongheaded people who say: "I'm glad that I don't know as much about music as a composer [or performer or critic]. I am lucky. I can just sit back and listen for the fun of it." But my normal state of sympathy is baffled by the equally

vii

wrongheaded people who say to anyone aware of the key a composition is in or able to distinguish between an oboe and a clarinet: "I envy you. You really understand music."

The people in the "just-for-the-fun-of-it" group would surely boggle at a claim that it is more pleasant to read a book in French if one understands the language only well enough to get a general idea of what it means. But at least these people have an opinion. Those in the second group are merely lazy, unless their professions of envy are automatic, and by their laziness they deny themselves enduring and increasing pleasure easy to come by.

Claims are often advanced that understanding and enjoyment of an art can be obtained in the way in which one studies a physical science: through an experimental approach. I do not mean to question the value of that approach to individual works of music. An enormous amount of information concerning the art could be extracted from a detailed analysis of, let us say, Tchaikovsky's *"Pathétique"* Symphony which dealt with it as an occurrence isolated from earlier and later music. But my underlying assumption in writing this book has been that by themselves technical analyses are of value only to creators, performers, or listeners already acquainted with large areas of the history, technique, and aesthetics of music.

Even if it were possible to approach the understanding and enjoyment of music by the experimental method in isolation from the constant changes in technique and form, that method would prove wasteful. An otherwise musically uninformed listener who had been helped to analyze the *"Pathétique"* to the point at which he could learn no more from it would have to repeat a similar process of analysis in different terms with each individual composition he wished to enjoy through real understanding. And, in fact, his first approach to Tchaikovsky's music would have been incomparably less difficult if he had been equipped with knowledge of many musical devices that Tchaikovsky took for granted. I have therefore deliberately combined essential aspects of the experimental approach with much more extensive documentation presented chronologically, emphasizing continually the pleasures of more conscious listening.

For an art is not a physical science. Scientific hypotheses and theories are constantly displaced by those of more advanced scientific eras; they lose their working value for practical science. Even such a magnificent intellectual advance as the Ptolemaic cosmology represented is now of little consequence except as material for comparative history. Later scientists have nearly always been able to do better exactly what their predecessors had attempted. But a later creative artist is not better able to do what earlier creators did or tried to do. He is differently able to do something new. Art is not an orderly series of evolving hypotheses, experiments, and theories, but a somewhat disorderly series of creations. The genuine achievements of artistic creators may fade or go out of fashion, but they cannot be rendered untrue. By comparison with scientific values, those of art are relatively permanent.

This book has been written in the belief that the best way to acquire understanding of the procedures of music as an art is to begin with the earliest compositions likely to be encountered in actual or recorded performance, and so to acquire technical and formal knowledge as the living art itself acquired its component parts. Thus, the book is not what is usually called a history of music. It relates only such historical and biographical matter as is essential to its central purpose. It employs a chronological scheme, but not to illustrate any theory of musical "progress" (there is no such thing), or for any reason other than convenience. The scheme removes the need for constant flashbacks, for explanation of the same technical or formal factors over and over. As adjuncts to the enjoyment and understanding of music as an art, historical considerations keep their importance only as they help to supply a logical picture of the evolution of musical means. I know that both history and biography have great values of their own: I am simply not concerned with them here.

Once we know what compositional techniques and formal aims composers or musical eras held in mind, we are better equipped to listen intelligently to their music. We are also in a better position to approach later music, for what we have already learned of methods and means—and of ways of listening—remains with us, serving as a point of departure. This technical knowledge, which is absolutely essential for the discussion or for the understanding of music, is most easily acquired cumulatively.

This book deals with the means that composers have employed, for more than five hundred and fifty years, to make their musical thought available to others. It assumes that music is not only the best, but the only, means for the communication of musical thought. It nowhere tries to re-create music in words; it never assumes that a description of music, however detailed, can take the place of music itself. It treats the musical art as a means of symbolic communication—in that sense, and that sense only, a language. The nature and processes of this musical language must be learned step by step, as a baby learns to use the speech it hears around it. Through use and the resulting familiarity, music must be allowed to become truly comprehensible in its own terms. Any attempt to translate it into a spoken or written language (or vice versa) is ridiculous and foredoomed, for whatever music may represent, symbolize, suggest, or present, it does so only in terms of *musical* discourse.

With a general knowledge of the parts of musical speech used by composers of the past and an acquaintance with the most important of their methods of arranging those parts of speech into significant discourse, an attentive listener can be well launched toward enlarged understanding and increased enjoyment. Subsequent alterations in musical language—the additions, subtractions, and reshufflings practiced by later composers—can become clear to him as he moves forward in time. Arriving at his own day, such an informed listener can come to a musical work in the state of readiness in which he ordinarily opens a book printed in a language he knows. He can be equipped to approach almost any meaningful composition (meaningless compositions and compositions of special difficulty exist) with the assurance that at least its component sections and their important interrelationships will be open to him. He can be ready to pass intelligent judgment, in the light of his own mental equipment and emotional predispositions, on what it is that a composer has intended to do and has done. He can, that is, have prepared himself to understand music as an art.

New York
May 23, 1953

CONTENTS

Music
as an Art

THE MEANING OF MUSIC

I should think that anyone with a more than passive interest in music as an art would want to have some conception of what music is, a description of it which is at least workable, though not necessarily (or even desirably) as exact as a mathematical formula. This question is complex and constantly unsettled. The theories and partial answers that philosophical and musical minds have brought to it demand the exercise of hard, sustained thought. I propose here to put forward my understanding of this problem and some suggestions toward its solution which I have encountered and evolved during years of reading, discussing, thinking, and writing about it.

Unless we are ready to deny that music is meaningful at all, in any sense beyond that of aural titillation, we shall have to accept temporarily some hypothesis of what it may mean. I learn from listening to music—equally music that I enjoy and music that I do not—that it both conveys significances somehow present in the arrangement of its tones and suggests other significances outside them. I am certain, that is, that arrangements of tones, like ordered sequences of words and ideas, can and do symbolize and suggest meanings. The processes through which such symbols act can themselves be explained only in metaphors, whether we decide to call them the evocation and satisfaction of physiological expectations or the setting up and release of motor tensions in the mind, or choose to see them as some less mechanistic variety of

3

rise and fall, cause and effect. For this inquiry it is more important
to acknowledge that such processes convey artistic meanings than
it is to analyze their working.

Listening to music also tells me that its meanings are not ideas
in the ordinary sense of that word: whatever else music may be,
it is not a vague substitute for spoken or written discourse or argument. Nor does it merely transmit pictures like a disembodied
television, though it is often allied to, often suggests, not only
ideas and pictures, but also a myriad other mental concepts and
sensuous data. But musical significance, the meaning of music as
an art, is something held among the tones themselves, something
different from the ideas or things they may suggest. This much
about music I am told by listening to it and at the same time
thinking about what I am hearing and how it is affecting me.

The largest obstacle to be circumvented in moving toward a
useful hypothesis of the meaning of music is the circumstance that
patterns of tone cannot on the surface appear to be an organization of previously existing subject matter—and that in this respect
music naturally seems closer to mathematics than to the other arts.
A book, in addition to any artistic values it may possess, is nearly
always "about" something that we can retell in our own words.
All but a few paintings, whatever their added qualities, are depic-
tions "of" more or less recognizable objects. Most sculpture is basically representational, commonly of human or other natural forms,
however altered. Architecture, lacking subject matter in the sense
that literature and painting and sculpture usually have it, is a
practical solution of physical problems. That part of it which is
not engineering, the "art" of architecture, consists in solving physical problems in such harmonious ways that the resulting structures
will show pleasing proportions to the eye, satisfying relationships
among lines, masses, and colors, and integrated or otherwise purposeful decoration. Music, however, is not in any immediately obvious way a practical solution of anything. One is tempted to say
that, unlike the other arts, music is all art. A stimulating but im-
precise figure of speech has claimed that music is "about" itself.
More suggestively still, though no more faithfully, it could be proposed that whereas the other arts possess no form separable from

their contents, music possesses no narrowly specifiable contents apart from its forms.

What, then, is music's power? Why should almost every human being everywhere find some variety of music pleasant, significant, even powerful? Why should so hardheaded a practical thinker as Confucius have said: "Music is intimately connected with the essential relations of beings"? What does music—not a certain composition, but music as an art—mean?

We shall protect ourselves from a large measure of confusion (some confusion appears inescapable) if we agree that to say "music means beauty" will get us nowhere. "Beauty" is one of the terms we use to symbolize the very significance or meaning for which we are searching: the word fails to help us forward. If we use it, we must next rephrase our original questions as: "In what does the beauty of music reside?" It will be better to leave to one side the valuable but troubling word "beauty."

Psychoanalytic theory has tended to explain all artistic creation, including that of music, as a symbolic satisfaction of "suppressed desires," those urges to love or power which, in varying extent, the creating artist—like everyone else—finds frustrated by social or individual circumstances and taboos. Such taboos, we are told persuasively, banish from consciousness elements of the urge to love and the will to power, drowning them in the unconscious activities of the mind, whence they well up in the vicarious guise, and even the shapes, of artistic creations, just as under other circumstances they float up in dreams and fantasies. If defining components of art are symbolic, sublimated expressions of such unconscious energy, it becomes easy to understand why artistic creations can arouse strong reactions in readers, beholders, and listeners. The individuals who comprise the audience for art, that is, are human beings whose minds harbor the same repressed urges toward love and power which the artist's mind had first censored and then symbolically released. Further, one group of psychoanalytic theorists believes that powerful unconscious drives endure from our primitive past. If we all perpetuate in ourselves such unrecognized survivals from earlier levels of human existence, the almost universal appeal of art can be partially explained.

That this psychoanalytic theory of artistic creation has solid foundations can be "proved" in a thousand ways. Intricate analyses have been made of the writing and painting of creative artists to demonstrate that elements of their power were drawn from sources not amenable to conscious control, and are therefore usefully to be thought of as products of the artist's unconscious mental activity. In one such analysis, for example, Carl Gustav Jung seems to prove that obscure, disturbing passages in the second part of *Faust* resulted from just such bubblings-up from Goethe's personal and racial unconscious. This type of criticism is revealingly applied to the plastic arts. It could possibly be made of music, though music's lack of sharply definable apparent subject matter may always baffle that sort of analysis.

Let us agree for the moment that the creation of music is, in important aspects, a symbolic activity of unconscious desire and repressed drive toward power and of emotional survivals—all forced into the unconscious by censor and taboo. Would not a satisfactory performing musician—conductor, singer, or instrumentalist—then be definable as one who (in addition to much besides) responds sensitively to the effective symbols and, in transmitting the sounds, selects for proper enforcement those elements by which the composer has symbolized the most widespread or most powerful unconscious forces? Might not the difference between superficial music and profound music, between "cheap" popular music and magnificent serious music, be in part a difference between the unconscious sources tapped and symbolized by the respective composers? Within the body of a single composer's work, might not the difference between a "great" composition and one merely adequate or downright bad be measured in part by the distance from his large ability at one time to tap the well of his unconscious to his small ability to tap it at another time?

Although the answer to these questions seems to me to be yes, I agree with Susanne K. Langer when she writes: "There are strong recommendations for the psychoanalytic theory of aesthetics. But despite them all, I do not think this theory (though probably valid) throws any real light on those issues which confront artists and critics and constitute the philosophical problem of art. For the Freudian interpretation, no matter how far it be carried, never offers even the rudest criterion of *artistic* excellence. It may explain why a poem was written, why it is popular, what human features it hides under its fanciful imagery; what secret ideas a picture combines, and why Leonardo's women smile mysteriously. But *it makes no distinction between good and bad art.* The features to which it attributes the importance and significance of a great masterpiece may all be found just as well in an obscure work of some quite incompetent painter or poet." [1]

The psychoanalytic theory of aesthetics, that is, may tell us why a composer fills music with significance, but it does not go nearly far enough to tell us how he does so. It fails to deal with the way in which the art—or, more exactly, the artist—organizes materials of whatever sort into the patterns or forms in which, alone, they can convey or evoke any but the most rudimentary meanings. To say that music is partly, or even wholly, a symbolic expression of the composer's unconscious, or that it speaks in part through the interpreter's unconscious to the listener's, is to beg our original questions almost as completely as we beg them by equating the meaning of art with beauty. For, even if we accept the psychoanalytic theories as valid, the unlocking critical question is: how does the composer symbolize, and thus transmit or evoke, hidden content or any content at all? I think that this question can be rephrased to read: what is artistic form, and why is it the criterion of artistic excellence?

Let us agree that elements in heard music are symbolic expressions of emotional energy in the unconscious of composer, performer, and listener, and that individual compositions are good or bad as their forms are successful or unsuccessful in transmitting or re-evoking such energy. And let us further assume what seems to be undeniable: that artistic form is good if it conveys both the ostensible contents (as in painting, sculpture, literature, song, and opera) and the hidden content—the only kind that music obviously possesses—conveys them in satisfying proportions, bodies them forth without slighting their important aspects or smothering those aspects in superfluous detail. With these working hy-

1 *Philosophy in a New Key* (New York: New American Library), p. 168.

potheses, we may be in a position to begin answering, however tentatively and partially, the basic questions of how, what, and why.

There can be no doubt that parts of both music's "content" and its "effect" are physical, the action on the human ear and mind of pure sound as such. It is easy to recognize, however, that this is not the salient, or even a very important, part of the meaning of music as an art, in which what is all-important is the web of relationships among tones. It is nonetheless sensible to notice that many supposed effects of music are in truth effects of mere sound, and by definition therefore not artistic, but strictly sensuous.

When opposed to phonetics as the science of sound, semantics is the science of meaning. It is in view of this distinction that Mrs. Langer writes: "If music has any significance, it is semantic, not symptomatic. Its 'meaning' is evidently not that of a stimulus to evoke emotions, nor that of a signal to announce them; if it has an emotional content, it 'has' it in the same sense that language 'has' its conceptual content—*symbolically*. It is not usually derived *from* affects nor intended *for* them; but we may say, with certain reservations, that it is *about* them. Music is not the cause or the cure of feelings, but their *logical expression;* though even in this capacity it has its special ways of functioning, that make it incommensurable with language, and even with presentational symbols like images, gestures, and rites." [2]

One need not be a philosopher or semanticist to understand that the meaning symbolized by the word "baby" does not reside in the four individual letters and their arrangement, each letter containing some portion of that meaning, but is one effect of the word as a whole. In the same way, the separate sounds that go to make up music do not, each in isolation, contain or "have" a small integer of meaning. Composers deploy them in planned interrelationships so as to symbolize pre-existing meanings and emotions. The word "baby" may be employed to evoke emotions or, as a signal, to announce them; but its primary function is to symbolize instantly the very young human animal, which existed long before the word, and which is symbolized otherwise in other lan-

---

[2] *Op. cit.,* p. 176.

guages. "Baby," in short, is one word "about" the young child, an expression of the fact of its existence.

Thus a word may hold meaning in solution, and can be combined with other words so as to furnish one element in the transmission of pre-existing meaning or the evocation of meaning freshly minted. It seems to me that smaller and larger combinations of musical sound too are meaningful because they symbolize, re-evoke, and express. They are deployed so as to present fresh meanings, to create pristine significance, just as, in the hands of a creative writer, words in new combinations are made to carve out meanings that could not have existed before.

Certain words, of course, imitate as well as symbolize. Such an onomatopoeic word as "bobwhite," being an imitation of the bird's two-note call, clearly makes use of two obvious kinds of symbolism, the word "sparrow" of only one of them. In an analogous manner, music can and does employ or approximate certain familiar sounds, such as those of bells, animals, thunder, and railroad trains, the denotative meaning of which is instantly accepted and clear. It also employs or imitates rhythms, such as those of breathing, walking, and dancing, which summon up for listeners both those activities and the emotions connected with them. In these usages music, though merely making use of extra-musical sounds and rhythms for connotative effect, momentarily becomes denotative. But such programmatic effects achieve truly musical significance only when, like any others of the art's techniques, they have been organized by the composer in symbolic, connotative, musically meaningful ways. When they are lazily or mistakenly employed as substitutes for real musical thought they inevitably weaken the formal structure and produce inferior music.

Music both conveys pre-existing meaning symbolically and creates new significance by employing its operative symbols in manners dictated in part by the physical make-up of sound. Our crippling difficulties in discussing the pre-existing meanings within a specific musical work arise chiefly from wrongheaded attempts to narrow down our immediate apprehensions of them into equivalent language; the problems of the freshly created meanings in each composition result from their being discussible only with the assistance of technical musical terms. I should like to look briefly at these difficulties and problems.

Some decades ago, an understandable reaction against the excessive claims of program music and against the nineteenth century's programmatizing of earlier compositions led to statements that music means nothing at all. Composers and critics were rightly sick to death of musical moonlight, biographies in tone, and orchestral philosophizing. Thus Stravinsky wrote in his autobiography that he considered music ". . . by its essential nature, powerless to express anything at all, whether a feeling, an attitude of mind, a psychological mood, a natural phenomenon. . . ." Nicely interpreted in context, Stravinsky's disclaimer may have considerable cogency. But our ears and the minds they serve will not agree that music expresses simply nothing at all. More recently Susanne K. Langer, Roger Sessions, Joseph Kerman, and Aaron Copland have been saying in various ways that its activity may parallel movements of emotion without describing or depicting them, may convey states of being without making use of the denotative data usually associated with such conveying in literature and painting. We are coming to believe that the very special quality and strength and universality of music derive from its ability to provide a natural, immediate, and direct symbolism of emotion.

Facing this problem where it is most thorny and complex—in a specific musical work—Joseph Kerman wrote of the first-movement *allegro* of Beethoven's A Minor Quartet, Opus 132, that it exhibits "an intensity of inconclusiveness," an attribution that I could accept because I can discern purposeful inconclusiveness in the technical layout of the *allegro*. But Mr. Kerman went on to say that every measure of the movement "deals with pain, but Beethoven's customary attitudes of fortitude, defiance, or deflection are replaced by a transcendent introspection, without self-pity, cleverness, or posturing." [3] And though I could feel in the music the attitudes and emotions to which he was giving definite labels, I accused him of the heresy that musical means can be made to convey narrowly definable non-musical meanings. I particularly objected to his use elsewhere in the same essay of such descrip-

[3] *Hudson Review,* Spring 1952, p. 34.

tions of the content of Beethoven's music as "pain," "terror," "grief," and "suffering." He replied in part:

"As you say it, music parallels, conveys, or evokes emotional motions. Can't it (in Beethoven's last period) do this so marvelously, so strongly, so accurately, psychologically speaking, that these emotional motions are specified at least to the degree that such unutterably lame words as 'pain' and 'terror' themselves parallel, convey, or evoke? The recapitulation of Beethoven's ninth [Symphony], first movement, really frightens me, just as the introductory tremolo is to me foreboding. I do not think, and I know that you don't think I do, that the recapitulation represents our terror at seeing a hero struck down in battle, or Beethoven's fright at learning of his deafness, or the way anybody has actually felt in any imaginable context. But 'terror,' yes! 'Music as a language autobiographical and exact'—no; but 'exact,' sure." [4]

On these terms I am ready to drop the accusation of heresy, though I do not feel any need to apply to the emotion symbolized by Beethoven's recapitulation the term Mr. Kerman chose—or, for that matter, any literally defining term at all. I believe that the memory of a strong, unwelcome emotion induced Beethoven to combine tones into melody, rhythm, harmony, and form that, for him, made it possible for his music to parallel, symbolize, or express what he had felt or was feeling. A just performance of that music transmits something of that feeling to Mr. Kerman or evokes it in his consciousness. But "terror" in itself is no more than one possible—and at best very approximate—symbol or name of the emotion that Beethoven felt. The emotion Mr. Kerman feels while listening to that recapitulation resembles the emotion he calls terror, resembles it by calling forth within him somewhat the same emotional-physiological reactions. But it may and does call forth in other listeners a physiological reaction paralleling that of sudden, immitigable despair—not the same emotion as terror. The words "terror" and "despair," like the musical symbols organized by Beethoven's genius, are expressions of an underlying emotional reality upon which we can all agree, but which there is no imperative need to name.

[4] In a personal letter dated July 11, 1952.

If we can agree that emotions, whose role is to lead us to action, are always exact and logically inexpressible, that even words and pictures, apparently realistic and specific, can convey or parallel emotions only symbolically, we shall perhaps be able to agree that music too can symbolize and convey them intensely even though it lacks the means wherewith to express factual, visible, and other data. Indeed, music's freedom from all necessity for such realistic appurtenances is exactly what enables its practitioners to speak to us without need of translation.

Critics often say of a song that its composer has written music inappropriate to his chosen text or has attached an unsuitable text to his music. Both the literal meanings of a poet's words and their symbolic significance may war with the meanings of the music. This kind of criticism is salutary when it is just, for it not only proves that music conveys meaning capable of being at variance with verbal presentation, but also invites us to criticism of a legitimate question of musical form. It requires us as listeners to decide whether the composer's judgment was flawed or whether he has set up a deliberate, and perhaps rewarding, tension between words and music. We must understand that one sort of artistic virtue may reside in a song whose text and music run parallel or present a stereoscopic double version of the same materials; that another sort of artistic virtue may reside in a song whose text and music diverge from, or deny, each other. But here it is most important to recognize that neither of these conditions could occur if music either meant nothing or were "about" nothing but itself.

The composer formulates and organizes what I have called his pre-existing meanings by the ways in which (very probably while consciously doing something else) he combines individual tones, arranges groups of tones into passages or movements. He is forging symbolic techniques of expression, not writing autobiography; he is setting down symbols of emotions that cannot be expressed in specific language, but which can be articulated in the relationships among tones. Music, that is to say, remains a connotative art rather than a denotative language.

The psychoanalytic explanation of the urge toward artistic creativity can remain; so, too, to some extent, can its description of the artist's unconscious choice of real subject matter. But the symbolic description of the meaning of music moves us an essential step onward. It tells us that the composer satisfies himself, the performer, and the listener by arranging ("composing") sounds in patterns of interrelationship; that it is the resulting forms which instantly symbolize to the trained or otherwise sympathetic listener the emotional, passionate, impulsive, specific—but denotatively unparticularized—meanings from which the music took its beginning. Like any other art, music deals fundamentally with matters inexpressible in direct discourse; it deals with them successfully (is "good" or even "great") when it works its symbols into self-justifying and satisfactory patterns. These forms—which in music are not merely melodic, harmonic, and rhythmic procedures, but the sum of all the means employed—are only in part separable for fruitful discussion by themselves. They are the very brain and blood of the art of music.

What I have spoken of with insuperable inexactness as new, more specifically musical, meanings are produced by the creation of form—not necessarily of *a* form, but certainly of form as defined above. A composer begins a piece with an arrangement of tones; at once that musical cell implies forward movement of a certain nature, requires him to proceed in one particular way—or one of several particular ways—if the expectations that his introductory phrase will arouse in listeners are not to be deceived and disappointed. For unless it is deliberate and purposeful, the deception or disappointment of this sort of expectation is always bad form and poor art: it is formlessness. And so with each succeeding phrase or other musical cell within a composition—both in itself and in relation to all the other sections and to the pre-existing extra-musical meanings being articulated. A successful musical composition, like every good work in any art, both expresses pre-existing meanings and by doing so creates meaning that could not have existed before.

What I understand by formal excellence has little or nothing to do with fugue or sonata, rondo or recapitulation, which are merely names for some of its possible shapes. It is the arousing of relevant and meaningful expectations and their complete satisfaction. Distinguishing between good and bad music cannot be the business of psychoanalysis or of any exclusive interest in the sources of subject matter or the reasons for its selection. That distinction is a judgment of the cogency with which the composer has organized *whatever* subject matter he was driven to employ. It is a measure of the ways in which he has articulated, organized, and disposed both his basic emotional energy and the meanings that he has evoked in the process of articulation and organization.

We shall always fall wide of the central mark when we ask music to be anything but a symbolic, immediate, and untranslatable presentation to our comprehension and response. Its power resides in its unique ability to dispense with portrayal, depiction, and exegesis, to strike directly to the mind and the heart by symbolic articulation. It may, of course, wield its power alone or in alliance with poetry, drama, gesture, and dance. Its condition as an art is determined by the relevance and internal strength with which the composer has woven the tonal web. Therein lies the meaning of music in so far as that meaning can be defined or comprehended in terms other than those of musical sound itself.

Music as an Art was written in constant view of this hypothesis as to the meaning of music. But the book deals only indirectly with the multifarious variety and shading of that meaning. For in it my purpose has been to examine and clarify the historic evolution of the methods, means, and techniques by which musicians have organized and presented the sounds that alone can carry, transmit, express, or evoke whatever significances of any sort their creations may have.

If music were nothing but organized sound it would not be the great art it has long been acknowledged to be. But the causal connections between *specific* organizations of sound and *describable* meanings are questions for psychology and philosophy. I have touched upon those disciplines here because I wanted this Introduction to give double testimony: to my belief that music always symbolizes human ideas, emotions, states of being, *and* to the certainty that music as an art can be most completely apprehended and most enduringly enjoyed when it is most consciously understood.

GREGORIAN CHANT · THE ECCLESIASTICAL MODES
EARLY POLYPHONY · ARS ANTIQUA
THE BACKGROUND OF EARLY SECULAR MUSIC

Although it has seemed reasonable to many writers to suppose that both speech and music evolved among primeval men from cries and howls, music almost certainly began to become an art after the discovery of its possible uses in religious rites. It is nonetheless difficult to believe that the powers of music as secular entertainment—communal and personal—could have been long in becoming evident. What is certain is that, at least until very recent times, music has tended to divide into two large categories, each with its own purposes and practices: the sacred or ecclesiastical and the secular, popular, or vulgar. In the first category lies the music that has helped men to adore, invoke, and placate the powerful forces they can sense and represent but never see, the mysterious, alternately gentle and terrible powers that have been their gods or God. In the second category lies the music that has expressed man's attitudes toward himself, his fellows, his dreams, and the visible universe.

For many centuries the dominating sacred music in Western, or Roman Catholic, Christendom consisted of a body of melodies known as Gregorian Chant. The first codification of this collection of purely vocal melodies probably occurred about the beginning of the seventh century, during the pontificate of St. Gregory, pope

15

from 590 to 604, who may have supervised or even performed the codification. The pre-eminence of Rome as seat of the papacy caused Gregorian Chant to supersede other, somewhat similar, bodies of Christian chant.

The huge collection of melodies recognized by the Roman Catholic Church as authentic Gregorian Chant consists of groups of chants used in connection with sections of the liturgy. All the melodies are referred to as plainsong. In most respects remote from the modern Western conception of music, plainsong is intended to be chanted without instrumental accompaniment. The fact that from early times the organ (and perhaps other instruments) supported the chant by duplicating exactly the tones being sung does not vitiate this statement, for the exact instrumental duplication of sung tones is not accompaniment in the modern sense.

Plainsong consists of a single vocal tone followed at an indeterminate time either by the same tone or by another separated from it by a predetermined interval in pitch, and then by another and another. It is not a succession of groups of tones sounded simultaneously or a combination of several melodies sung together. It consists of single-tone melodic strands in which only the pitch relationships among the tones are definitely fixed. The duration of these tones is not (or was not originally) fixed, but depends largely upon the length or brevity of the vowels in the syllables of the texts sung. The volume and timbre of plainsong in its pure form are functions of the voice or voices of the priest or chanting group, traditionally entirely male.

Most modern listeners are psychologically ill-prepared to hear unaccompanied single-tone melodies without feeling instinctively that almost every tone implies one or more related simultaneous tones. We have become accustomed, that is, to hearing melodies move forward on the support of chords or as parts of them. In much of the most familiar music, in fact, the successive tones that make up the most noticeable melodies are simply the highest notes of a succession of chords. We think of music as at once horizontal and vertical: a melody or melodies flowing along in time or moving from left to right on a printed page *and* a series of chords, each sounded all at once and read up and down on the page. This habit of thinking about and hearing music is what makes it difficult, if not altogether impossible, for us to hear the sinuous melodies of Gregorian Chant as they must have sounded to listeners at the time of their codification and for some centuries thereafter.

Very many Gregorian melodies are in themselves entirely satisfactory entities. The effort to apprehend them purely, as melody and nothing else, can be highly rewarding even if it falls short of complete success. Although the expressive or functional superiority of one melody or succession of tones over another is a matter of such complexity that no satisfactory explanation of it has yet been devised, the reasons for the musical effects of plainsong can, within limitations, be sought and discovered in its technical procedures. But the total effect of the Chant as one element in the religious rite for which it was and is intended depends on factors outside the competence of a musical historian or musicologist. That total effect is dissipated when the Chant is heard outside a Roman Catholic church—in a concert hall or at home by way of radio or phonograph—for it depends upon the Chant's being part of a divine mystery celebrated under perhaps the most solemn conditions and auspices that men can imagine.

Only a Roman Catholic hearing Gregorian melodies as part of the service that supplies his contact with God can apprehend the total effect of those melodies. It is reasonable to doubt that today even he, accustomed outside the Church to later, more complex music of many sorts, can apprehend the Chant exactly as his ancestors sensed it a millennium ago. To most of us today plainsong in pure form sounds, not natural, but peculiar, as though stained by a special religious antiquity. It is as different from the sounds (including the music) of everyday life as the odor of incense among stone is different from the odors of secular places.

In musical terms this "peculiarity" of the Chant resides in the absence of definite, measured rhythm and of chords, chordal sequences, harmony, and accompaniment. It resides, too, in the intervals by which the Gregorian melodies proceed and in the frequent use of several tones to a single text syllable. It is foolish to say that plainsong has *no* rhythm: music wholly devoid of rhythm is inconceivable. In modern terminology, the rhythm of plainsong is like the meter of prose, whereas the rhythm of most later music resembles that of poetry couched in recurring patterns of accents or feet. Almost all the Western music with which we are now familiar—whether symphony or opera, ragtime or mambo, classical sonata or ultramodern piece—has a repetitive rhythmic pattern, as have blank verse, the sonnet, and many other poetic forms. The rhythm of the Chant is like that of prose or *vers libre.*

In addition to the strangeness with which we are impressed on hearing unaccompanied melody without harmonic support moving in proselike meters, the Chant brings us the strangeness of music outside our system of keys and scales. The conception we now call key is essentially the idea of building music on the framework of a seven-step scale in which every tone exists in an established or customary relation to one chief tone, called the principal or tonic (*i.e.,* tone-ic). This procedure became important in European music after 1500 and began to lose its sovereign power only after 1875. The salient fact about the scales at the heart of this system is that they are of two chief sorts, either of which (major or minor) may begin on any tone. The only important difference between one major or minor scale and another major or minor scale is that of pitch. The arrangement of intervals between the successive tones in, let us say, the B major scale is identical with that in the F major scale and the same identity of arrangement exists among minor scales.

Gregorian Chant, however, long antedates our major-minor system, being constructed on a system of eight-tone scales known as modes, almost certainly Oriental and Greek in origin. The modal system [1] was codified between 800 and 1000 into the so-called eight ecclesiastical modes, each of which was for a long time considered to have a special ethical significance. Here the important fact about the ecclesiastical modes is that the differences among them are in the arrangement of successive intervals within

---

[1] The medieval modes should not be confused with the extremely theoretical ancient Greek modes, not here dealt with.

19 O.T.R.

each, and not necessarily in pitch. One mode differs from another, that is, not as one major scale differs from another major scale (the same arrangement of intervals at a different pitch), but as any major scale differs from any minor scale (a different arrangement of intervals at whatever pitch).

Working strictly in one of the ecclesiastical modes, a musician had to pay special attention to the four modulations within it. In our modern use this word indicates transitions from one key to another, but in modal terminology it refers to four significant tones within each mode: the final, dominant, mediant, and participant. A melodic phrase might begin or end on any of the four modulations of the mode in use, but the concluding phrase had to close on the final because it would also conclude the melody. This sounds confining, and from the point of vantage of some later practices it was, though the stricter rules of academic nineteenth-century harmony or of the twelve-tone system as practiced by Arnold Schoenberg and his disciples look no less confining at first glance.

But the modal rules were not ironclad, and all varieties of deviation from them were increasingly condoned and even tacitly legislated. Although modern students believe that when the codification of the ecclesiastical modes was in process, many melodies were altered to fit the rather strait rules, not all Gregorian melodies can be analyzed strictly according to the codified system. Some of them either could not be altered or simply were not. Also, it is certain that the melodies were sung differently at various places and times.

The developing notation in which Gregorian Chant was set down differed from our modern notation not only in appearance, but also in significance. With something approaching exactness, our notation can indicate pitch, duration, accent, volume, speed, and several other desired characteristics. The neumes, as the signs in Gregorian notation were called, indicated much less. Nor were they always intended to be read literally even within their limited field of indication. At a very early date musicians felt the need for "accidentals," intervening semitones roughly equivalent to the black notes of our piano keyboard. Before the tones represented by these accidentals were considered quite permissible, and therefore before signs indicating them were introduced, it was nevertheless understood that at certain melodic junctures they were to be sung instead of the tones actually called for by the notation. The mere profile of a melody might seem to the ear—which makes all musical "laws" that are obeyed—to require a semitone where the mode did not permit one. The cause, in that case, would have been an incipient feeling for the harmonic occurrences that we moderns feel to be implied by any melody. The neumes are scarcely more than a mnemonic device, it being unlikely that anyone not already familiar with a Gregorian melody in performance could have sung it properly merely by interpreting the neumes on a parchment before him. He would have known the melody or its component procedures already; the neumes merely recalled its shape and general progress to his mind.

The theoretical purity of the liturgical music of the Church, already sullied by the customary use of accidentals, was further marred, probably after 700, by a custom said to have been imported from Byzantium. This was the interpolation of new melodic phrases into existing Gregorian melodies. These additions proliferated rapidly in response to the creative urge of musicians, and it was not long before they were being included in the chanting of most sorts of liturgical song.

The liturgy of the Roman Catholic Church consists largely of the Mass and the special services for the Canonical Hours, the texts for which are found respectively in the Missal and the Breviary. The Mass is divided into two sections: the Ordinary, consisting of those parts of the text which are unchanging, and the Proper, those parts of the text which change with the season or with the saint being commemorated. The Mass is not usually set to music complete. The musical portions are customarily for all sections of the Ordinary, and it is only in the special case of the Requiem Mass that numerous non-Gregorian settings have been made of sections of the Proper.

The practice of interpolating new melodic phrases soon spread even into the Ordinary of the Mass, formerly the strictest division of the Chant, as well as into the music for the Canonical Hours.

The new phrases were known as tropes, and it was not long before tropes began to flower within tropes. One variety of trope, known as a sequence, gradually attracted text words to itself. Sequences became so elaborate as to threaten the sacred text with incomprehensibility, and in the mid-sixteenth century the Council of Trent ordered nearly all of them expunged. The *Dies irae* and the *Stabat mater,* sung respectively on the Friday of Passion Week and the third Sunday in September, are the best known of those remaining.

From early in the Middle Ages on, there has been an evident tendency to tamper with the isolated purity of plainsong. That tendency, inherently related to the structure of sound itself, was for a long time questionable from an ecclesiastical point of view, but for six or seven centuries it nonetheless provided the chief great method of the art music of the West.

The groups performing Gregorian Chant in churches were made up, from relatively early times, of both men and boys. The result was that the differences in pitch between the pre-adolescent and post-adolescent male voice produced the same melody in simultaneously sung octaves. It is altogether probable that a man singing a C, let us say, and a boy singing the C one or two octaves higher thought that they were singing the same tone. This is one of the most curious of musical phenomena, not to be explained entirely by the fact that the vibrations producing "the same tone" an octave higher are exactly twice as rapid as those producing the lower tone. The sensation that tones separated by one, two, or even seven or eight, octaves are all the same tone, but in differing pitches, survives intact. Only psychologists collaborating with physicists may be able to produce an explanation of it at once credible and inclusive.

At other periods, and in various regions of Europe, the distance between the two voices or groups of voices simultaneously singing the same melody was less than one octave, sometimes a third, a fifth, or a sixth. But the performing singers did not think of the result of singing two simultaneous tones as, in our sense, a chord, for they were all engaged in singing one melody, the same melody. The practice of singing plainsong in constantly parallel octaves, fifths, or other intervals did not significantly dilute the purely melodic conception. The combinations of tones that inevitably occurred at certain junctures were not deliberate or intentionally important. To us they must often sound purposeless, if not ugly, particularly in the order in which they were allowed to occur. They might have sounded so to the singers if their ears had been accustomed to hear music as we customarily hear it: both vertically and horizontally. But they had no reason to hear or think that way, being engaged consciously in the production of one unaccompanied melody.

But coincident with the developing importance of semitones not originally native to the modes and with the spread of sequences and other tropes, there began to be introduced into church music the simultaneous singing of two or more *different* melodies. The mere existence of polyphony naturally hastened the existing tendency to drift farther and farther from the strait purity of Gregorian Chant.

It was in all probability as a result of creative experimentation with temptations inherent in the very structure of sound that musicians gradually learned the attractions of singing different melodies together. In Church music one melody, thought of as fundamental, was usually from the Gregorian compilation. To it was added another melody—or several other melodies—adapted from secular music or composed for the purpose. And the singing together of two or more different melodies created problems for the singers. The changing solutions of those problems, by performers and composers, comprised a large part of the music and the musical history of the Church up to roughly 1600.

A melody to be sung simultaneously with another melody had to be measured out in divisions of duration which could be matched against corresponding divisions in the other or others. Singers could no longer depend for their tempo, as the singer of a single melody could, on individual interpretation of the length-emphasis required by the vowels of the words sung. This fact brought about, in Church practice, new developments in notation. The music marked off into regular divisions of time was called *musica mensurata* (measured music), a term that survives in our use of the word measure for the space between two of the vertical lines in printed music. By about the middle of the twelfth century, six so-called rhythmic modes had been established, the effect of which was to make it possible to fit together, as of equal duration, musical measures corresponding to distinct sorts of poetic feet: trochee, iamb, dactyl, anapaest, spondee, and tribrach.

Real polyphony did not emerge all at once. Rising out of performances in which two voices were separated by an unchanging interval—that is, were actually singing the same melody at an unchanging distance from each other—polyphony soon began to deviate from the parallel, especially at the openings and closes of melodic phrases. The voices began to end frequently "in unison" (on the identical tone). The intervals between the two singing voices at first had tended to be preponderantly fifths and fourths, but both voices were often also duplicated at a distance of one octave. When strictly parallel motion between the *tenor* (fundamental melody) and the *duplum* (added melody) began to be avoided, the motion often became oblique: one voice remained relatively stationary in pitch, repeating the same tone or tones immediately adjacent, while the other voice moved closer to it and farther from it in pitch, thus constantly altering the width of the interval between the two voices. Still greater freedom enfranchised contrary motion: the voices moving toward or away from one another. In some eleventh-century polyphony, in fact, the two voices, at first widely separated in pitch, not only met in unison, but actually crossed, thus in effect exchanging relative positions.

Another important development was the appearance of music in which the singing of one tone against another tone—literal counterpoint—was cast aside in favor of singing two, three, and even four tones in the *duplum* against each tone in the *tenor*. As the twelfth century wore on, in fact, the *duplum* flowered into groups of tones, each group sung against one tone in the basic plainsong *tenor*. In the works of the twelfth-century musician Perotinus, a *triplum* and *quadruplum* were added to the *tenor* and *duplum,* thus producing four-part polyphony. The inevitable result, at least at first, was that rhythm had to become more and more strict (it was limited to versions of what we now call three-beat or triple time).

During the years up to about 1300—the period which later musicians called the *ars antiqua*—music moved very far indeed from the unencumbered single-tone melodies of plainsong. The secularization of the musical art was developing with constantly increasing speed. In one sense, the *duplum, triplum,* and *quadruplum* melodies set against all or, in some later forms, part of a Gregorian melody were already secular despite their sacred texts: they were not in themselves Gregorian Chant. But in many pieces from the *ars antiqua,* secularization had advanced farther still: all of the melodies were non-Gregorian. Even the *tenor,* now usually called *cantus firmus* or *canto fermo,* was in itself newly composed or adapted from secular music.

The most important of the numerous polyphonic forms elaborated toward the close of the *ars antiqua* was the motet. It came into existence when one of the added voices, instead of vocalizing on a vowel from one of the text syllables being sung by the chief voice, sang words of its own. The added text or texts—for a *triplum* and *quadruplum,* each with its own words, soon became common—nearly always commented on the immediately preceding text of the *cantus firmus.* By the end of the thirteenth century, however, a new step toward complete secularization of the motet had been taken. Motets were by then numerous in which the *cantus firmus* was taken from Gregorian Chant and retained its liturgical text, but in which the added voices sang profane, sometimes obscene texts. These motets, largely French, were of bewildering complexity, for in addition to having its own text, each of the two, three, or four melodies was often in a different rhythmic mode or variant of a rhythmic mode from its companions.

By the end of the *ars antiqua*—the so-called *ars nova* period began about 1300—polyphonic music was an extremely conscious, complex, and self-sufficient art. It had not only begun to absorb secularity, but in another sense had begun to admit the possibility of becoming entirely secular in itself.

Before glancing at the music of the *ars nova,* it would be wise
to note some large facts about the wholly secular music that undoubtedly existed during the Middle Ages.

The exact nature of very early Christian secular music is all
but unknown. The reason is clear. The learning that had begun
to lead to the effective noting-down of music was almost exclusively in the hands of monks and other churchmen. These men
had no reason to preserve the songs and other music of the high-
roads, market-places, and pleasure resorts of the laity. The fact
that this popular music existed, though vouched for by the find-
ings of literary and social historians—as well as by the exercise of
common sense—has often been overlooked or implicitly denied
by historians of music. The result of this falsification has been a
treatment of medieval Church music as though it had existed and
evolved, until just before the Renaissance, in a vacuum disturbed
only, from about 1100 on, by the music of the troubadours, minnesingers, and trouvères. The result of that treatment has been
a picture of musical development crowded with palpable nonsense.

All the musical practices of the modern Western world have
inherited largely both from the music of the medieval Church
and from the secular music of the Middle Ages, including that
of itinerant goliards, minstrels, and lowly jongleurs. But the earliest important body of non-Church music of which large remnants
survive is naturally that of the first secular musicians educated
enough to have been able to note it down: the troubadours. These
aristocratic, often princely, poet-musicians flourished in Provence
and Catalonia from about 1100. The models from which they
developed their intricate poems and their melodies are not clearly
known, but they were almost certainly various. The geographical
position of Provence and Catalonia, as well as details in the surviving troubadour works, suggests influences from Spain and, via
Spain, from North Africa. The love poetry cultivated at the court
of the Carolingian rulers between 750 and 950, and the cult of
ecstatic adoration of the Virgin were other possible sources drawn
upon.

Although one of the foremost early troubadours, Marcabru, was a commoner, most of them of whom we have reliable information were nobles or princes. It is believed, however, that they were importantly assisted, even in part supplied with the works bearing their names, by minstrels of the lower classes. The art of the troubadours was gallant, intricate, and flowery. The fact that pictorial representations of their singing often show the performers with instruments was at one time thought to prove that their poem-songs were accompanied instrumentally in the modern manner. Later students, however, are now all but sure that when instruments were used, they merely duplicated the sung melodies (strictly or with trifling divergences) or were employed for brief, purely instrumental preludes, interludes, and postludes extemporized on the spot. There is no indication whatever that troubadour music was ever anything but monophonic—*i.e.*, single-voiced—but there are many indications that it disregarded the ecclesiastical modes and tended toward the use of a scale much nearer to the major scale as we know it.

The musico-poetic achievements and practices of the troubadours appear to have spread gradually to Spain proper, to Portugal, Italy, England, northern France, and the German states, in all cases unquestionably as infiltrations into already existing forms of secular poetic music. The most immediately fruitful of these offshoots of the troubadour art were those in Germany and northern France, where they helped to germinate respectively the art of the minnesingers and that of the trouvères.

The flowering, in the minnesingers (German *Minnesänger,* love-singers), of the only known important German music of the Middle Ages dated from about 1156, the year in which Friedrich I ("Barbarossa"), Holy Roman Emperor, married Beatrix, heiress of Upper Burgundy. With this princess, French manners and influences penetrated the German court. While the names of the Provençal troubadours are now familiar only to specialists, those of three minnesingers—Tannhäuser, Walther von der Vogelweide, and Wolfram von Eschenbach—are widely known because Richard Wagner seven centuries later wove into a popular opera supposed incidents from their lives and an actual song-contest that was held during the thirteenth century. The surviving minnesinger melodies are more closely restricted to the ecclesiastical modes than most troubadour songs.

The trouvères of northern France date from the mid-twelfth century, with Blondel de Nesles and Quesnes de Béthune, both aristocrats. They included Thibault IV, King of Navarre, and died out with Adam de la Halle, a commoner, in 1287. About eight hundred of their poem-songs survive complete as to text and melody. The texts are often classified by subject. The musical forms related to these poetic manners became so important that in fact text patterns began to be adapted to them. For this reason certain of the trouvère patterns have been spoken of as the first independent musical forms.

Both as to classifications and as to interpretations of the exact manner of performance, the surviving songs of troubadours, minnesingers, trouvères, their counterparts elsewhere, and their immediate successors (including the fifteenth-century *Meistersinger*) still occasion scholarly quarrels. The niceties of historical placement and details of performance may safely be left in the eager, disputatious hands of specialists. What is important for the musical amateur to remember is that, so far as scholars can determine, the music of all these men was monophonic, consisting like Gregorian Chant entirely of single-note melodic lines devoid both of harmony in our sense and of accompaniment as we understand it. This wholly secular music was, in this respect at least, as far distant from our present musical conceptions as was the Chant, to which it remained, in fact, much closer.

Although it is self-evident that sacred and secular music could not have existed in non-communicating separate compartments, it was when they began to interact deeply and constantly that music as the art we think it began to come into existence.

By the end of the twelfth century, polyphony was firmly rooted in Church music, where it had produced musical creations of enduring strength. Within polyphony, music was abandoning the purely horizontal view (of however many melodic strands moving simultaneously in whatever manner) for a mixture of the horizontal and the vertical view, a mixture prefiguring the close relationship between harmonic practice and the physical constitution of sound. As much attention would, not very much later, be expended upon chords and the logic of chordal succession as upon the forward motion of separate or polyphonically combined strands of melody. Chords and their implications, that is, were to be examined and employed for their own power in musical construction and logic. Instrumental music would come into its own (this does not mean that it had not already a long, if mostly unknown, history). And with independent instrumental music, ancillary to it, would emerge the conception of melody supported by a chordal, non-polyphonic accompaniment. For these reasons, it is no mere whim to look upon the two centuries that began with the year 1301 as the first era of a new musical dispensation.

ARS NOVA · MACHAUT · IMITATION · LANDINO
"SUMER IS ICUMEN IN" · DUNSTABLE

Defining periods in the history of an art is a convenience for easy identification in discussion. If such periods are mistaken for a series of separate happenings, their use becomes misleading and dangerous. In music, as in other arts, forms, usages, influences, and manners flow along without interruption, intermingling, dying away, coming to birth or rebirth. The date 1301, for example, is a significant signpost along the way. But the new varieties of music which came to full bloom immediately following the turn of the fourteenth century did not issue suddenly in that way from the garden of a single composer or group of composers. They happened to blossom at a given time, but their roots were deep in the past and their stems had been maturing for decades, unnoticed in gardens of other plants in other stages of growth, flowering, and decay.

The fourteenth century may conveniently be considered as a period during which the fifteenth was gestating. But it was also the time when the twelfth and thirteenth centuries were dying away, and it produced astonishing and admirable flowers of its own. During its early decades writers on the practice and theory of music began to indicate awareness of musical change by referring to the art of their immediate predecessors as the *ars antiqua*. Philippe de Vitry (1291-1361), Bishop of Meaux, near Paris, was

probably the first poet-musician-theorist to call the music of his
own period the *ars nova*. Viewed from a distance of six centuries,
the most noticeable differences between the "old" and the "new"
arts supply one key to the condition of Western music in the age
of Dante and Giotto.

Despite the encroachments of a variety of semi-secular usages,
the music of the *ars antiqua* had remained largely Gothic, sacred,
and ecclesiastical. But the gay courtly music of the troubadours
and trouvères had begun to drift into it, affecting its patterns, its
rhythms, and its urge to freedom. This secularizing tendency,
with other influences, helped to produce the *ars nova,* much
more than the *ars antiqua* a music of laymen.

Flourishing especially in France and Italy, with related developments in England and elsewhere, this music of the early fourteenth century was (if judgments based on surviving music are
just) most expressive in the hands of Guillaume de Machaut, a
French poet-composer who lived from about 1300 to 1377, and of
such Italians as Jacopo da Bologna, Giovanni di Cascia, and the
somewhat later Francesco Landino (or Landini). There were significant differences between the French and the Italian manifestations of the *ars nova*. South of the Alps neither the *ars antiqua*
nor the trouvères had flourished. Italian musicians were therefore not required, as their French contemporaries were, to follow
and digest such well-defined achievements in style. They developed more independently, and therefore differently.

Despite regional distinctions, the typical music of the *ars nova*
differed from that of the *ars antiqua* most notably in that it increasingly naturalized measures in duple time in company with
the previously sanctioned measures in triple time; succumbed to
an increasing desire to think music horizontally *and* vertically;
extended the function of the full triad (C-E-G, F-A-C, *etc.*), later
the radiating heart of harmonic activity; and was even freer than
its predecessor in admitting what it considered to be dissonances
on all but the first beats of measures and those which closed
melodic phrases or musical units.

Guillaume de Machaut was as much poet as composer. Chaucer,
about forty years his junior, was acquainted with his poetry, from

which he quoted. In his person Machaut brought together for a remarkable late flowering the traditions of the trouvères and the manners of the Gothic ecclesiastical musicians of the *ars antiqua.* He was himself in holy orders, and he composed the earliest known polyphonic setting of the Mass to be the work of a single individual.[1] He also wrote numerous secular songs. He handled his materials with ease and unmistakable originality, bringing an immense musical erudition to the aid of a fresh conception of music as an art.

Not all of Machaut's compositions were polyphonic. Of eighteen surviving *lais,* for example, sixteen are composed for a single voice, as are twenty-five *virelais.* So many of Machaut's surviving pieces have one vocal melody and one, two, or three simultaneous melodies for instruments that it is possible to consider him one of the first composers to write melodies with instrumental accompaniment, a novelty often attributed to the early seventeenth-century initiators of opera. Machaut's rondeaux, deviating widely from his trouvère models, resemble to some extent later art songs for a single voice accompanied by two or three instruments. These "accompaniments" are still, of course, polyphonic; they do not serve the purpose of chordal support fulfilled by most modern song accompaniments.

In his motets Machaut strove for all-over patterns of rhythmic unity through isorhythms, a system codifying a few set patterns of time value, the number of repetitions of a pattern within a composition depending upon the desired length and character. He also employed widely a constructive principle that has continued to be one major form of musical syntax ever since: imitation— which, needless to say, he did not "invent." Imitation is what occurs in polyphonic texture when a melody or melodic fragment that has just been sung or played is repeated (in the same pitch or a different pitch) by one or more other voices or instruments while the first voice or instrument goes on to other materials. It is the ruling syntactical principle of many musical forms, including canon, round, catch, and fugue. The round, simplest of these,

---

[1] The only earlier Mass that may possibly have been composed by one man is now generally thought to have been the work of several men.

is familiar to anyone who has ever taken part in singing "Oh how lovely is the evening," "Scotland's burning," or *"Frère Jacques."* One voice begins the melody. When it has advanced a predetermined number of beats, the second voice comes in with the beginning of the same melody. The third (and fourth) voice enters similarly.

The principle of the round is imitative, rhythmic, and repetitive—for as soon as the first voice completes the entire melody, it may begin it again, and thus the voices may continue to go round and round until, after a predetermined number of repetitions, each voice, beginning with the first, stops singing as it reaches the end of the melody. In the round, the imitating voices sing either in the same pitch as the first voice or at an interval of one octave from it. In a strict canon, the imitating voices may repeat the melody at the interval of a fourth, a fifth, or some other distance from the first voice. In the canon, too, the imitating voices do not always wait for the completion of a musical phrase by the preceding voice, as they do in the round, but may enter at a variety of different points.

Machaut made extremely clever use of canon in his motets, while in some of his rondeaux he foretold the almost unbelievably complex "puzzle-canons" of a later era. Originally a dance-song of fresh simplicity, the rondeau could, in Machaut's hands, become an intellectual game requiring the close attention necessary to the solution of a rebus. The most renowned of his compositions of this sort is, with literal truth, called *"Ma fin est mon commencement"* (My end is my beginning). In modern notation, as quoted by Gustave Reese in *Music in the Middle Ages* (W. W. Norton & Company, Inc.), it looks like this:

This amazing composition is for one voice and two instrumental parts. The melody of the vocal part (upper line on bottom staff) is also used for one instrumental part (top staff), where it is reversed note for note, proceeding backward throughout. The other instrumental part (bottom melody on bottom staff) has a distinct melody; this reaches a conclusion halfway through the rondeau (at the double bar-line), after which it proceeds backward to its own first note!

"Ma fin est mon commencement" also displays another characteristic of the *ars nova* which continues to be an important means of musical construction: syncopation, the temporary displacing of regular, expected accents. In the third and fourth measures of the music, upper staff, one sort of syncopation is produced by the absence of notes on the first, most important beats. Here the expected first-beat accent is subtly shifted to the second half of that pre-eminent beat. In the eighth measure, upper melody on bottom staff, another variety of syncopation is produced by the holding over *through the important first beat* of a note first sounded on

the weak fourth beat of the preceding measure. Machaut used syncopation in motets organized isorhythmically, producing extraordinary rhythmic elaboration and interest. In this special kind of complexity some of his compositions were scarcely matched until the twentieth century.

Machaut made notable use of freedoms new to music. In polyphony he often composed all the melodies himself. In his view, that is, the art of musical composition was rapidly becoming the conscious activity we think it today: the creation of an entirely original whole rather than the imbedding of a borrowed element in newly devised additional material. Later composers, of course, have at times reverted to the earlier practice: Tchaikovsky wrote his *Mozartiana* Suite around melodies used by Mozart; Edvard Grieg composed for a second piano original pieces intended for performance while Mozart sonatas were played at the first piano; Igor Stravinsky built his ballet *Le Baiser de la fée* around materials borrowed from Tchaikovsky. Sets of variations on borrowed themes are common.

Machaut sometimes treated all voices or parts as of nearly equal importance. Looked at vertically, his many-voiced compositions seem to the modern eye to pay strict attention to consonance at certain important junctures and to disregard it at others. As in some earlier and many later pieces, the voices are likely to begin by producing a perfect consonance—that is, are likely to be separated as they start by an octave, a fifth, or a fourth. They are likely to return to one of these perfect consonances for points of rest or finality, such as the closes of melodies or melodic phrases. Between any two of these consonant points, however, the intervals are very often not only dissonances, but dissonances in sequences that would have been anathema to most eighteenth-century and nineteenth-century musicians. Although the intervals between simultaneously sounding tones were becoming more and more important, melodic profile and strictly melodic motion forward remained of more interest than vertical, chordal structure or chordal succession and forward motion.

Most important, of course, such gifted musicians as Machaut and Landino produced expressive and (without reference to past or future) satisfying musical structures by using the newly found freedoms of the *ars nova* in conjunction with older procedures. In composing his Mass for four voices, Machaut might hew as closely to the older manners of ecclesiastical polyphony as, being a fully living man of a later day, he could. But composing other pieces he was interested in creating, by whatever available means would render it pleasing and expressive, music that would support and display the texts he had selected or written.

Landino moved farther still from earlier practices, allowing the *ballata, caccia,* madrigal,[2] and other forms to be shaped by the sensuous, lush turns of melody somehow native to his homeland, and to this day spoken of as Italian. These pieces were almost certainly not intended for performance by voices alone. Stringed instruments (mostly of sorts now no longer in use), both plucked and bowed, the small portable organ known as *organetto,* recorders (end-blown flutes), and possibly other wind instruments may have been meant to play with the voices or, in some cases, to replace them.

In Landino's surviving compositions, especially as they must have sounded when he himself took part in performing them (he was an accomplished player on organ, lute, flute, and other instruments, including one of his own devising), music was slipping altogether from its Gothic period. It was shedding, that is, its hieratic medieval rigidity, its purposeful and often powerfully communicative narrowness, and was preparing to take on some of the graciousness, the curving, soft, almost fleshly charm of the Renaissance. Landino, the last great figure of the *ars nova,* died in 1397. By that year Donatello and Fra Angelico had been born and the wonderful English musician John Dunstable was a grown man.

In the British Isles, from the mid-seventh century on, the ways of dealing with plainsong and of singing were much like those of the Continent, the chief differences being caused by differences in

---

[2] The madrigal of the *ars nova* was not what composers of the sixteenth century and later indicated by that word, being a much more strictly applied poetico-musical form—of which the later madrigal was a liberally interpreted imitation.

folk music and by a tendency, apparently more advanced in Britain than in France or other Continental countries, to make use of the local or national language in addition to, or instead of, Latin. A number of special practices naturally developed, but they were refinements, now of interest only to scholars. Also, though the islands were somewhat isolated geographically, communication with Continental centers of culture was constant, and influences flowed in both directions across the Channel and the North Sea.

Few documents on the early history of music survive in Britain and Ireland, and less is therefore known of insular than of Continental developments. Yet the earliest preserved example of written-out polyphony is a musical illustration in *Musica Enchiriadis,* a theoretical treatise written in England or Ireland in the ninth century. And by the early decades of the fourteenth century (possibly, though improbably, before the middle of the thirteenth) there had been written out in England one of the most enduringly famous of musical compositions, "Sumer is icumen in," known as the "Reading *rota*" (round).

Unless this astonishingly elaborate and expressive piece is to be regarded as an isolated upthrust of individual genius of an unparalleled sort, it inescapably suggests that the techniques of polyphonic composition were, by the date of its noting-down, more advanced in England than elsewhere. The piece is frequently sung today because of the lively beauty of its melodic material, whose springtime freshness has remained undimmed by six or seven centuries of time and change. As an early example of imitation it is all but incredible; it is made up of two simultaneous rounds, the upper for four voices, the lower for two.

Technically, "Sumer is icumen in" is of enormous interest. The voices of the upper, four-part round enter successively at intervals of four measures. When the fourth voice comes in, there are actually six voices singing together, and they do so for thirty-four measures (or perhaps more, for though the piece seems intended to end when the first voice has completed the melody once, there is no intrinsic reason why it could not continue until the final voice has completed the melody, the other voices, mean-

while, having successively fallen silent). Also the piece appears to
be in what we know as the major mode: each staff of the manu-
script has a B♭ set down at its beginning—in our modern system,
the indication ("key signature") of F major.[3]

Further interest is given "Sumer is icumen in" by the fact that
it employs a ground-bass or *basso ostinato,* a compositional device
still in use. This indicates a melody or melodic fragment used as
the lowest part of a composition, where it is repeated over and
over, usually below changing melodic and other occurrences in
the other voices or parts. In this piece, the two lowest voices
actually constitute a double ground-bass that is in itself a round!
And the "Reading *rota*" is, of course, not only secular, but in a
local (Wessex) dialect: its opening words mean, in modern English, "Summer is coming in. The cuckoos sing loudly." True, it
also has a Latin text. Written under the lines of the upper round,
absent from the lower, this begins: *"Perspice Christicola."* It does
not fit the melody nearly so smoothly as the English words, and
it was possibly added so that the music might be sung in Reading
Abbey, where the famous manuscript, now in the British Museum, was discovered.

"Sumer is icumen in" contains no notable dissonances. If sung
from a replica of the manuscript, it ends on a chord containing
the three tones of the full tonic triad of F major (F, A, and C). It
is exceedingly smooth in texture and harmony. Above all other
qualities, it displays the euphonious sweetness that was to be
singled out a hundred years and more later by Continental musicians as being English. This element, so remote from the stiffly dissonant angularity of much earlier polyphony, was to help fertilize
the great Burgundian-Flemish schools of contrapuntal composition, schools initiated by men who had either studied with John
Dunstable (1370?-1453) or were his indirect disciples.

The surviving compositions of Dunstable differ from the
French works of his period chiefly in their tendency toward later
evolutions of vertical, harmonic thinking. When they employ
three voices, the resulting three-note chords are preponderantly
consonant; they move forward with something of the harmonic

[3] Or D minor, clearly not intended here.

motion that—codified and then legislated—would govern musical architecture in the seventeenth and eighteenth centuries and the early part of the nineteenth. John Dunstable was what scarcely a composer before him could be called: a great inventor of persuasive melody. And there is evident in his compositions a consideration for sonority in itself, for the full, pleasing *sound* of the music, that was either something new or something Dunstable had acquired from now unknown British musicians and then himself startlingly advanced. It has often been suggested that Dunstable's suave and charming style represented the preservation and evolution of a native English taste for euphony which had somehow escaped the pointed, powerful influence of Gothic Continental polyphony. Yet Dunstable's taste for melismata approaching the purely decorative *colorature* of later Italian music appears to indicate that he was acquainted with very similar arabesques in the music of the late Italian *ars nova*.

Although nothing is known of John Dunstable's life, it is generally believed that he died in 1453, at an advanced age, and that he had served for a time as master of a musical establishment kept in Paris by a brother of Henry V. Almost as much as his native genius, his presence on the Continent in the early decades of the fifteenth century would explain both his great fame and the fact that most of his surviving compositions have been discovered outside England. It would likewise explain the clear evidence of Continental procedures in his music and his own profound and enduring effect on his Continental contemporaries and immediate successors. He seems to have come at the end of a long period of vital development in British music, to have combined its procedures with certain Continental habits to the advantage of both streams of creation, and to have turned the resulting fusion over to Continental composers rather than to his compatriots, who were soon to be put into long eclipse by Burgundian and Flemish masters.

The compositions of Dunstable and of such of his British contemporaries as Lionel (or Leonel) Power do not bespeak a fully evolved harmonic system. But many of them do show a feeling for chords and for the logical progression of chords—the elements that would lead later to the formulation and practice of such a system. Abandoning exclusive attention to melodic strands, composers had long since begun to insist on the musical significance of the intervals between tones sounded together. In earlier polyphonic usages, to be sure, consonant combinations were expected at openings and closes, and sometimes at other important musical junctures. But there had been no prevailing sensation that a certain sort of dissonance ought to be resolved—that is, succeeded by a specific, defined consonance. This belief—that there is an inherent logic of chordal succession—is the chief tenet of the system that obtained in most eighteenth- and nineteenth-century music. It had not become conscious by Dunstable's time. But that system is in part derived from unchanging mathematical relationships in the physical make-up of musical sound itself, and long before its codification men responded to instinctive feelings about some of its components. One expression of this was the procedure called *faux bourdon* or *faulxbordon*, false bass, a variety of which —called English discant—was natural to Dunstable and his British contemporaries.

The reasoning behind *faux bourdon* was complicated; its effect in practice was a series of parallel sixth-chords (such as F-D followed by E-C, F-D, G-E, *etc.*). Between the outlying voices, the third voice remained at an interval of a third above the lower tone (F-A-D, E-G-C, F-A-D, G-B-E, *etc.*). And the acceptance of these resulting thirds as constituting a pleasant, "consonant" interval was what marked *faux bourdon* as an important step toward the harmony of later days. Furthermore, if we transpose the top voice (which the complex theory of *faux bourdon* considered to be "the real bass") down an octave to its "lawful" position at the bottom—as it was unquestionably "heard" by the performing singers—we get a series of full triads (D-F-A, C-E-G, D-F-A, E-G-B, *etc.*). And the full triad was to supply the very armature on which the later system of harmony was to be modeled. English discant, though arrived at (or explained) by a different, equally complex, sort of theoretical reasoning, resulted in much the same sort of chords as *faux bourdon,* and was therefore as likely to lead toward the elaboration of harmony.

Both *faux bourdon* and English discant as employed by Dunstable imply a heightened sense of the independent and interrelated natures of chords. Similarly, the constant employment, if not in writing music, then in performing it, of accidentals, though primarily a melodic procedure, indicated an increased tendency to think harmonically. This was particularly so when an accidental was used to produce a semitone between the seventh tone of a scale and the final tone, invariable in our modern diatonic scales, both major and minor. These musical methods were used in response to demands by the listening ear, which instinctively understood more about the physical nature of musical sound than earlier compositional practices had demonstrated.

The awakening of this sort of consciousness marked a long step from earlier polyphony toward what is now thought of as the classical system of harmony. It defined the available store of forward-tending, almost-harmonic devices available to European composers during the first decades of the fifteenth century. Music was still preponderantly vocal, but instruments were increasing their importance. Music for the organ and other instruments, notably plucked and bowed strings, stood on the verge of idiomatic independence from the human voice. Compositions were already widely performed on instruments: in actual performance some or all "voices" in polyphonic pieces were played rather than sung. In the continuing ebb and forward surge of these intermingling usages and means, Europe was, during the succeeding century, to move into one of its great periods of musical creation.

Three

BURGUNDIAN SCHOOL · DUFAY · BINCHOIS
INSTRUMENTS · OKEGHEM · THE CHANSON
OBRECHT · JOSQUIN DES PRES · THE MADRIGAL

"Burgundian School" is a name given to a group of composers who lived during an interregnum between the musical manners of the *ars nova* and those of the Netherlandish masters. In another view, it is merely a comfortable label for two great musical creators who fit poorly elsewhere: Guillaume Dufay (1400?-1474) and Gilles Binchois (1400?-1467). It was chiefly these two men who first combined in their working methods the best of the *ars nova* and the sweetening flavor of Dunstable. The result was music of sensuous tenderness.

Cambrai and Dijon were the centers of a musical style that turned from the complex, extraordinarily learned music of the *ars nova* toward more direct expressiveness. The turn was occasioned by a preference for orderliness and consolidation, for rule over experiment. Looked at in cross section, the history of Western music may be viewed as a series of alternating emphases, swings between experimentation and summation. The *ars nova* had been fertile in novelty; its motion was centrifugal or onward. The Burgundian School cared little for novelty in that sense; its movement was centripetal and inward. Its achievement in creating beauty was large, but except for its gradual development of a few harmonic devices, it was, from the historical point of view, almost re-

42

actionary. It could have been followed only by stagnation, gradually devitalized aping, or another period of experiment.

Dufay and Binchois carried forward the establishment of the full triad as the foundation of logical chord-progression. Their feeling of the relative importance of the steps within a scale came closer than that of their immediate forerunners to what came to be considered, late in the seventeenth century, as normal—and was so considered until very recently. Besides ceding a prominent role to the full triad, the Burgundians developed a strong feeling about the melodic use of the seventh degree of a scale.

A harmonic pattern that moves to a sensation of finality or repose is called a cadence, and the last chord of a closing cadence must have the key-tone (that is, the first tone of the scale native to the key) as its chief constituent. Melodically, this tonic is most often approached through the tone immediately below it, the seventh degree of the scale in use, what we call the "leading note." But in approaching this final tonic, the Burgundians often employed what amounts to two leading notes: first the seventh degree of the scale and then the sixth. Thus, if the tonic was C, the melody notes at the close of a Burgundian composition might be B, A, C (the opposite—A, B, C—would be a more common eighteenth- and nineteenth-century way of ordering these same notes in the same location). Landino had made some use of this double leading note, producing what is sometimes called the "Landino cadence," but with Dufay and Binchois it became customary, lending their cadences, to modern ears, a curious instability.

The new importance of the full triad (an interval of a third superimposed on another third) insisted on the basic importance of the third as an interval. The triad was interpreted by Dufay, Binchois, and their Burgundian colleagues according to the principles of *faux bourdon*. When looked at vertically, therefore, their music often contains long clauses made of chords like CEA, GBE, which contain both a third (CE, GB) and a sixth (CA, GE). This produces a chordal series remote in effect from the octave-fifth angularity of earlier days. A mixture of Gothic and later manners, it tends toward the curving, softer-textured idiom of the Renaissance. Melodically it accompanied the advance into a new day.

In writing sacred music, the men of the Burgundian School displayed a new interest in setting the Proper of the Mass, thus finding new musical materials in the changing sections of the liturgical text. In their settings of the Ordinary, or unchanging sections, the Burgundians often lent over-all musical unity to the whole by using one basic theme or melody in various forms throughout. Dufay, for example, was one of the earliest composers to adapt the secular song *"L'homme armé"* to this purpose, thus helping to establish a vogue that endured into the seventeenth century. In structural intention, these thematically unified Masses resemble those symphonies of the nineteenth and twentieth centuries in which all or part of a single theme or melody appears "cyclically" in each movement.

With the Burgundians the motet occupied a ground halfway between sacred and secular practices. No longer was the usual motet multitextual; no longer was it usually rested on a *cantus firmus.* Becoming the celebratory music performed as a grand tribute to a victory, coronation, royal wedding, or other public occasion, it began to employ the same text in all its voices and either to employ no pre-existent *cantus firmus* at all or to use fragments of one, not in the bass, but in the highest voice.

Dufay was a composer of sacred music who also wrote some secular music. But Binchois's three-part secular songs have such an eminent place among his works as to make him appear more a secular than a sacred composer. These chansons are almost exactly songs in the modern sense, the musical clothing of a poetic text. Binchois's chansons are softer, less harsh, less male music than almost all earlier Continental music. Burgundian music in general most often summons forth such adjectives as plaintive, sensuous, mellow, sentimental and feminine. Of the two foremost Burgundians, Dufay appears the more vigorous.

In both sacred and secular compositions the Burgundians naturally admitted acquaintance with the technical innovations of Machaut and his contemporaries. Particularly, they became adept at formal construction by use of imitation, and especially of canon. In this they remained content to do superbly what their predeces-

sors had done well. Theirs was no challenging, restless search for
new methods. Yet their sheer dexterity can amaze us, not only
for its own sake, but also for its expressivity. In one example
of close-meshed imitation, an *Agnus Dei* from Dufay's *"L'homme
armé"* Mass, the quoted melody, used as a *cantus firmus,* is first
sung backwards and then reversed, to be sung forward in diminution (*i.e.,* in notes half as long as those first used). In the four-
voice texture of the *Agnus Dei* it could be thus recognized only
by a highly trained and attentive ear. To recognize it, even if
only through the eye, is to add something to our understanding
of how music was made by Dufay. For the musical value is only
incidentally dependent on this learned device: the musical point
is that this reversed melodic line has been fitted into relation with
other melodic lines in such a way as to produce good music. Both
the cleverness *and* the musical interest increase when, nineteen
measures from the end of the *Agnus Dei,* the same melodic line
appears moving in its original direction (*i.e.,* forward), but in
shortened notes.

When this *Agnus Dei* is sung, it becomes so difficult to distinguish the *cantus firmus* from the other voices that it is fair to say
that its very presence—not to mention that it is one phrase of
"L'homme armé" sung forward after being sung backwards—is
for the admiration of the eye and the composer's own satisfaction.
The totality of the *Agnus Dei* is for the ear and the glory of God.

Although it is impossible to determine exactly the assignment
of melodic lines to voices and instruments in many surviving Dufay and Binchois scores, the Burgundians certainly made wide use
of instruments. Indeed, instruments had by their era taken on
such importance that we must know something about them in
order to imagine, however approximately, the real character of
Burgundian music as originally performed.

The end-blown flute known as the recorder occupied a prime
post in the instrumental parts and few wholly instrumental pieces
of Dufay and Binchois, as did the organ in several sizes and forms.
Of other wind instruments, perhaps the most widely used were
the shawm and the trombone.

The shawm, ancestor of the modern oboe, English horn,[1] bassoon, and contrabassoon, was a wind instrument in which the sound-producing element was a pair of flexible reeds so placed within a wooden tube that the pressure of the player's breath caused them to vibrate against each other. The shawm was made in several sizes, from one with about the pitch of the present oboe to one not too far removed from the modern contrabassoon.

The fifteenth-century trombone differed little from the one used today in bands and orchestras. Evolved in part from a medieval instrument called a sacbut, the trombone is really a deep-voiced trumpet. When the mechanisms of most other wind instruments were still insufficiently developed to allow them to produce all the tones required for wide usefulness in musical performance, the trombone had already been equipped with the slide that allows the player to produce all the semitones within the instrument's range. It could, therefore, all but match the human voice in flexibility and was not restricted, as many other wind instruments were, to use for fanfares and military calls.

Of stringed instruments, the Burgundian composers particularly favored the viols. These incarnations of such medieval bowed instruments as the rebec, vielle, and lyra entered their heyday about 1500 and had been largely superseded by the violins by 1650. They differed from the modern violin family chiefly in that their backs were customarily flat rather than gently rounded; in that their upper body sloped away from the neck on both sides instead of springing straight out from it; in that they had six strings instead of the violins' four; in that they had horizontal frets like a guitar instead of a smooth neck; in that their bridge—and therefore their alignment of strings—was almost flat instead of being rounded (this facilitated the bowing of more than two strings at a time); in that even in their smallest sizes they were held downward between the player's knees or on them instead of being placed in a semi-horizontal position against the player's neck and shoulder; and in that

---

[1] The modern orchestral instrument called "English horn" is actually, like the bassoon, a larger oboe. In modern usage a horn is a brass instrument lacking the vibrating reeds characteristic of the oboes and usually having a conical bore, *i.e.,* an air column whose circumference increases away from the mouthpiece. "English horn" as the designation of an oboe is therefore merely a well-established misnomer.

the stick of their bow was curved outward rather than made straight or nearly straight. The chief difference in sound between almost any viol and almost any member of the violin family of comparable size is that the viol, though possessing a suave, delicate tonal color, lacks brilliance and is easily covered by the sounds of other instruments. Violin, viola, violoncello, and contrabass,[2] the leading violins, are incomparably more assertive and brilliant than their viol ancestors.

With these and other instruments, Dufay, Binchois, and the lesser Burgundians delighted to employ the upper register of the male voice. They cherished the crying, impersonal color of vocal tone produced in the throats of boys and high tenors, and even the "artificial" tone known as falsetto. Because falsetto is produced high in the throat, it affects many modern listeners as unpleasantly nasal, but when sensitively used it has, even in small volume, a color distinct from any other, and therefore useful to a composer, particularly to one not otherwise equipped with the widest choice of timbres.

The Burgundians composed motets and Masses expressive of the chivalric, medieval-into-Renaissance elegance of a ducal aristocracy. Their secular music was apt entertainment for the courtiers of Philip the Good and Charles the Bold. Either their application of wide musical erudition was not so self-conscious as that of the later *ars nova* masters or to us it simply does not seem so elaborate because it is almost constantly at the disposition of an aristocratic mode of expression. The charming music of Binchois and Dufay brings us a glimpse of the elegant way of life that was to disappear (along with Burgundy itself as an independent entity) before the fifteenth century was over. It is the way of life made familiar to the eyes in the paintings of the Van Eycks.

Jean de Okeghem (1430?-1495?), high musical servant to Charles VII and to Louis XI, was an all but exact contemporary of François Villon and Jean Fouquet. He has a good claim to being con-

---

[2] The contrabass, or doublebass, is sometimes classified as a viol. Indeed, its correct full name is double-bass viol. It is, in fact, half a viol and half a violin, with its viol descent most noticeable in its sloping shoulders.

sidered foremost among all teachers of musical theory and practice. Himself perhaps a pupil of Binchois or Dufay, he would in turn attract one pupil—Josquin des Prés—who would outshine all his predecessors in personal expressiveness and the sort of innate musicality of which Mozart is the best-known exemplar. Scholars regard Okeghem as a founder of a school of Netherlandish composers who inherited a fabulous legacy from the Burgundians, and with it rapidly expanded the technical resources of the art of music.

If the comparison of Josquin des Prés to Mozart is useful, so also is that of Okeghem to the great modern methodologist and composer, Arnold Schoenberg. For Okeghem was an intellectual, fascinated by the mathematical possibilities in musical relationships, wonderful at designing musical puzzles that latter-day theorists delight to solve. But he was no more a desiccated academician than Schoenberg, for he wrote music that some of his contemporaries regarded as marvelously beautiful and expressive. But it was his destiny, influenced in large part by his musical character, to be outshone by Josquin his pupil, and to go down in musical history as an innovator and setter of patterns. "With Okeghem, in fact," as Cecil Gray wrote in *The History of Music,* "the art of polyphony goes to school and is set to perform tasks, frequently dull and thankless in themselves, but constituting the discipline and exercise which are a necessary preliminary to any fruitful development."

Okeghem composed numerous Masses; about twenty of them survive. He also left motets, chansons, and canons—including puzzle-canons noted down in cryptograms permitting several solutions. One of his Masses is entitled *Cujusvi toni* (In Whatever Mode). It purposely lacks clef-signs, the result being that for whichever mode the singers choose they must so supply clefs that pleasant relations will be maintained among the individual voices —this in addition to the fact that they must insert accidentals!

Notorious among Okeghem's displays of technical dexterity is the canon *Deo gratias.* This is essentially "paper music," more to be admired by the astonished eye than heard by the unconvinced ear. But it is an indicative example of the learning and virtuosity of technique at which fifteenth-century musical crea-

tors had arrived. *"Deo gratias"* is repeated and repeated throughout the canon, which requires thirty-six singers, nine each of altos,
sopranos, tenors, and basses. The altos start the complex pro-
ceedings, entering one by one for nine successive measures, each
beginning the melody anew, though not always at the same pitch.
When all nine of the altos are singing together, the sopranos enter
similarly, one by one, measure after measure, until eighteen
voices are singing eighteen fragments of the same melody at once.
When the tenors begin to add their voices, however, the altos fall
silent; when the basses begin to enter, the sopranos desist. The
thirty-six voices never sing all together, but even eighteen voices
singing sections of a melody make, structurally speaking, a musical fabric of very considerable complexity. To avoid fierce outbursts of unwanted dissonance, Okeghem had to select or design
his melody with a degree of care that resulted in parched
monotony.

This game among experts is a world removed from Gregorian
Chant or its first simple adaptations intended to exalt the glory
of God. Josquin des Prés was to play it successfully for even
higher stakes in *Qui habitat in adjutorio,* a canon to full text: in
it six each of sopranos, altos, tenors, and basses finally succeed in
singing together twenty-four sections of a melody.

In 1501, when Ottaviano dei Petrucci, expanding the young
process of printing music from movable metal type, issued the
first important musical book ever thus printed, he included no
pieces by Jean de Okeghem. But of Okeghem's more winning and
musically gracious contemporary, Jacob Obrecht, he put into his
Harmonice musices odhecaton A two secular compositions. Eight
of Obrecht's Masses, as well as many of his chansons and motets,
were printed later.

The polyphonic chanson, though likely to be cast (or partly
cast) in one of the patterns that had come down from the troubadours and trouvères, was inclining toward a new simplicity. It
was also signaling a tendency to evoke new patterns, often used
but once and then discarded, which were related to the demands
of the texts selected. Okeghem and, particularly, Obrecht put
into secular chansons some of their most winning and persuasive

ideas. Although these were probably conceived either as purely vocal pieces or as largely vocal pieces with instrumental support, conclusive evidence exists that the possibility of wholly instrumental performances was not ruled out. There were readings of these scores in which the melodic line of each voice was played on an individual instrument.

Like many of his Netherlandish and other northern contemporaries, Obrecht helped spread the new virtuosity to Italy by living and working there. He served both Ercole d'Este—the patron of Ariosto—and Lorenzo the Magnificent. He had no musical protégé so famous as Josquin (who often seems more influenced by Obrecht than by Okeghem), but at one time numbered among his pupils the great scholar Desiderius Erasmus. Most of his works are set to Latin texts, but his French chansons uncover a lively secular temperament: one of them has the timeless subject *Tant que notre argent durera* ("As long as our money lasts"). On the basis of one setting, for use during Holy Week, of the Passion of Christ —including the Seven Last Words—Obrecht was long cited as a forerunner of Johann Sebastian Bach in his great Matthew and John Passions. But this large polyphonic structure (in which there is no attempt at the Bachian dramatic differentiation of roles) is no longer believed by scholars to be Obrecht's work.

The Netherlands School [3] was partly a reaction against the increasing secularization heralded by Dunstable, Machaut, Dufay, and Binchois. If assessed quantitatively, it was more sacred in emphasis. It concentrated on the Mass and the sacred motet. Using scriptural texts, the Netherlanders habitually composed motets for four, five, six, and even more voices. Although Okeghem's surviving motets indicate a preference for a *cantus firmus* in long-held notes, with the other voices uncoiling melismatically, Obrecht and his followers developed the more specifically harmonic manner of conceiving the voices together vertically, in chords. Known as the "familiar" style, this concept resulted in a

---

[3] Various groupings of the northern-born composers of this era have been designated "Late Burgundian School" and "Middle Flemish School," but "Netherlandish" seems more accurate when the group is made to include Belgians, Hollanders, and belated Burgundians.

texture allowing the Latin syllables to be understood. All the singers pronounce the same syllables simultaneously, to notes held for equal durations. In both manners the most accomplished and talented of the Netherlanders wrought motets of enduring beauty expressing with certainty the religious attitudes of an epoch in which such men as Botticelli, Leonardo da Vinci, and Dürer were painting and Christopher Columbus was sailing west in search of Cathay.

The Mass quoting all or fragments of a secular melody continued to hold the creative attention of the Netherlanders. The long-popular *"L'homme armé"* continued, for example, to challenge the repeated ingenuity of composers in the *"cantus firmus* Mass," so called because the adapted melody was used in the *tenor.* Both Okeghem and Obrecht employed other secular melodies that were popularly known to accompany familiar amorous or narrative texts in the national language. Both men also composed what appear to be wholly original Masses in which no previously existing melodies are imbedded.

So complex and absorbing had the available techniques of vocal polyphony become, so adept were choristers in the great churches of the Netherlands, France, and Italy, that independent instrumental music advanced little in those countries during this period. Music for instruments was, of course, both composed and performed, but its comparatively feeble development—except, perhaps, as the alternate method of performing primarily vocal music—proves that it did not enlist the full energies of the most accomplished composers of the time, who continued to be more attracted to the turreted castles they could design and erect out of language and vocal sound.

It is doubtful that any instrumental music fully comparable in scope to the best vocal works of Okeghem, Obrecht, and Josquin made its appearance before the seventeenth-century days of the surpassing Northern organists. Instruments continued evolving and differentiating themselves, notably early or ancestral forms of the harpsichord (string plucked by plectrums activated from a keyboard), the clavichord (strings vibrated by wedges fastened to the back of leverlike keys extended from a keyboard, the wedges also serving to "divide" the strings into lengths and thus determine their sounding pitch as the fingers do on violin strings), and various sorts and sizes of horns, flutes, recorders, and viols.

This was the musical world in which Josquin des Prés (1445?-1521) reached resplendent maturity, the most honored and glittering individual in the history of music to his day. Not primarily an experimenter or innovator, Josquin (in this resembling Bach) most fully exploited the technical resources of his era, putting them masterfully at the service of an intense poetic sensitivity and a copious imagination. His Masses and motets are not very different in technique from those of his contemporaries and immediate predecessors: they are simply better achieved and more expressive, whether judged obliquely as appropriate settings of text or squarely as music. Ronsard, the foremost French poet of the time, placed Josquin at the head of "excelling workers in the art [of music]," while Henricus Glareanus gave him in music the rank that Vergil held in poetry. His works were published widely while he lived, and were performed all over Europe. Martin Luther, a musically learned man, said: "Musicians do with notes what they can. Josquin does with them what he wishes."

Josquin was worldly and sophisticated. His music gleams with wit, with lively humor. He could play musical paper-games with the best of his contemporaries, but he was more interested in sound, its effective manipulation and its beauties. It is known that he was sometimes dissatisfied with one of his new compositions when he heard it sung and would then alter its notes to make it *sound* better. For sheer glory of sounding voices, his six-part masterpieces may never have been exceeded. He contributed little to the history of musical technique, much to music as a means of expression. Except for influencing his pupils and imitators, he changed music's direction little—much less, for example, than Okeghem. But the repertoire of vocal polyphony would be more impoverished by the deletion of his surviving works than by the loss of Okeghem's.

Josquin blazed like a sun. In that brilliance, the lesser lights of his most talented and craftsmanlike contemporaries now seem to have paled. It would be a mistake to forget those others or to leave their music unperformed. But in a study devoted to musical *means,* to the understanding of music's parts of speech, Josquin himself has a small place and they have none. Their names retain a flowery charm—Loyset Compère, Pierre de la Rue, Jean Mouton, Antoine Brumel, the Huguenots Claude Goudimel and Claude le Jeune—or a fine strength—Heinrich Isaak. But the practices of music were not materially modified in their hands.

In the middle years of the sixteenth century, the evolution of the chanson in France was paralleled in Italy by that of the later, now more familiar, type of madrigal. This was at first—and for some decades—chiefly the work of Flemings living in Italy and of Italians. Not by any measurement a strict musical form, the sixteenth-century madrigal was a vocal composition for three, four, and later five unaccompanied singers. Its texts dealt with nature, love, and death. The manners of madrigal performance suggest later chamber music, for the singers most often sat at a table with their music before them, and the entire atmosphere was intentionally intimate.

Although madrigals composed in the 1530's by such Flemish musicians as Jacob Arcadelt (1514?-1570?) and Philippe Verdelot, and such native Italians as Girolamo Carlo and Costanzo Festa (?-1545) were preponderantly homophonic in texture, consisting of a primary melodic line accompanied by the other voices, the pieces shortly thereafter became much more polyphonic. The finest motets of the Venetian Flemings like Adrian Willaert (1480?-1562), Cipriano de (or van) Rore (1516-1565), and Philippe de Monte (1521?-1603) contain five voices of substantially equal interest. In their hands, in fact, the madrigal was becoming the secular counterpart of the motet.

The later sixteenth-century madrigal evolved into a highly integrated poetico-musical means of expressing intense personal emotions. The high Renaissance was at hand, and many of these flowery madrigals show the defining characteristics of what we call romantic music. Their eager search for emotional expressiveness led such men as Willaert, Rore, and the later Carlo Gesualdo (1560?-1613) to previously unheard-of melodic use of semitone intervals not native to the scale employed: chromaticism.

The combining of several chromatic melodies inevitably produced chromatic chordal progressions. It is this chromaticism which still lends the madrigals of Willaert, Rore, Gesualdo, and others their peculiar, intense, plaintive quality.

In Italy the madrigal became constantly more complex, at last giving rein not only to so idiosyncratic a style as that of Gesualdo, but also to the virtuoso singer and to programmatic, coloristic effects. Scarcely an important Italian musician of the last half of the sixteenth century and the opening years of the seventeenth but wrote in madrigals some of his most personal and characteristic music. Too, the madrigal spread to England (where it was optionally called ayre, canzonet, sonet, or even just song), to Spain, and to the states of Germany. Of these offshoots, by far the most fruitful was the English, of which the first surpassing master was the greatest composer Britain had yet produced, William Byrd (1543-1623), a somewhat older contemporary of Shakespeare.

FURTHER EVOLUTION OF POLYPHONY

ORLANDO DI LASSO · PALESTRINA

VICTORIA · BYRD · INSTRUMENTAL IDIOM

The techniques of Burgundian, German, and Netherlandish composers were spread across Europe by their practitioners as they labored in the chapels of kings, princes, popes, and dukes. As the period now called the Renaissance began, the Netherlands proper witnessed a decline in the supremacy of local music as Netherlandish inheritors, altering their teachers' practices in national, local, and personal ways, began preparing another of music's great periods. This time the light was to blaze chiefly in Italy, Spain, and England. Vocal polyphony was to have its freest and its most formally successful manifestation, after Josquin des Prés, chiefly in the work of four men. Only one of them was a Fleming by birth, and by career he was as international as Igor Stravinsky. The other three were an Italian, a Spaniard, and an Englishman.

The Fleming Roland de Laittre (whose name is usually Latinized into Orlandus Lassus or Italianized into Orlando di Lasso), Palestrina, and Victoria are often erroneously exalted above both Josquin and William Byrd. Perhaps they were individually superior in certain respects, but such superiority is at most a matter of shading. What matters here is what each composer did to alter the language of music and how each used it—both as he encountered it and as he changed it in the process of adapting it to his

own purposes. We shall find that it was Palestrina, Orlando di
Lasso, and Victoria who brought a period in music to a close,
not Josquin and Byrd. We shall find Byrd clearly foreshadowing
the future by being almost equally attracted by—and adept at—
vocal and instrumental practices. Never again since Orlando and
Palestrina died in 1594 and Victoria in 1613, have the greatest
composers worked primarily in vocal polyphony.

The year of Victoria's death marked one of the most definite
boundaries in the history of music. On the other side of it, music
had meant singing; on this side, in most of the civilized world, it
would mean music for voices and music for instruments in varying proportions. For centuries on the other side of it, music had
meant polyphony; on this side, music would mean, in varying
proportions, polyphony (or its parallel, instrumental counterpoint) and chordal harmony and accompanied melody. On the
other side of it, music had meant largely sacred music, with composed secular music comparatively unimpressive in quantity; on
this side of it, music would mean secular and sacred music in
varying proportions, with secular more and more predominating.
Before 1613 was at hand, however, the musical era that first
reached its height in Josquin's maturity was to produce in unaccompanied vocal polyphony one spate of the most magnificent
of all musical creations.

Melody, basic to music from any discernible beginnings of the
art, basic today, was meanwhile being forced to share its leading
role more and more with harmony. A brief backward look will
recall that the earliest forms of polyphony contained the germ of
what we have come to call harmony, the germ that has always
lived in the physical make-up of sound and of overtones. In many
of the earliest known examples, a *duplum* exactly paralleled the
tenor, thus (if looked at vertically) producing simultaneous combinations of tones which were almost, but not quite, chords.[1]
Usually at intervals of a fifth or a fourth, but additionally in
octaves and thirds, this type of parallel *órganum* was not, in our

[1] The word chord is now customarily reserved for combinations of three or more
simultaneously sounded (or implied) tones.

modern sense of the term, harmony. But it made harmony inevitable unless music was mortally to limit itself. How closely
the gradual acceptance of intervals as consonant was related to
the physical nature of sound becomes clear when we recall that
the first natural overtone is removed from the basic tone by an
octave, the second from the first by a fifth, the third from the
second by a fourth, and the fourth from the third by a third—
approximately the historical order in which the octave, fifth,
fourth, and third were accepted as consonant and therefore as
widely useful.

By the end of the tenth century the parallel phase of *órganum*
had begun to give way to the freer type, in which the *duplum,*
often by then the higher of the two voices, moved in oblique and
contrary motion and broke into several successive tones to each
tone in the *tenor.* This was still not harmony, for the forward,
horizontal movement of distinct melodies remained the ruling
factor in the minds of composers and singers. Although some
combinations of simultaneous tones—some intervals—were felt to
be more pleasant, more permissible, than others, there was as yet
no well-defined structural concept based on the manner in which
one interval might best succeed another. This is the essential
difference in meaning between chord (two, or more strictly three,
or more different tones sounded at once) and harmony (the
arranged, orderly succession of chords and of the relationships
among them).

Free *órganum* split, during the first half of the twelfth century,
into variants of itself. One of these was different only in rhythm:
instead of moving by the free meters of earlier *órganum,* determined by the length of syllables in Latin texts, it was regulated
by the rhythmic modes. In other variants, a *triplum* and *quadruplum* were added to the *tenor* and *duplum,* thus producing
what resembles, but is not, three- and four-part harmony. It is
not harmony because it is still a succession of incidentally related
chords, each of which occurs only because several melodies hap-
pen to come together thus at given points. Melismata had become
elaborate: the principal voice was often slowed down so that the
other voice or voices could sing whole groups of notes to each of

its tones. Music was yearning toward harmony, making use of many of its future materials without truly becoming harmonic. There is not any doubt of an increasing awareness of vertical, chordal structure, but a succession of chords is not in itself harmony unless the relations among them have an important effect on the choice of tones employed. The status of *órganum* during the twelfth century was semi-harmonic.

Feelings about consonance and dissonance meanwhile developed and changed, as they always have. Consonance is the name given to the pleasant or restful effect that certain intervals and successions of intervals produce; dissonance is its opposite, the relatively unpleasant, dissatisfied, and therefore unrestful effect that certain other combinations of tones produce. These feelings are in large part subjective; they shift constantly, not only from century to century, but even individually, as experienced by a single listener at different stages in his musical awareness. These feelings are, however, also the response of the ear and the mind to aspects of the constitution of sound itself. Some ears, some eras, some minds, are more tolerant than others; some find *this* pleasant, *that* unpleasant, while others reverse *this* and *that*. This agitated and endlessly discussed subject is a physico-psychological mixture as little explicable by present-day knowledge as is the difference between a cheap tune and a noble melody.

There is proof in the earliest *órganum* that singers and listeners of the time found both the fifth and the fourth to be pleasant intervals. Further, as the voices remained parallel for most of the duration of a piece, it is certain that singers and listeners were not jarred by sequences of fourths and fifths. By the early nineteenth century, however, though the fourth and fifth were both still held to be consonances, a series of parallel fifths was considered by schoolmen (who had their reasons) to be a compositional sin. The octave was certainly a consonance always: it is impossible to conceive of its being considered dissonant. But, again, scholastic harmony would find in that very fact sufficient reasons for considering a series of *parallel* octaves sinful.

During the eleventh and twelfth centuries such previously ostracized chordal intervals as the sixth and the third began to assert their usefulness. But they were considered, if not dissonant, less consonant—that is, restless and relatively unpleasant—and were therefore avoided at the openings and closings of compositions, as they were until the twentieth century. Further, intervals still regarded by many musicians as dissonances, such as sevenths and seconds, occurred where they could immediately be erased by a following consonance. This is a straight harmonic concept: that the presence of one chord may make desirable (or be retroactively excused by) the presence of another. Even though such dissonant-consonant sequences occurred because the forward movement of simultaneous melodies produced them incidentally, the fact that they are numerous shows that the harmonic sense had begun to be one of the architectural means of music.

Sometimes a composer felt that he could heighten interest in the profile of a melody by decorating one of its tones—that is, by preceding a tone with a briefly sounded nearby tone (usually the tone just above or just below it). Known as an *appoggiatura*, from the Italian *appoggiare*, "to rest on," this incidental tone often formed, with a tone sung simultaneously in another voice, a dissonant interval. As the *appoggiatura* was sounded very briefly, however, it produced only a very temporary dissonance. Or a dissonance might occur between two consonances because of a composer's feeling of the way his melodies must advance. When harmonic practices came to be codified, this sort of non-harmonic tone was denominated a "passing" tone because it occurred in passage from one consonant or basic interval to another and because any dissonance of which it formed a part was thus quickly succeeded by a healing consonance.

Constantly the listening musical ear was enlarging its awareness. Insensibly, but certainly, it was also increasing its hospitality. An interval that one century felt to be dissonant, the next century might hear so often as to come to accept it without any sensation of restlessness or unpleasantness. It would then decide to call that interval consonant. Theorists, listeners, composers, and performers became constantly more tolerant, until in our own time there have been many to say that though consonance and dissonance have temporary realities, they are unimportant abso-

lutely, and should be disregarded in favor of other more important musical facts. Not all ears and minds travel at the same
speed or to the same regions, and the complaint of many music-
lovers that too much modern music is "discordant" really means
that modern composers have found formerly dissonant junctions
and sequences of tones both pleasant in themselves and worthy
of prominence, "consonant" in every sense but that implied by
abstruse technical explanations. To their own satisfaction and
that of some listeners, they have reduced "consonant" and "dissonant" to purely historico-technical terms.

Those of us who have been formed largely on the music of the
eighteenth and nineteenth centuries cannot help finding the masterpieces of the true golden age of vocal polyphony a little exotic
in texture. They remain on the other side of what was, until
music's yesterday, the farther limit of our own age. Palestrina
sounds modern when contrasted with Dunstable or Binchois, but
he sounds ancient, somehow loose and texturally indecisive despite the surpassing loveliness of his melodies, if we listen to him
with mental ears that have been conquered by Bach, Handel,
Haydn, Mozart, and Beethoven. Of Palestrina, Orlando, Victoria,
Byrd, and their contemporaries and less mighty followers what
was true of Gregorian Chant is still true: if we are to attempt hearing them almost as they heard themselves, we must make every
effort to listen to their music as melody upon melody moving
forward in time.[2] For despite its proto-harmonic features, their
music was still intentionally melody before anything else.

With the Italian Giovanni Pierluigi da Palestrina (1525?-1594),
the Flemish Orlando di Lasso (1530?-1594), the Spanish Tomás
Luis de Victoria (1535?-1613), and the English William Byrd
(1543-1623), unaccompanied vocal polyphony reached its Hima-
layas, points so high in accomplishment that to rise beyond them
became quite simply impossible. Of the three great Continental
composers, only Victoria strikes today's average ears as notably
original, and that semblance of originality is partly a result of

---

[2] This is not true of all of Byrd's music, some of which, as will shortly be shown,
had stopped being polyphony.

our unfamiliarity with his Spanish predecessors. For these great composers added astonishingly little to the materials, the historic evolution, of musical means. They were summations. In their compositions they brought to a final ripening the developments with which this book has thus far been concerned. They did not, in any important positive sense, point toward the future or hint what their most important successors would do to and for the art of music. In their air of finality they belong, not with path-finders like Okeghem, Haydn, Beethoven, Wagner, and Stravin-sky, but with the monumental composers who satisfied themselves and their listeners by doing superbly what others had already done, men like Josquin des Prés, Bach, and Brahms.

Palestrina, who was invited by Gregory XIII to edit the body of Gregorian Chant in the Gradual and the Antiphonary (a task he did not live to complete), was endowed with unsleeping good taste. Devoting himself largely to Church music—nearly one hun-dred of his Masses survive, for example—he composed nothing excessive, almost nothing that was not superbly devotional, noth-ing that was not right and just in whole and in detail. His worldly positions gave the most highly trained chapel singers into his hands more often than not, and for the greater glory of God he strained their capabilities to the limit, but never beyond it.[3] He most often seems as impersonal, as non-subjective as Gregorian Chant itself, but that is because his passion, his large emotional energy, has been wholly transmuted into the terms of religious music as the best musicians of his era understood it—polyphonic and modal, but with occasional clauses and sentences all but fully

[3] Curt Sachs has pointed out that these singers, notably those in the Papal Chapel, "were famous for their skill in dissolving the plain notation on their music sheets in fluent graces and coloraturas." We must not, that is, suppose that actual per-formances of Palestrina's music—or that of his contemporaries—were confined to the notes set down by the composer. The Renaissance was in blossom, and the day was still far distant (Dr. Sachs himself sets it as late as 1800) when performers would be required to produce only the notes in the score before them. I cannot agree, how-ever, with those who bewail the fact that (to quote Sachs again) "the solemn, stately voice parts of Roman polyphony were never heard in the sober form that the scores suggest." It is senseless to apply a Protestant prejudice in favor of simplicity to Ro-man Catholic music of the Renaissance—and the real point is that the great ex-amples of Roman polyphony are so magnificently conceived that no amount of expert decoration could effectively mask their structural strength and beauty.

harmonic. He composed some secular music, including madrigals
honoring the glories of Italian women, but his major effort went
into the weaving of religious musical fabrics strong enough to
resist time. With good reason he is regarded as one of the greatest
of composers.

A man of altogether different cast was Orlando di Lasso. A
minor statesman of importance, the friend and confidant of the
politically powerful, he somehow found time to become one of
the most productive composers of all time. His known compositions run to nearly two thousand. In one sense, he alone in his
time points toward the future: he is often dramatic to the point
of theatricality, and thus seems to suggest the imminent emergence of opera. But he is more clearly the summation and climax
of the musical traditions of the North. Beside Orlando's brawling
vigor, Palestrina sounds at first a little pallid; beside the incredible variety of Orlando's motets, madrigals, villanelle, psalms,
French chansons, German lieder, and other forms, Palestrina's
scope appears at first a little narrow. But Orlando, for all his
suave mastery, did not come close to Palestrina's unbroken purity
of style, which finally gives the Italian's music the strength that
resides in any perfectly proportioned structure. Only in his
Masses and his powerful Seven Penitential Psalms did Orlando
equal the religious fervor and formal perfections of his foremost
contemporary.

Victoria was the first great mystic to be a composer. He was,
too, a Spaniard. He alone of the sixteenth-century geniuses wrote
no secular music whatever: he looked upon his compositions as
manifestations of mystical religious devotion. To modern ears
tuned to hear them well, his Masses, motets, and great *Officium
defunctorum* (Requiem) swirl with a heady, curious mixture of
the sacred and the not-quite-sublimated fleshly, with an almost
neurasthenic intensity. In the melodic ways by which they somehow hint also at the African and gypsy turns that have given more
recent Spanish music its peculiar quality, we can locate one of
the causes of an unquestionable originality not always distant
from eccentricity. Certainly religious passion has seldom been suggested by music of such direct intensity. It is an appropriate and

suggestive fact that Victoria was a contemporary both of El Greco and of those God-driven Spanish mystics, Teresa of Ávila and Ignatius Loyola.

It was to these peaks that the innate necessity to do something to plainsong and other simple melodic lines had led. For centuries composers had been celebrating the Christian God and helping their fellowmen to worship Him through the beauties of many voices lifted together. Instrumental music had seemed less effective for their purposes, and most of them had developed it only incidentally. But while Palestrina, Orlando, and Victoria were living and dying there occurred in Italy, Spain, the Netherlands, France, and the Germanies, and across the Channel in Britain, a number of feeble beginnings of developments that would shortly leave in the past many of the techniques they had employed.

The first master composer to divide his creative efforts appreciably, in quality if not in quantity, between unaccompanied sacred vocal polyphony and secular instrumental music was, in fact, a slightly younger contemporary of the great completers. He was England's foremost musician after Dunstable, William Byrd.

It was the opinion of François-Joseph Fétis, expressed in the course of his eight-volume *Biographie Universelle des Musiciens* (1837-44) that "Byrd was the Palestrina and the Orlando di Lasso of England." This in itself would indicate that if Byrd had composed nothing but his three Masses (one each for three, four, and five voices), he would still lay claim to an exalted position in the history of his art. His contributions to *Cantiones quae ab argumento sacrae vocantur* (1575), the earliest known book of Latin motets to be published in England, are also marvels of expressive contrapuntal composition for as many as eight voices. Although this book was in part the work of Thomas Tallis (1505?-1585), possibly Byrd's teacher and certainly his colleague for a time in the Chapel Royal, Byrd later published collections of sacred songs entirely his own. Among these, the two groups of *Gradualia* (1605, 1607) are wonderful amalgamations of self-sufficiently expressive music and the apt, incisive setting of Latin texts.

Byrd also composed sacred music for use in the Church of

England. Here, encountering few set patterns on which to mold
his materials, he had to evolve the necessary musical forms from
the hints and trials about him. He succeeded so brilliantly that
English liturgical music kept for a long time (perhaps too long
a time) the patterns he set. From his teeming imagination and
untiring hand there poured psalms, anthems, *preces,* sacred songs,
and whole services. Of these last, the so-called Great Service is a
masterpiece as impressive as his Catholic Mass in Five Voices.

This protean Englishman was deeply and permanently marked
by the manners of the Italian madrigal. This influence is easily
apparent in his Church music, whether Latin or English—in frequent imitations of non-musical sounds, in a dramatic boldness
as striking as Orlando's. The English madrigal was to have a
variegated flowering, and Byrd's contributions to it added to the
strength of its colors and the sweetness of its perfume. Beside the
firmest and most vivid of Byrd's own madrigals, in fact, even the
piercingly tender pieces of such other Englishmen as Thomas
Morley (1557-1603?), Thomas Weelkes (?-1623), John Wilbye
(1574-1638), and Orlando Gibbons (1583-1625) seem to lack
vitality.

Byrd's vocal compositions would more than suffice to establish
him as a sovereign musical creator. But what more clearly helped
to shape the nature of the musical future was his understanding,
sure-handed writing for instruments. To his songs for solo voice,
for example, he composed accompaniments for four viols, accompaniments that astonish by the real instrumentality of their style.
In texture they are almost string quartets, far more original in
conception than the lute accompaniments to the ever-charming
songs of John Dowland (1563-1626). Byrd went farther still, composing instrumental fantaisies for groups of three, four, five, and
six instruments (there is even one for seven) which may well be
the oldest composed string music entirely independent of vocal
style. Although he was adept at writing for the various sizes of
viols, he also helped to formulate the future of the later-developed
violin, viola, and violoncello, using them together, composing
chamber music of a charm comparable to that of the later string
trios and quartets of Haydn.

What music had been composed earlier than that of Byrd and his younger contemporary, John Bull (1562-1628),[4] for early forms of the clavichord and harpsichord had been largely polyphonic vocal music directly transcribed, or at least music conceived as a parallel to vocal polyphony. But Byrd, writing probably for the primitive harpsichord known as the virginal or "pair of virginals,"[5] found ideas and time to delineate a style and a texture derived directly from the capabilities of its keyboard. Here he deserted polyphony for homophony, the musical texture in which a melody is supported on accompanying tones or chords. He created the keyboard variation, a form that, undergoing constant extensions and change, remains viable today, having evoked enduring music from, among many, Bach, Handel, Haydn, Mozart, Beethoven, and Brahms. Some of Byrd's virginal pieces are adaptations of previously existing vocal music, but these have been translated wholly into idiomatic keyboard terms. He employed dance forms (*"pavana," "galiardo"*) on the keyboard too, prefiguring the dance-form suites of Bach and Handel. Although Byrd was a great religious and vocal composer, his historical influence was most germinative in the direction of the increasing secularization and instrumentalization of music. In his own person he bridged the golden age of religious vocal polyphony and the first great era of music that dispensed with the human voice.

[4] It was partly through Bull's friendship with Sweelinck and their exchange of compositions and musical compliments that the discoveries of the English keyboard composers influenced the fertile school of North German organists which was to culminate in Johann Sebastian Bach. Bull himself was an accomplished organist and composer for the organ.

[5] The derivation of the name virginal for this harpsichord is uncertain. It may have become attached to the instrument because it was considered particularly appropriate for playing by young girls, or it may have reflected the Latin word for the rod or jack that was animated by the virginal's keys, *virga*. The idea that it honored Elizabeth, "the Virgin Queen," is disproved by the occurrence of the word before her reign. Equally uncertain is the confusing phrase "pair of virginals" as referring to a single instrument.

THE ORGAN · INSTRUMENTAL FORMS · FUGUE
SWEELINCK · SCHEIDT · EARLY HOMOPHONY

Although the organ traditionally descends from the syrinx, or pipes of Pan—a small row of mouth-blown pipes bound together side by side in a flat triangular shape—it first attained something of its modern character in Alexandria about the middle of the third century B.C. Its history is as complex as its structure. Its basic principle is that air under pressure is released through a series of graduated pipes, producing tones of varying pitch and timbre. In modern organs, the release of air is controlled from one or more keyboards, by foot-operated pedals, and by hand-operated pistons. Various mechanisms have been evolved to make possible the sounding of two or more pipes at once by the operation of one controlling unit. Handily the most complex of all musical instruments, the organ occurs in uncounted variations of size, make-up, and flexibility.

In Western Europe the organ, increasingly up to about 1300, supported or doubled the single melodic line of plainsong or the *vox principalis* in such early polyphony as *órganum*. Technical limitations and both the audibility and the multiplicity of its jangling overtones long kept the organ from use in purely instrumental polyphony: on organs of the earlier periods, the performance of almost any polyphony would have evoked an unsortable blur of unwanted tonal relationships. During the thirteenth and four-

66

teenth centuries, however, in part as the result of improvements in the design of the instrument, a variety of the vocal sequence-trope began to be written for the organ alone.

Known as the *estampie,* this polyphonic organ form varied in pattern. Most commonly it consisted of from four to seven melodic sections, each played twice in succession. These sections, called *puncti* (points), each had two different endings or closes, one for the first statement, the other for the second. The evolution of the *estampie* from secular vocal music is clearly suggested by this verselike pattern. In all probability the form developed first as accompaniment to dancing.

While the organ was becoming constantly more complicated and more flexible, English, Italian, and German organists and composers were working out methods of noting down music to be played on it. Tablatures, as these notations were called, were also increasingly used for the music of such other instruments as virginals, flutes, lutes, guitars, and viols. They differed from the notation for vocal music chiefly in that they substituted alphabetic letters, numbers, or conventional symbols for notes. Also, when used for keyboard instruments, the tablatures were intended to be read as successions of vertical groupings rather than as distinct lines of horizontal melody.

During the fourteenth century, *estampies* and instrumental motets were set down in organ tablature, for the instrument had begun to be used for the solo performance of complex music. The German organists employed tablatures widely during the fifteenth century, and later wrote out not only such transplanted Italian vocal forms as the *ricercar* and *canzona,* but also free preludes, examples of a quasi-improvisational form wholly native to the keyboard. In the free preludes preserved in tablature from about 1450 on, German organists composed brief pieces that were not consistently either monophonic or polyphonic. Their alternations of chords with passages in single notes were to become standard practices of the first half of the eighteenth century, when Handel and Bach flourished. These organists also built into increasingly massive instrumental compositions the Protestant hymn melodies called chorales, evolving such instrumental forms as the chorale prelude and chorale fantasia.

The first important name in German organ composition is that of Conrad Paumann (1410?-1473). Although born blind, Paumann became a performer of extraordinary proficiency on, among other instruments, organ, lute, and flute. He was honored by emperors, princes, and dukes, and was decorated by the pope. A relative handful of Paumann's organ compositions survives, and of them most appear to be simple two-voice exercises for the training of other organists. Another blind organist, Arnolt Schlick the elder (1460?-1517?), composed instrumental arrangements of chorales which are already almost chorale preludes.

A very remarkable—though little known—school of organ composition flourished in sixteenth-century Spain. Its towering figure was Antonio de Cabezón (1510-1566), still another blind organist— the organ has always been *par excellence* the instrument of the blind. Cabezón resembled Byrd in his strong feeling for the idiomatic nature of keyboard composition, as also in his development of variation techniques. Serving both Charles V and Philip II as organist and harpsichordist, he evolved a courtly instrumental art of enormous originality. In Italy, meanwhile, another important school of organists evolved. Its most prominent members were the Venetian Gabrielis, Andrea the uncle (1510?-1586) and Giovanni the nephew (1557-1612), and the most renowned organ virtuoso of his time, Girolamo Frescobaldi (1583-1643), a composer of very great talent. In France, too, Jean Titelouze (1563-1633) initiated a national school of the organ.

But the surpassing period of organ music was inaugurated by a Netherlander who may, when very young, have studied with Andrea Gabrieli: Jan Pieterszoon Sweelinck (1562-1621). Sweelinck, a musician of genius, gave increased importance to the pedals, thus helping to enlarge the organ's resources for both composer and performer. From the *ricercari* and fantasias composed by his antecedents and contemporaries, Sweelinck evolved real fugues for organ, thus setting a pattern as important as the free prelude.

The fugue is the most richly organized form of imitation. In a fugue, a short melody or melodic fragment is first stated by one voice or part and then taken up, in imitation, by other voices or parts, traditionally three or four in number, though other numbers occur. The voices or parts enter in quick succession, and the melody or fragment of melody eventually appears in all of them. Other melodic figures are often added to employ voices or parts when they are not occupied in pronouncing the chief theme; in this the fugue diverges from the strict canon or round, in which no material other than the theme is used. As developed and altered by both major and minor composers, the fugue became malleable enough to emerge as one of the most fruitful and widely used musical patterns as long as counterpoint ruled. Its usefulness diminished in the first era of homophony, but resurged when counterpoint and harmony began to be mixed skillfully. To our own day, even in the hands of extreme modernists, the fugue has continued to delight composers by its unremitting challenge to ingenuity, listeners by its expressive and climactic potentialities.

Sweelinck also borrowed the variation principle from the earlier clavier and virginal composers, made superior creative use of purely instrumental figurations, and in general prefigured the organ and harpsichord compositions of Bach. Although he was also an accomplished creator of sacred and secular vocal music, in which he combined a learned use of imitation and a forward-tending sense of rhythm, Sweelinck is known best now as a composer for organ. His pupils and emulators formed a real constellation of stars. One of them, Samuel Scheidt (1587-1654), reacted in irritation against the superficial "coloristic" tablatures being issued all about him—coloristic here indicating a manner of composing in which musically meaningless *colorature* were appended to almost every important note. In the third volume of his history-making *Tabulatura nova* (1624), Scheidt disclosed sacred organ music of sober, powerful expressiveness. Making extensive use of fugal forms, Scheidt also prepared the way for the Northern Baroque, the so-called "Gothic" style, which expanded the length of organ compositions, including the toccata, another instrumental form of enduring usefulness.

Although the exact meanings of musical terms alter with time, it is instructive to note the differences originally implied among *sonata* (in which instruments were sounded), *cantata* (in which voices sang), and *toccata* (in which sounds were touched into vibration through a keyboard). Andrea Gabrieli had composed toccatas in which, as in free preludes, chords and single-note passages were alternated with chords. In the toccatas of the Gothic style, there are also contrapuntal passages in *fugato,* fuguelike matter imbedded in music not strictly fugal. The toccata, that is, was becoming an extended keyboard composition in which composers felt increasingly free to lodge the most varied musical thoughts.

In large outline the genealogy that led from Scheidt to Johann Sebastian Bach was double, consisting of a North German line and a Middle German line. The Gothic style was chiefly the province of the Northerners, outstanding among whom were Johann Adam Reinken (1623-1722), Dietrich Buxtehude (1637-1707), and Vincent Lübeck (1654-1740). The Middle German line began with Heinrich Bach (1615-1692), grandfather of Johann Sebastian, and included Johann Pachelbel (1635-1706), Johann Kuhnau (1660-1722), and several members of the prolific Bach family. These men tended to content themselves with shorter, simpler organ compositions than those which satisfied their Northern comtemporaries.

A little to one side of this double genealogy stood the South German school of organists. Predominantly Roman Catholic (in contrast to the mostly Protestant lines from Scheidt to Bach and Handel), the South Germans absorbed Italian and French manners, and naturally proceeded without the Protestant chorales so basic to the music of the other Germans. The earliest important South German organ-composer was Johann Jacob Froberger (1616-1667). A pupil of the magnificent Frescobaldi, Froberger favored the toccata, several varieties of *canzona*-with-variations, and the capriccio, which he interpreted as still another sort of variation-*canzona.* He was intimately familiar with the keyboard compositions of his contemporaries in France, and he imported many of their novel practices into German organ music. In his harpsichord compositions, indeed, he followed the French manner of combining short, dancelike movements, developing the keyboard suite, a varied and important form later cultivated by both Handel and Bach. Froberger's influence on other South Germans shows most in the fact that his successors nearly always preferred Italian and French practices to those of other parts of Germany.

Both Netherlandish and German organists also wrote vocal music, sacred and secular, and pieces for rapidly evolving forms of clavichord and harpsichord. In whatever medium and in whatever patterns they cast their musical materials, they were unknowingly hastening the end of polyphony's sovereignty. All felt free to introduce homophonic passages into polyphonic textures. Most showed disregard of, even unfamiliarity with, modal usages. Coming into view in the faded leaves of their published music is the major-minor division of classic harmony.

More important than the willing acceptance and employment of an increased variety of chords was the increasingly strong underlying assumption that some chords naturally "resolve" into others, evoke a desire for other chords to follow them. Certain chords are relatively static, seem not to bespeak onward motion. Others ask for fulfillment, require other combinations of tones for the release of the psychological tension, however small, that they themselves set up. The profound assumption that there is a natural logic of chord-progression is, as already pointed out, a theorem of harmony as understood in the eighteenth and nineteenth centuries.

Once the modal system had been all but entirely left to the past, once the sensation of chordal logic had diluted the belief that music, when not a single unaccompanied melody, was a fabric of disparate melodies moving forward in time together, then the classical system of harmony had become inevitable. But anti-modernists who speak as though that classical system of harmony were established forever, who claim that artistic sanity requires its present dominance too, forget that it achieved its perfections slowly, in response to the changing demands of the listening ear. When the listening ear no longer demands change in response to outward and inward logic and stimuli, the only predictable fate for the art of music is stultification.

Another proof of the drift toward classic harmony marks the music of the sixteenth and seventeenth centuries, whether among the German organists or among their Italian, French, and English contemporaries. It is the waxing prominence of the first (tonic), fifth (dominant), and fourth (subdominant) degrees of any given diatonic scale. This incipient hierarchy among the scale-tones was closely responsible for the increasing desire and ability to move, in the midst of a composition or section, from one tonality (key) to another, though this "modulation" was still achieved with some difficulty and under limited conditions.

Music, still thought of in part as consisting of forward-moving autonomous vocal lines or instrumental parts, was falling under semi-codified vertical regulations. The very profiles of composed melodies began to be occasioned to some extent by a wish to employ chords in logical succession and—at important junctures of grammatical and syntactical force—to base them on certain tones of the diatonic scale being used. Also, non-polyphonic music was being composed with the influence of certain scale-degrees and specific chordal progressions dominant in the composers' minds. What it is reasonable to call harmonic considerations had started to displace purely polyphonic or contrapuntal concepts. Music had already moved light-years away from plain chant: it was scarcely recognizable as the art that, only a few centuries earlier, had consisted of melody and of nothing else.

The formulation of what is here referred to as classic harmony was a development during many centuries, a slow definition by small adoptions and codifications, rather than the abrupt product of one man, one group of men, or even one school or century. In a wide, loose, but real sense, that slow formulation began at the mythical instant when the first elementary polyphony thrust out of monophony and the physical constitution of sound. In a useful sense it may be said that the keystone of its central structure, the major and minor scales and keys, had been installed by 1722, when Johann Sebastian Bach completed the twenty-four preludes and fugues—one of each in every major and minor key—that make up Part I of *The Well-Tempered Clavier*.

But classic harmony is more than just that central structure. For its complete definition it had to await the heyday of Haydn, Mozart, and all but the latest Beethoven. During the entire seventeenth century it was coming more and more to hold sway over musical creation, but without being spoken of or even foreseen as quite what it at last became.[1] For then it was still co-existing on something like even terms with the last blossoms of pure polyphony. And pure polyphony is, except as an occasional device, by definition inimical to classic harmony. In one sense, to be sure, the two textures cannot co-exist.

It is clear, for example, that many so-called polyphonic or contrapuntal compositions of the eighteenth, nineteenth, and twentieth centuries are not in reality polyphonic or contrapuntal. In fact their texture is homophony: they consist of a dominating or principal melody supported on pseudo-contrapuntal accompaniment consisting of present or implied chords. The essential difference between monophony and polyphony is simple to state and easy to understand: it is the difference between a single melody and two or more simultaneous but independent melodies. But the essential difference between polyphony and homophony is more complex, residing as it does largely in intention and understanding. Homophony is easy to detect in simple compositions, where it can be seen as a single melody accompanied by chords that are not accidental results of the superimposition of two or more additional, independent melodies on one another. When, however, homophony becomes complex to the degree at which almost every tone of the melody is one constituent of a chord, we often encounter a musical texture that has most of the visual signs of polyphony.

This kind of apparently polyphonic or contrapuntal music must often be listened to with detailed attention if we are to determine what its primary texture really is—and therefore whether the interpreter is performing it, and we ourselves hearing it, properly. If the composer's intention was homophonic, then the separate "melodies" that can often, by ingenuity, be detached from the forward-moving chords by the process of reading one interior tone from one chord, one from the next, and so on, are incidental. If this is the case, any insistence on polyphonic performance or lis-

[1] At the exact (mythical) moment when classic harmony was complete and supreme, of course, it began to become something else. The parlor game of nominating that moment has been played often, producing widely separated answers. One composition often named as the *locus classicus* of pure classic harmony's special euphony is Mozart's Symphony No. 39, in E♭ major.

tening falsifies the composer's intention and devaluates his music.
If, however, two or more independent melodies assert themselves
together, the composition (or passage) is polyphonic even though
the chords accidentally formed can be interpreted by strict rules
of academic harmony. Such compositions or passages must be performed with some emphasis on the separate melodies, and must
be listened to with similar emphasis, for to perform or listen to
them with the diminished attention to interior details usually desirable with homophony is to mistake the significance of their discourse.

We have seen polyphony unconsciously weakened by increased
recognition of the powers, duties, and interests of chords; by the
wasting away of the Church modes; by the gradual assertion of
modern diatonic scales; and by the seductions of melody with accompaniment. A further telling blow against polyphony as music's
ruling texture was struck consciously at the opening of the seventeenth century. It came from an unexpected and relatively weak
quarter. For a time, nevertheless, it was decisive. It altered both
the fabric and the history of music, not abruptly, but with results
that persist today. The scene was Florence, the immediate occasion the self-conscious birth of opera as an artistic form.

OPERA · MONTEVERDI · MONODY · RECITATIVE

SONATA · CONCERTO · ARIA · CONTINUO

BASSO OSTINATO

For more than a millennium musicians and theorists of music have been disputing the philosophy, nature, techniques, and ethics of the music of ancient Greece. The surviving evidence, mostly literary and sculptural, is pathetically inadequate, and the disputes have therefore produced spun-out ratiocination, alternately of the most fascinating sort and the most boring. By deciding, during the years just before 1600, that they knew precisely how music had acted as the partner of the Greek drama, a group of largely amateur musicians in courtly Florence produced by far the most vital and long-lived offspring of the argument. It was in this attempt to re-create the conditions under which they supposed Greek plays to have been linked to music that the men who met in the palace of Giovanni Bardi, Count of Vernio, evolved the opera.

The honor of being the first opera is usually conceded to *Dafne* (1597) by Jacopo Peri (1561?-1633?). Its music, however, has been lost. Its immediate successors were a *Euridice* by Peri and one by Giulio Caccini (1558?-1615?). Both were musically thin, pallid, and stiff. Their importance in the evolution of musical style (in contradistinction to their obvious importance in the history of opera) lay in their being all but entirely homophonic, in conform-

75

ity with the theories held by Count Bardi's courtiers, known as
the *camerata* (men who met in a room). What prevented these
earliest operas from being vital musico-dramatic wholes was not
their almost total avoidance of polyphony, but the fact that their
composers were hobbled by the self-conscious novelty of their
procedures and by a decisive lack of musical talent.

Peri, Caccini, and their friends were convinced that Greek
tragic actors had recited on tones of prescribed, varying pitch, accompanied in a simple manner by instruments. They conse-
quently laid out musical lines dictated by the spoken rhythm of
the Italian words of their chosen texts, with accents falling as
they would in normal, or slightly heightened, speech. They referred to this musical prosody as *"stile recitativo,"* or reciting
style, and thus bequeathed to operatic terminology the word recitative, later applied to something rather different. Their meager
semi-melodies were supported on chords sounded by a small scattering of instruments—notably lutes and varieties of harpsichord—
whose business it was to pronounce this *basso continuo* (thorough-
bass) as long as the singing voices pronounced the text. Only at
the end of important dramatic scenes was this monotonous half-
song, half-speech varied by the introduction of choruses and songs
in regular musical meters or by an attempt at autonomous melody. These choruses and songs were intended to accompany small
pantomimes or ballets—so early had opera learned its manners.
Otherwise the poverty-stricken, supposedly Greek, "drama with
music" went helplessly on.

The following excerpt from Caccini's *Euridice* displays (in
modern notation) the bones of the *camerata*'s procedure. The
notes here printed in the bass clef were simply shorthand indications to the instrumentalists of the chords desired; in some
cases, it will be noted, this bass is "figured"—has small superior
numbers to indicate the chord to be built on the note. The excerpt is the beginning of the Prologue sung by Tragedy:

Io che d'al - ti so - spir va - ga, e di pian - ti

Spars' or di do - glia or di mi - nac - cie il vol -

to Fei negli am - pi - te - a-tri al po - pol fol- to Sco-lo-

rir di pie - tà vol- ti e sem bian - ti

After the indicated *ritornello*—the only purely instrumental passages were these brief sections—six additional verses were sung, apparently without the smallest variation in the music! Yet much of the future of music can be seen in this impoverished excerpt, for here in full clarity are the two assumptions that melody rests on an accompanying bass and that a logic of chordal succession must be recognized and obeyed.

Polyphony played only a very small role in these Florentine
operas, and then usually in the simplest note-against-note manner.
In the hands of any but a master composer, in fact, polyphony and
theatrical action mix poorly, the dramatic poet's ideal musical
texture usually being accompanied melody. Earlier than the Bardi
camerata's experiments there had been some curious, often musically interesting, madrigal comedies, by, among others, Orazio
Vecchi (1550-1603) and Alessandro Striggio (1535?-1587). These
were polyphonic settings, in chains of madrigals, of complete
plays. Earlier still there had been the liturgical musical dramas
of the Middle Ages and the mysteries of the Renaissance, but
modern scholarship reasonably refuses these places in the immediate family tree of opera.

No single person or *camerata* could have invented the symphony or the concerto, but members of the Bardi group deserve
the honor usually accorded to them, of having invented opera.
Italian dramatic poetry happened in their time to have evolved
exactly the sort of play which could then best be set to music:
the pastoral eclogue. The poets were Torquato Tasso, Giovanni
Battista Guarini, and Ottavio Rinnucini. Their works—intact,
excerpted, revised, adapted, and imitated—became the sources of
opera librettos in numbers now beyond computation. Rinnucini
was the author of the books of both the first two operas, *Dafne*
and *Euridice*. Such texts as Tasso's *Aminta* and *Rinaldo* and
Guarini's *Il Pastor Fido* were set to music again and again. Whole
generations of opera librettists, in fact, mined the rich veins of
Tasso's *Gerusalemme Liberata,* finding that they could isolate
from its epic structure the dramatic episodes they craved and
could employ.

No more than Christopher Columbus did these men realize
that they had discovered a new world. The Greek performance of
tragic drama was the Cathay they sought, and they almost certainly died believing that they had reached it. Their operas, however, were musically sickly, and but for the accident of their
being also intensely fertile, their kind would have died out with
them, forgotten and unsung. Peri and Caccini had the gift of
serendipity: inadvertently they had hit upon a form that their

musical betters would raise to greatness. For their secure place in history they are indebted in part to happy chance.

Early in 1567 a composer of genius had been born in Cremona. Claudio Monteverdi (1567-1643) took up the Florentine novelty and used it to prove himself a musician seldom surpassed in dramatic power. Monteverdi lived to be nearly seventy-seven, and in the course of accomplishing much else he refashioned the Bardi *camerata*'s pseudo-Greek play-with-music into a genre endowed with seemingly eternal vitality. His *Orfeo* (1607), with a libretto by Alessandro Striggio the younger (son of the composer mentioned above), is the earliest opera that still repays performance.

Orfeo has proved to be so symptomatic of opera's subsequent career that Monteverdi, though not the inventor of opera, is rightly considered its preceptor. The score begins with a "toccata" played by the instrumental ensemble; though this consists, as Donald Jay Grout pointed out in *A Short History of Opera,* of nothing more than "a dressed-up version of the customary opening fanfare," it led directly to the operatic overture and prelude. There are twenty-five more purely instrumental pieces in the five acts of *Orfeo.* Monteverdi desired a full-bodied accompaniment, much richer in color, harmony, and contrapuntal development than the Florentine fathers had allowed. Peri, who sang the role of Orfeo when his own *Euridice* was performed at the Pitti Palace on October 6, 1600, was content on that occasion that the opera be equipped with only four instruments. These he himself, in the preface to the printed opera, calls *gravicembalo, chitarrone, lira grande,* and *liuto grosso.*[1] Monteverdi's *Orfeo* calls for at least forty instruments, including violins, viols, harpsichords, harps, lutes, small organs, trombones, and trumpets. Although the opera contains no passage in which most of these instruments sound together, and though more use is made of them in the frequent purely instrumental passages than as accompaniment of the singing, this was rich, heady fare if contrasted with the thin instrumentation of Peri.

[1] *Gravicembalo* indicates a form of harpsichord; *chitarrone* a long-bodied bass lute; *lira grande* a collateral relative of the violin, but larger, with numerous strings so placed as to make chord-playing easy; *liuto grosso* a short-bodied bass lute.

Far from consisting of a string of recitatives lightened by occasional strophic songs or choruses, Monteverdi's *Orfeo* is a musical whole as elaborately planned and unified as a fine symphony or concerto. Each of its five acts has a scheme both of color and of layout which helps to give it over-all unity. Fragments of the same instrumental music appear several times and in various acts, again contributing to unity. The musical texture is astonishingly responsive to the atmosphere and situations of Striggio's poem, sensitively shifting its texture and coloration in response to the emotions and fortunes of its characters. Here, very early in the career of opera, is a realization of the drive toward music both implicated and characteristic rather than merely decorative or self-sufficient. Monteverdi did not out of cold theory disdain any available musical device: he used all the applicable resources of his era and his learning (which was vast), employing them as means toward full-bodied musico-dramatic entity.

In Act III of *Orfeo* occurs *"Possente spirto,"* the supplication of the underworld spirits, the most renowned of Monteverdi's operatic excerpts except for *"Lasciatemi morire,"* all that remains of his second opera, *Arianna*. *"Possente spirto"* is an elaborately organized unit, consisting of a melody presented and then followed by four strophic sections, each of which might be described as *coloratura* variations on it. Each section has its own sympathetic accompaniment, such as two violins, two cornetts,[2] two harps, and two violins with one *basso da brazzo,* a form of violoncello. At times the instruments support or reinforce the voice; at others they compete with Orfeo in a manner that later degenerated into the standardized contest between soprano and flute. Listened to as expressive music apart from its context, *"Possente spirto"* is no less impressive than that more familiar aria of Plutonic supplication of a later day, *"Divinités du Styx,"* from Gluck's *Alceste*. It is nonetheless primarily an instrumentality in the evocation of Orfeo's tragedy: not merely beautiful dramatic music, but also successful theater.

---

[2] The cornett—so spelled to prevent its confusion with the cornet (a small variety of trumpet)—was an eight-sided wooden or ivory instrument with six finger-holes in a row; it flared slightly outward from its mouthpiece.

Few modern listeners could sit joyfully through a complete performance of Peri's *Euridice*. In recent years many have found Monteverdi's *Orfeo* deeply moving. Few facts better illustrate the chasm between intention and genius than that these two operas (as well as Caccini's *Euridice*), composed within one decade, are settings of the same Greek legend dealing with the power of music.

In 1602 Caccini had published a collection of vocal pieces in the monodic manner of his operatic recitatives, and with thorough-bass accompaniments. Called *Nuove musiche* (New Music), this became not only the manifesto of the anti-polyphonic movement, but also the source of the name now generally given to it. The "new music" found its purest expression in the hands of inferior composers—for Monteverdi simply combined its procedures with those of polyphony, adding variants of his own devising—because it was basically a demand that music serve poetry faithfully and without asserting its own autonomy. It was partly a rebellion against the overelaborated polyphonic manners of motets and madrigals in which musical complexities rendered any understanding of the text all but impossible. The "new music" was the brother of opera. It aided the inception of the great baroque forms of cantata and oratorio. And it erected a barrier between Netherlandish traditions of vocal polyphony and the music of the seventeenth century and after.

But the "new music," if faithfully interpreted and evolved, could only have reduced a once-great art to servitude. Monteverdi was one of those who put music first and thus saved his art from that future, keeping it free in the cause of expressiveness. In his dramatic cantata *Il Combattimento di Tancredi e Clorinda* (1624), with text derived from *Gerusalemme Liberata,* he announced what he called the *"stile concitato"* (literally "excited style") for the rendering of rage and agitation. This amounted to the free use of string tremolo, the rapid repetition of one tone by fast, short bowings. In this important forerunner of the myriads of not-quite-operas satisfied with cantata state, he also indicated the striking together of swords by the use of string *pizzicato,* a plucking of strings by the player's fingers.

Although the musical forces required by *Il Combattimento* are

fewer in number than those for *Orfeo,* its musical expressiveness
is much more clearly achieved for its own sake, a sign of the
gradual reassertion of the power of music even when used to illustrate a text. And in Monteverdi's last opera, *L'Incoronazione di
Poppea* (1642), composed when he was nearly seventy-five, further
important developments become obvious. The exact instrumentation cannot now be determined because the only surviving copy
does not specify it, but what is clear is that this is primarily an
opera to be sung. Every ounce of Monteverdi's energy has been
concentrated on compacting an effective, unified musico-dramatic
whole. The perfect balance among text, music, and theatrical
viability he achieved was as far removed from the text-overbal-
anced experiments of the Florentine *camerata* as from the music-
overbalanced operas of a later day, in which composers sank their
texts in favor of show-off singers or of their own overweening
assertiveness.

The history of opera can be translated into a graph, with a line
wavering between extremes of domination. All the so-called "reforms" of opera have been reactions against one or another of
these excesses. The ideal itself has been certain since Monteverdi's
time. It is the assumption, as in *L'Incoronazione di Poppea,* into
a new, living unit of the text and the music that underlines and
bodies it forth. This assumption must be so complete in the ideal
opera that no tag ends of text, music, or mere theatricality extend
beyond the area occupied by the newly created unit.

Opera had been initiated with mythological subjects. Although
similar subjects were always to be composed, *L'Incoronazione,*
making use of a pseudo-historic episode from Roman history,
initiated the human opera with a masterwork. In it the personalities of Nero, Poppea, and the other protagonists—including Val-
letto, a page boy destined to reappear in many guises in later
operas—are portrayed in music with the sort of psychological
verisimilitude which was to reach a splendid fullness in Mozart's
The Marriage of Figaro and *Don Giovanni.*

Despite—or perhaps because of—its development of opera, cantata, and oratorio, the seventeenth century, whatever its prolifera-
tion of magnificent musical creations, now necessarily appears

somewhat shadowed by the towering musical centuries it lay between. Happening, as it did, after the most glorious achievements of pure vocal polyphony and before the powerful graces of the high baroque and classic Viennese periods, it reveals an understandable tentativeness, the uncertainties of any experimental era. To understand its most important accomplishments in changing and enlarging musical materials, we had best look at the seventeenth century region by region. In experimental vitality, in tentativeness, and in regional specialization, it much resembles the first fifty years of the twentieth century.

Through the extremely complex history of music in Italy between roughly 1575 and 1700 run the threads of several struggles whose outcomes proved of first importance to the whole vocabulary of music as an art. First was the challenge of the weakened government of polyphony by the alliance of monody and homophony. Then there were the attempts to balance the architectural roles of instruments and the human voice. Additionally there was an unremitting determination to develop formally satisfying relations between melody and accompaniment. Underlying and suffusing all of this alternately revolutionary and reactionary activity—with most musicians oscillating between or combining the two—was an irregular march toward the unsuspected land of classic harmony.

In the Northern countries, the florescence of polyphonic organ music and the consequent evolution of such noble instrumental forms of polyphony as the organ chorale and the fugue may be interpreted as a final attempt by the organism of polyphony to adjust itself to the new environment of non-vocal and harmonic music. The best compositions of Sweelinck and Buxtehude proffer melodies of fine emotional power, themes wholly distinct in profile and procedure from those of earlier times. They often tempt us to listen to them as melody with accompaniment, but melody with accompaniment was not their chief constructive principle, and to yield to that temptation is to miss their true character. They were still a web of many-voiced construction which denied pre-eminence to any single line of melody.

In Italy, to the contrary, though contrapuntal usages, far from vanishing, continued to produce extraordinary and vital music, accompanied melody more and more advanced recognized claims to first position among expressive means. From the point of view of musical architecture, this was the chief significance of the melodically poor Florentine operas. It was likewise the chief meaning of many Italian developments of instrumental and vocal-instrumental music, of the emergence of purely instrumental melodies in many varieties of sonata and concerto, as well as of such vocal genres as *aria* and *arioso*. *Basso continuo* supplied one method of freeing melody from its cloak of many voices, of displaying its true form. The *continuo* did not become lost in the harmonic fabric of eighteenth-century music before it had influenced forever all music consisting entirely or in part of accompanied melody.

Let us examine the relative and shifting emphases that these usages, manners, and forms suggest. This examination is of first importance: an awareness of a composer's intentions is essential both to listening to his music and to judging the rightness with which it is performed. To listen to polyphonically intended music it is essential not to concentrate attention on a single thread of melody; to listen polyphonically to music designed as accompanied melody is about equivalent to expecting to experience tragedy in watching a farce.

SONATA

When looking at the historic and evolving meanings of the term sonata, it is necessary first to cleanse the mind of all additions to its meaning since Haydn's time. The word did not originally bear the chief significance we now automatically find in it: it did not, that is, describe a composition for one or more instruments which was divided into three or four separate movements, each constructed according to a more or less established pattern.

As explained earlier, the word sonata originally indicated a composition "sounded"—in contrast to one "sung" (cantata) or one "touched" (toccata) on a keyboard. From the middle of the sixteenth century to about the middle of the seventeenth, sonata was the generic label for many sorts of pieces intended primarily for instruments other than organ, clavichord, or harpsichord. During this hundred years, many "sonatas" were composed which bear no relationship whatever to the specific pattern of composition to which the label was transferred shortly later.

On the other hand, early forms of the musical patterns to which the word sonata was later applied were originally known under other names. Musicologists commonly find one of the earliest of these in certain Franco-Flemish chansons of the early sixteenth century, composed by such men as Claude de Sermisy (1490?-1562) and Clément Jannequin (sixteenth century). Jannequin—a composer noted for his remarkably naturalistic imitations of the noises of barnyard, hunt, and battlefield—frequently constructed four-voice chansons on a tripartite (ternary) ABA pattern, two statements of the same section separated by a contrasting middle section in another mood and another tempo.

These Northern chansons achieved great popularity in Italy, where the fact that their texts were either French or Flemish, added to the current tendency to transfer vocal compositions to instruments, led composers to arrange them for solo instruments or instrumental ensembles. Andrea Gabrieli, the great Venetian, published, in 1571, *Canzoni alla francese per l'organo,* French chansons for organ. Not content thus to give new raiment to the works of foreigners, Italian musicians began also to compose pieces of this genre directly for instruments, calling them usually *canzoni da sonare* (chansons to be sounded). These were written for both keyboard instruments and small groups of non-keyboard instruments, some of the earliest of them apparently being intended for performance either way *ad libitum.* They were couched in variants of ternary form—ABA, ABB, occasionally even AAB—and in expanded patterns such as AABC. Gradually, however, a real difference was established between *canzoni* for keyboard instruments and those for ensembles (which often included a keyboard instrument). Keyboard *canzoni* tended to lose the overtly sectional architecture. Becoming more compact, and retaining their predominantly polyphonic texture, they contributed to the emergence of the keyboard fugue. In Germany, in fact, pieces that in Italy would have carried the generic designation *canzona* were often headed *Fuge*.

Canzoni composed for small instrumental groups gradually drifted toward the pattern we know as sonata. Of many varieties and patterns as created by composers of the late sixteenth and early seventeenth centuries, they attained their most (in our sense) sonata-like shape in the hands of Frescobaldi. His *canzoni* freely mingled homophonic passages with contrapuntal passages making large use of imitation. In them, a change from polyphonic to homophonic usually indicated an alteration in tempo, with greater swiftness of performance desired for the polyphonic sections than for those in homophony. Frescobaldi's *canzoni* published between 1623 and 1634 were definitely sonata-like, especially in their contrasts between sections. In them, and in the *canzoni* of his contemporaries and immediate successors, the *canzona* began to contract toward the A, B, and A of perfect ternary form. After the middle of the seventeenth century this sort of *canzona* was increasingly called sonata, the older word being applied more and more to fugal compositions or to the one fugal movement in a preponderantly homophonic sonata in several movements.

Giovanni Legrenzi (1626-1690) and other Venetians produced, during the late seventeenth and early eighteenth centuries, *sonate* related even more closely to the classic Viennese sonata. Instead of being one-movement pieces deployed in continuous, contrasted sections, these were highly organized compositions in several movements. One pattern employed was AbCdA—A being a rapid movement in fugal texture, C a homophonic movement in triple time; b and d brief contrasting slower sections. Giuseppe Torelli (1658-1708) worked out a variant of this pattern, four movements arranged slow, fast, slow, fast. Known as *sonata da chiesa* (church sonata, in complex and uncertain contrast to the so-called *sonata da camera,* or chamber sonata [3]), this proved to be an extremely fertile pattern. It was favored by the great Italian violinist Arcan-

---

[3] Primarily a development of the less organically unified suite of separate pieces, the *sonata da camera* tended toward the classic sonata only as it also tended to merge with the *sonata da chiesa.*

gelo Corelli (1653-1713) and many other composers of the era. Later Italians were likely to compose *sonate* in three, five, six, and even more movements; they only occasionally returned to the four movements of the *sonata da chiesa*. It was left to German composers, notably Handel and Bach, and to the great French violinist Jean-Marie Leclair (1697-1764) to carry the four-movement ABCD *sonata da chiesa* pattern to the very threshold of the classic Viennese period.[4]

CONCERTO

Like the English word concert, the Italian *concerto* is derived from the Latin verb *concertare,* meaning to contend or to debate, with an implication of contending co-operatively for common results, of debating with a peer in friendly fashion. The term was used first to distinguish accompanied vocal music from *a cappella* ("for the chapel," *i.e.,* unaccompanied, choral) singing. It was used by many Italian musicians after 1575, notably by Giovanni Gabrieli, who in 1587 published a book of pieces by his uncle and himself as *Canti concerti a 6, 7, 8, 10, e 16 voci* (Concerted Songs for 6, 7, 8, 10, and 16 Voices). The term became attached to both polyphonic and monodic vocal music supported either by organ or by small ensembles of instruments. It persisted in this sense for nearly one hundred years, even Bach having labeled certain of his cantatas *Concerten.*

Only when forms of the word *concerto* began to be applied to instrumental music did it begin to indicate pieces that, however uncertainly, we should be likely to recognize as concertos. With music for instrumental ensembles, *concerto* at first literally indicated contention or debate. Within the ensemble one division of instruments would alternate with another, "struggling" or "debating" for the privilege of contributing most to a satisfactory unit. Many such compositions were labeled *concerti* in Italy; but many that might justly have been so labeled were called *canzoni,*

4 Further discussion of the sonata and its changing terminology, noting the sonata for four stringed instruments as the string quartet, that for orchestra as the symphony, will be found on pages 137-147.

sonate, and even *sinfonie,*[5] having been looked at for other characteristics.

Under whatever label it appeared, the musical principle of concerted playing became a major aspect of formal architecture. Italian composers of the early seventeenth century often classified it as the *"stile moderno,"* as when, in the 1620's, Dario Castello issued groups of *canzoni* for keyboard, winds, and strings, as *Sonate concertate in stilo moderno.* Throughout the 1600's, numerous Italians composed these concerted pieces, mostly single movements divided into sections by alternation of the instruments or groups of instruments employed. In the last quarter of the century, however, compositions in the concerted manner—increasingly called concertos—tended to break up into several movements and to be preponderantly homophonic, consisting of melody with chordal accompaniment. The term *concerto* nevertheless continued capaciously to house several distinct musical genres. Of these, the concerto for a soloist and an ensemble, did not emerge fully developed until the eighteenth century. Two other late seventeenth-century sorts of concerto require mention here.

The so-called *concerto-sinfonia*[6] failed to survive intact, but expanded into other forms. Its basic principle was alteration of sections in differing styles, but all performed on the same instruments. It followed, for example, a solemn passage in which all the instruments were sounded together with a passage in which a few of them exerted all their technical brilliance while the rest sounded a somewhat recessive background. It required virtuosity of instrumental technique, particularly from players of instruments that could be made to stand out from the general concourse. In part at least it produced, and was produced by, the first virtuoso violinists; it evolved almost directly into the *concerto grosso.*

A *concerto grosso* is a composition for instrumental ensemble

[5] As late as 1873 the French composer Lalo gave the name *Symphonie espagnole* to a large composition for violin and orchestra which has many of the determining marks of a concerto for solo instrument and orchestra.

[6] The Italian word *sinfonia,* derived from the Greek *symphōnia,* indicates simply two or more tones sounded together, but implies that they are sounded together harmoniously.

in which a small group of instruments plays in contrast against the full group. The smaller group is called the *concertino* or *principale,* the whole ensemble the *tutti, ripieni,* or simply *concerto.* Early composers in this genre were Corelli and Alessandro Stradella (1645?-1682). Their *sinfonie* or *concerti* still hung backward toward the fragmentary architecture of *canzoni,* often being constructed of many brief, highly contrasted movements. By the beginning of the eighteenth century the distinction between a *concerto grosso* and, say, a concerto for solo violin and orchestra was becoming definite. By then the *concertino* of a *concerto grosso* commonly consisted of two violins with cello and harpsichord thorough-bass, the *ripieni* of a string orchestra and harpsichord, to which still later practice at times added both woodwinds and brasses. Corelli himself, having composed earlier in rudimentary forms, lived to write—in his so-called "Opus 6," of which the eighth piece is the familiar *Christmas Concerto*—superbly assured masterpieces that differ from the final development of the *concerto grosso* only in that they have five and more movements.

Another Italian violin virtuoso, Francesco Geminiani (1687-1762), consistently confined the *concerto grosso* to the four-movement dimensions of the *sonata da chiesa.* Still another violinist, Antonio Vivaldi (1675?-1741), favoring an ABA sequence of movements, fast, slow, fast, established a pattern that was followed by Bach in four of the best-known of all *concerti grossi,* the six of his "Brandenburg" set. Frankly imitating Vivaldi, a very great composer, Bach also adapted the Italian's brilliant style, whereas Handel, in his scarcely less remarkable *concerti grossi,* preferred the five or more movements and less advanced style of his friend Corelli.

During the late eighteenth and nineteenth centuries the *concerto grosso* was to drop out of sight, but its texture was retained in movements of suites, symphonies, and solo (especially double and triple) concertos. The solo concerto, however, was to become a typical genre of the nineteenth century, which was strewn with hundreds upon hundreds of piano and violin concertos, to name only two varieties. The twentieth century, however, has witnessed a return to the past for formal usages. So modern a composer as

Ernest Bloch labeled as *Concerto grosso* one of his pieces, for string orchestra and piano. Other modern composers have used the appellation; still more, including Stravinsky, have composed *concerti grossi* under other names. After its period underground, the form has emerged alive and vital.

ARIA AND ARIOSO

Aria is the Italian word for air, often with the secondary meaning of breath. Its application to song is easy to understand, as is the English use of "air." The Italian word is now generally reserved for a lengthy accompanied solo song not in strophic form—that is, not repeating music to differing textual sections, but being one continuous unfolding of music. It did not always bear this significance.

Aria as a musical term is said to have appeared in print first in the *Arie di canzon francese,* published in 1579 by Marc' Antonio Ingegneri (1550?-1592), a teacher of Monteverdi. Ingegneri used the word to differentiate certain textless but still polyphonic songs among his madrigals. In the *Nuove musiche,* Caccini placed the word above examples of monody which were brief and were built on strophic principles.[7] During the seventeenth century, however, the aria underwent a bewildering series of incarnations and metamorphoses.

During the first half of the 1600's the aria was often that compromise between true song and the recitative which later composers called *arioso.* Like the instrumental *concerto grosso* and sonata, the aria also borrowed and altered patterns from the *canzona,* organizations erected out of rapidly contrasting brief sections. Still other *arie* were constructed of a chief melody soaring above an accompanying bass consisting of a brief semi-melody constantly repeated: a *basso ostinato.*

The first variety of aria to be preferred above all others was

[7] Willi Apel, in the *Harvard Dictionary of Music,* points out that *aria* in this sense was used by German composers of the seventeenth and eighteenth centuries for songs that were direct ancestors of the strophic German lieder of the eighteenth and nineteenth centuries. Thus one sort of early *aria* descended to a rich musical form often cited, somewhat foolishly, as inimical to its other important descendant, the full-fledged opera aria.

in the ABA ternary pattern that, in a myriad ways, pervades music. This was the *aria da capo* ("aria from the head," in the sense of beginning), in which, after a contrasting middle section, the first section is repeated. In later *arie da capo* the relationship between A and B was often that between a major key and the minor key having the same number of sharps or flats, called the relative minor. Sometimes A and B were sternly contrasted in nature; more often the difference between them was less dramatic.

The *aria da capo* captivated composers and singers, and, through them, listeners. Monteverdi hinted at it in both his first and his last opera. Other Italian composers cultivated it with constancy. Alessandro Scarlatti (1659-1725), not bothered by the unlikelihood that a real person would express thoughts or show emotions in ternary form (he knew the difference between life and art), filled his many operas with characters singing *arie da capo*. Every *prima donna* (literally, first lady) and leading *castrato* (castrated male soprano or alto) attempted to triumph by using the *aria da capo* as a platform for the performance of superhuman vocal tricks. Operas, in fact, became simple chains of *arie da capo,* often of excelling beauty in themselves, but at last entirely detrimental to the poetic or dramatic component. This excess helped to incite one of the several "reforms" of opera.

Composers and librettists, bent on reducing the arrogance of singers and restoring the significance of the libretto, tried to move back toward an improved variety of the Florentine operatic concept. First they attacked the *aria da capo* for its lack of verisimilitude. Then, more sensibly, they insisted that the aria, of whatever pattern, be fitted more intelligently into an operatic fabric. The renowned eighteenth-century "reformer of opera," Christoph Willibald von Gluck (1714-1787), reacted against the aria (of which his earlier operas had been full) in favor of a variety of lied. Wagner, another reformer, attempted to banish the aria altogether in an effort to make music dramas uninterrupted wholes. The *Pelléas et Mélisande* of Debussy contains nothing that can be called an aria.

Yet this form of extended song has produced not only some of the most attractive operatic music, but also apparently unoperatic wonders dotting the oratorios, cantatas, and passions of Bach and Handel. It has also been composed for its own sake, apart from any larger framework, as in the concert arias of Mozart and Beethoven. To denounce it or refuse it careful attention because of the gymnastic excesses to which pandering composers and vacuous star singers have led it is both futile and foolish.

CONTINUO, BASSO CONTINUO, THOROUGH-BASS, FIGURED BASS, BASSO OSTINATO

Continuo, an accompaniment in the form of a submelodic element continuing throughout a composition; *basso continuo,* a bass accompaniment so continuing; thorough-bass,[8] an English translation of *basso continuo;* and figured bass, an accompaniment of this nature notated in a sort of shorthand, with figures or musical signs to indicate desired chords—these terms represent important musical means evolved during the sixteenth and seventeenth centuries. Like the concepts of sonata, concerto, aria, opera, cantata, and oratorio, they were available to those eighteenth-century musicians who were to sum up the immediate past in a massif of final achievement and to those (Carl Phillipp Emanuel Bach, Haydn, Mozart) who were to evolve the manners we have come to call classic.

In a motet dated 1587, Alessandro Striggio the elder wrote out a part for the organist, really the merest suggestion of the supporting chords required. In slightly later similar parts some single notes are topped by sharps and flats to suggest that major or minor triads are desired. In the earliest surviving operatic scores, the *Euridices* of Caccini and Peri, there is a similar *basso continuo,* but with Arabic numerals to indicate the chordal combinations desired. This "figured bass" became, and for a long time remained, the usual way of notating the thorough-bass. Some form of *continuo,* figured or unfigured, became so integral a part of composition that the high baroque period of music—roughly from the beginning of the seventeenth century to Handel's death in 1759—is often called the "thorough-bass period."

8 Thorough is here an early form of through.

The musical significance of the *continuo* lies in its being the foundation of a harmonically logical structure, in which chordal succession supplies an important element of the logic. In religious music, the *continuo* was often to be played by the organ, but in secular compositions thorough-bass parts were soon intended for a harpsichord and—to lend additional strength to the substructure—a cello, viola da gamba, or bassoon. The use of one or more melody-carrying instruments was essential as long as the bass retained a melodic life of its own, but in the eighteenth century the bass began to lose that life, tending toward chordal accompaniment *per se.* Then the harpsichord gradually took over the accompaniment without any other instrument, and the orchestra was usually conducted from it, a practice followed by Haydn as late as the 1790's.

Where a keyboard *continuo*—figured or unfigured—is called for, the modern performer must either be equipped to improvise discreetly or be ready to play some editor's arbitrary "realization" (that is, writing-out) of what he is to play. When, for example, we listen to a Handel violin sonata, we should understand that of the notes being played by harpsichord or piano Handel indicated only the bass, while the performer is either improvising the treble or playing a version of it supplied by an editor. This means that there may be as many versions of the sonata as there are players—and that the "rightness" or "wrongness" is a function of the individual performer's education and taste.

Although these practices grew out of improvisational ways of using instruments with polyphonic music, they asserted their full value when applied to monody. All were signally important in helping to evolve musical ways by which melodies could be harmonically supported.

Basso ostinato, a device as old as polyphony and still often used, is of a different nature. *Ostinato* (persistent) is applied to a fragment of melody or submelody which recurs quickly and often, on the pitch and in the voice or part of its original appearance. It may occur in any voice, but because it proved peculiarly useful in the bass, the term *basso ostinato* has become familiar.[9] Its English

---

9 See the discussion of "Sumer is icumen in," pages 37-38, for one of the earliest surviving examples of *basso ostinato.*

equivalent is ground bass or ground. Like imitation, it is a form of repetition, of which variation is also the child. But *basso ostinato* involves a new conception of structural and aesthetic value: that of continuous variation or new creation against a repetitive, unchanging, and customarily simple background. Grounds made up of nothing more than four successive tones repeated over and over have supported music so elaborate that unwary listeners will fail to hear the accompanying reiteration.

The most renowned of all passacaglias, Bach's in C minor—but not every passacaglia—is built on a ground bass. So are two of Brahms's most satisfying finales, that of his *Variations on a Theme of Haydn* and the passacaglia last movement of his Fourth Symphony. So is the magnificent lament of Dido in Purcell's opera *Dido and Aeneas*, "When I am laid in earth." Purcell's use of *basso ostinato* is so especially effective that it is worth examining here as one demonstration of the technical means by which an accomplished musical craftsman can wring emotional power from an apparently dry-as-dust device. Here is the ground that is stated seven times in "When I am laid in earth":

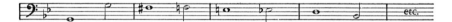

In its predominantly descending one-octave (G to G) motion, this semi-melody evokes pathos. This is enhanced by the fact that the descent from G as far as D is made by semitones. Not musically very meaningful by itself, this five-measure ground was flawlessly designed for Purcell's tragic purpose.

One all-but-complete presentation of the ground serves as an introduction: Dido begins to sing only on its closing note. Her melody, rhythmically more varied than the ground, and of stronger musical interest, having greater variety of up-and-down motion, is exquisitely meshed with it. The stately progress of the constantly falling ground is relentless. Yet Purcell did not interfere with the logical relation of text and vocal line even to avoid what—if looked at without regard for dramatic or over-all musical effect—are clearly dissonances. Most of these are quickly resolved, followed by assuaging consonances, so that in performance they scarcely project from the mostly consonant combinations. But they occur, and by occurring intensify the emotional atmosphere. In creating a vocal melody sensitively related to the contour of the ground bass, then, Purcell by no means confined himself. On the contrary, he used the device to compose one of his greatest arias.

Purcell could, of course, have composed a continuously unfolding bass accompaniment to his melody, a more varied support than this constantly repeated ground. But here he wanted exactly the grave, stately effect evoked by the ground even when the listener, attending to the aria as a whole, is not directly aware of its separate existence. Also, there is more than a mere probability that the melody actually arose out of the ground—that, having selected the ground, Purcell sketched in a melody that would both mesh with it and symbolize the emotional urgency expressed by the text. He was not performing a learned stunt, but composing music out of an imagination freed of restriction by the very handling of this useful musical device.

Sonata, concerto, aria, *arioso, basso continuo, basso ostinato*— these and other methods, forms, and performance devices were instrumentalities in the continuing emergence of homophony, monody, melody chordally accompanied along proto-harmonic lines. They provided typical roads to the future. All reached a high development in Italy, though not exclusively there. They flourished through those seventeenth-century changes of musical syntax and grammar which a schooled musician of 1675 could consider natural, whereas his forerunner in 1575 would have thought them either devoid of meaning or full of a different meaning. All discussions of the rich musical life of seventeenth-century Italy is necessarily crowded with the terms used to designate them.

Seven

SCHÜTZ · GABRIELI · CHROMATICISM · ORATORIO
LULLY · BALLET · RECITATIVE · OVERTURE
SUITE · KEYBOARD COMPOSITION
COUPERIN · PURCELL

In the states of Germany during the 1600's differences of musical background, local taste, individual talent, and religious observance continued to produce music with emphases and formal procedures different from those burgeoning in Italy. Some of the remarkable Northern developments of keyboard music have already been discussed: the appearance of free preludes, toccatas, fugues, variations, capriccios, and suites with textures distinct from those of vocal music. But the most intensely German musician of the seventeenth century was not primarily an organist or instrumental composer. His main contribution to musical evolution was a fusion of older Northern polyphonic practices and some of the newer manners of the South. He has been called the "father of German music" because some of his compositions seem to lead directly to Bach. He was born an exact century before Bach. He was Heinrich Schütz (1585-1672).

Schütz's talent having been noticed by his employer, the Landgrave of Hesse-Cassel, he was sent to Italy in 1609 to study under Giovanni Gabrieli. That his studies were pursued at Venice under an organist of St. Mark's Cathedral had peculiarly direct results

both in the style of Schütz's compositions and in their forms. St.
Mark's is laid out in a Venetian adaptation of Byzantine church
architecture: its ground plan is that of a Greek cross, so that its
transept and nave divide each other into halves. Because its con-
gregation could not stand in relation to the choir as it stood in
churches laid out in the form of the long crucifix or Latin cross,
its choir was divided into two sections, one placed in each arm of
the transept. Each half-choir, further, was supplied with its own
organ. By the time Schütz arrived to be Gabrieli's pupil, St.
Mark's was the home of a form of choral music making a virtue of
this necessity. Gabrieli had composed choral works for two groups,
works that took constructive advantage of all the possibilities of
contrast and response thus given him. Nor had he been satisfied
by manipulating only two choral groups: some of his pieces were
polychoric—for three and four separate choirs.

Gabrieli's polychoric compositions are roughly like paintings in
which all the resources of chiaroscuro are summoned to heighten
emotional impact. His choral groups, truly "concerted," compete
for the honor of contributing most to the realization of his musico-
religious intentions. He loved the widest contrasts, those between
very high and very low human voices, between single voices and
one or more choirs, between soft (*piano*) and loud (*forte*), between
the timbres of voices and those of instruments, especially brasses.
He was enamored of pure splendors of sound: his employment of
the voice, whether solo or in masses, is instrumental. In his creative
imagination the human voice was becoming one instrument
among many—perhaps, with the organ, the most important, but
no longer a ruler in isolated supremacy. Gabrieli joined glinting
and shattering brass sounds to those of organs and voices in a
firmly controlled avalanche of sonority not matched for monu-
mentality until the oratorios of Handel.

Into this musical climate the twenty-four-year-old Schütz moved
as a pupil of the sixty-two-year-old Gabrieli. It was 1609, when in
the Germany from which he had traveled the homophonic, monodic, not-quite-harmonic music budding all across Italy was
scarcely realized. Schütz himself, returning to Cassel after Gabrieli's death in 1612, successfully imported that music into the North

and mixed it with the North's own music. In 1619, while living at
Dresden, Schütz published twenty-six settings of the Psalms. He
had scored them for eight and more voices or solo parts, two, three,
and four choirs, and a *basso continuo* for one or more organs, with
lutes, strings, trumpets, and other instruments as further accompaniment. Students find in these, besides the obvious external
signs of Gabrieli's mastership, the indirect influence of the Florentine opera-makers' concept of vocal declamation. In them, too,
homophony, monody, and polyphony have been combined and
alternated toward expressive ends.

Four years after publishing the Psalm settings, Schütz supplied
the Electoral Chapel at Dresden with a setting, for use on Easter,
of the story of Christ's Resurrection. In a number of German
churches it had been customary for many years to sing the story
of the Passion during Holy Week, that of the Resurrection on
Easter. One of Schütz's predecessors at Dresden, the Italian Antonio Scandello (1517-1580), had provided settings for both. Surviving copies and partial copies of these prove that they were unaccompanied choruses, recitative solos, duets, trios, and quartets.
The individual characters in the stories are not, except for the
Evangelist—whose part is a recitation for solo voice—assigned in
theatrical manner to a single singer: Peter, for instance, is represented by a trio from the choir, Christ by a quartet.

Schütz's setting of the Resurrection story is for accompanied
singing, there being instrumental parts. He has moved in the direction of theatrical verisimilitude, too, in that when composing the
music for an individual protagonist as more than one melodic line,
here continuing a motet procedure, he indicates that one of the
parts might be omitted or played on an instrument. His Three
Marys sing three separate vocal lines; two angels perform a duet.
That the eleven Disciples do not have eleven interwoven melodic
strands, but perform a six-voice chorus, indicates no diminution
in dramatic realism, but only that Schütz was more interested in
musical truth than in performing a prodigy. His Resurrection setting is a boldly taken step away from pure vocal polyphony of
strict liturgical cast toward that balance of polyphony and homophony, of liturgy and realistic drama, which was to flower in all ma-

turity in the cantatas and Passions of Bach and the oratorios of Handel.

Schütz's Resurrection oratorio dated from 1623. Two years later he published a collection of forty-one *Cantiones sacrae* (sacred songs), their Latin texts set for four voices with a *basso continuo* for organ. His formal usage here was a compromise between the motet (polyphony) and the concerto (polyphony-homophony). It was also an attempt to preserve some of the antique strength of the ecclesiastical modes in the face of chordal motion, the latter often suggesting a harmony moving by semitones, *i.e.,* chromatically.

Diatonic, it will be recalled, describes an octave-wide scale (for example, C-D-E-F-G-A-B-C) made up of seven steps, some of them whole tones, some semitones. The chromatic scale, on the other hand, covers an octave in twelve semitone steps (for example, C-C♯-D-D♯-E-F-F♯-G-G♯-A-A♯-B-C).

Scales, whether diatonic or chromatic, are usually about as important as the alphabet is important to a poet: what matters is what the composer builds out of combinations of tones selected from the scales. Using mostly the tones native to the diatonic scale dominating a given passage, the composer writes a diatonic passage containing diatonic intervals making up diatonic chords involved in activities of diatonic harmony. If, on the contrary, he freely *and structurally* introduces tones not native to the prevailing diatonic scale, he writes a chromatic passage containing chromatic intervals making up chromatically moving chords involved in chromatic harmony.

Composers habitually introduce chromatic intervals into diatonic chords without obliterating the predominant diatonicism. Similarly, chromatic chords may be introduced into diatonic harmony without destroying it, and passages in chromatic harmony do not inevitably destroy a predominant diatonic harmony. The question of whether a given passage, chord, or harmony is diatonic or chromatic is often open to several answers, but is generally decided on the basis of the prevailing wind. A mostly chromatic example is chromatic with diatonic aspects; in reverse, a mostly diatonic example is diatonic with chromatic aspects. A composition without at least tinges of both is now all but inconceivable.

Oriental music is, and has long been, richly chromatic. But Western European music was all but exclusively diatonic until the middle of the sixteenth century. As remarked before, the first European composers to make free use of chromaticism were Flemings living in Italy: Adrian Willaert and Cipriano de Rore. Many Italians composing during the second half of the sixteenth century used chromaticism experimentally. Notable among them was one of the most spectacular and talented eccentrics in musical history, Carlo Gesualdo, Prince of Venosa. Inhabiting a brightly illuminated cul-de-sac of his own, Gesualdo so sensitized his music to nuances in his madrigal texts that his harmonic practice fled entirely beyond what his contemporaries considered reason. He composed chromatic melodies and then wove them together with disregard for diatonic probity. Historical development happened to leave his expressive madrigals to one side: his contemporaries and their immediate successors were much more conservatively diatonic. Three centuries later the composers who could have found Gesualdo's example useful had forgotten his existence.

Sweelinck, almost exactly Gesualdo's contemporary, but quite uninfluenced either by him or by the slightly less daring Luca Marenzio (1553-1599), let himself wander into chromaticism chiefly when composing fugues. He enjoyed the problems and solutions presented by a chromatically evolving principal subject for a fugue; even more, his followers and some of his German coevals introduced such chromatic semi-melodies as answers or countersubjects in fugues still mostly diatonic. But Schütz, in his *Cantiones sacrae* of 1625, was, in a sense, going back behind Sweelinck to the apparently moribund ecclesiastical modes for a basic substance onto which to graft the newer, more directly expressive chromaticism inherent in concerted music of the melody-with-accompaniment type evolved in Venice, particularly by Gabrieli.

Still acting the persuasive ambassador, Schütz in 1627 composed—or arranged and composed—the first German opera. Rinnucini's text of the first opera, *Dafne* (1597), had been translated into German in the expectation that Peri's music could be sung to it when the opera was produced at Torgau in 1627 for a royal wedding. Peri's music, however, married to the Italian syllables, would do nothing of the sort. So Schütz apparently composed a new score for the translated text. That score, like Peri's original one, is now lost.

In 1629, Schütz returned to Italy in his forty-fifth year, going to a Venice musically much altered since he had first visited it seventeen years earlier. The vogue of the solo voice, carrying a melody to intense dramatic effects, had increased notably. Harmonic textures were more seasoned with dissonance expressively employed. Instruments were supplanting the earlier accompaniments by massed voices. While still in Venice, Schütz published the first of his three collections of *Symphoniae sacrae,* this one containing twenty settings in Latin of Biblical texts. Some of these "symphonies" (a term very vaguely employed at the time) are in reality cantatas or oratorios.

Opera, originating almost exactly at 1600, constituted the first formal achievement of the monodic manner. Near the hour of its birth that manner found, in the cantata and its larger extension, the oratorio, non-theatrical forms of equal durability. The cantata existed in embryo in collections issued by both Peri and Caccini before 1610, where it appeared as a monodic substitute for the polyphonic madrigal of the preceding century. Tightly wrought pieces of sectional, often strophic, construction, some of these cantatas consisted of alternating passages for voices and for instruments, the voice pronouncing both recitative and almost-arias deserving the name *arioso.* Related by ancestry and patterns to forms of the instrumental *canzona* that led to both the fugue and the sonata, this sort of cantata became a favorite with such Italian composers as Luigi Rossi (1598-1653),[1] Marc' Antonio Cesti (1623-1669), and, above all, Giacomo Carissimi (1605-1674).

In Carissimi's hands the third great formal genre of monodic music was brought to maturity. The oratorio, descended somewhat indirectly from so-called "dialogue tropes" of the years between 925 and 1075, from the resulting Biblical plays with music, from the later "mysteries"—from which the serious drama of Western

---

[1] Patronized by Cardinal Mazarin, Rossi spent some time in Paris. His opera *Orfeo,* translated into French as *Le Mariage d'Orphée et Euridice,* one of the earliest such works to cross the Alps, was sung in Paris in March 1647.

Europe also in part evolved—and from other semi-liturgical musical plays, achieved its name and much of its enduring nature in the middle 1500's. It was then that St. Philip Neri founded the Order of Oratorians, with headquarters in a Roman oratory (literally a place for prayer). Part of the services in the Oratory were semi-theatrical presentations intended for popular approval, adaptations in polyphonic vocal style of the earlier mysteries.

Many religious musico-dramatic works of the turn of the seventeenth century remain difficult to classify. The *Rappresentazione di anima e di corpo* (1600) of Emilio de' Cavalieri (1550?-1602) is alternately called the first oratorio and one of the earliest true operas. We no longer think of oratorio as having such elaborate stage settings and costumes as were given to the performance of this work by a friend of Peri and Caccini, but it was an oratorio in spirit. Carissimi, however, composed works that, even as produced then, would have fallen completely within our present understanding of the term oratorio.[2] In his sacred music dramas for performance without settings or costumes, but articulated with devotion and musical strength out of chorus, recitative, *arioso,* solos, groups of soloists, instrumental passages, monody, homophony, polyphony, concerted voices and instruments, and free use of the then most advanced harmonic idiom—in these Carissimi left models on which many future composers, including Handel, could exercise their ingenuity and genius.

Acquainted with the music of Monteverdi and Carissimi, aware through direct experience of the Italian cantata and oratorio, Schütz spent most of the rest of his long life in the Germanies. He went on pouring out compositions combining the older strengths of Northern polyphony with the sensual dramatic allurements of the younger Southern monody, varying the proportions accurately in view of particular purposes. Of his later works the most important were (1645) the *Seven Words of Christ on the Cross;* (1664) the *History of the Joyous and Merciful Birth of the Son of God*

---

[2] Many Masses and Passions are distinguishable from oratorios only in that their texts are liturgical. But this distinction breaks down when confronted with oratorios having scriptural and liturgical texts. It is useful to consider Masses, Passions—even such a work as Bach's *Magnificat*—as varieties of oratorio intended for use in church services.

and Mary—an oratorio; and (1665-6) musical treatments of Christ's Passion as set forth by Matthew, Luke, and John. Brought down to us imperfectly, these last intensely sensitive works, composed two decades before the birth of Handel and Bach, are in no way stylistically inferior to *Messiah* and the *St. Matthew Passion,* from which they differ notably in dispensing entirely with instruments. They were first fruits of the consummation of the wholly remarkable marriage of Germanic and Italianate musical genius which has come to be called the German baroque.

Seventeenth-century France, lying between the Italy of Corelli, Alessandro Scarlatti, and Carissimi and the Germanies of Schütz and the great organists, asserted its national character in its manner of absorbing one or both foreign influences. French music became more Italianate than Teutonic, but remained French. In the compositions of a Gallicized Italian and a quintessential Frenchman, France contributed forms, musical atmospheres, and technical practices of the first importance—as well as music that, if properly listened to, remains wholly delightful. These men were Jean-Baptiste Lully (1632-1687) and François Couperin (1668-1733), called *"le grand"* to single him out from the numerous composers in his family. Lully's talents filled ballet and opera with fresh emphases, molded the overture, and significantly developed the instrumental suite. Couperin was a major formulator of keyboard manners.

Lully's proficiency as a violinist, then unexampled, at least in France, attracted the attention of Louis XIV. As the leader of the King's ensemble known as *Les Petits Violons,* Lully wrote instrumental music rich in contrapuntal effects, but tending to harmonic poverty. He gradually abandoned the texture made by assigning chief melodies to one instrument; he increasingly favored a more even distribution of notes among the instruments employed, and finally arrived at an over-all balance that may be called orchestral. In ballet he carried on the already established tradition of theatrical presentation of largely mythical and allegorical stories by means of a group of dancers, a tradition that in France dated from the 1400's. By his time both the costumes and the scenery of ballet were lavish; the stage machinery was often far more impressive than either the music or the dancing. One of the best-known of the earlier ballets of which the music has survived, the *Ballet Comique de la royne,* was first danced in 1581.

In Lully's versatile hands the music for ballets, beginning with the *Ballet de la nuit* in 1653, consisted more and more of sharply defined brief dance forms. Enduring and often used among these were the minuet, *rigaudon, bourrée,* gavotte, and *passepied.* Grouped into suites (or, later, composed specifically for that use), these musical forms proved central to the evolution of both orchestral and keyboard music. In the history of ballet as such, Lully remains significant because he enlivened the previously monotonous stately movements with rapid steps and because he made the importance of the star *danseuse,* complete with pirouettes and other twinkling attractions.

When Lully began to compose operas, his genius led him to become a key figure in the entire story of French art. With his setting of Philippe Quinault's *Les Fêtes de l'Amour et de Bacchus,* staged on November 15, 1672, the long and various pageant of French opera was inaugurated. This was the first of twenty operas by the two men. To subjects pseudo-historical or mythological, Lully matched music of understanding variety and suppleness. Not satisfied with the recitative manner of his operatic predecessors—the "dry" recitative or *recitativo secco,* a semi-song, semi-declamation accompanied only by harpsichord or a related instrument—he treated the connective tissue between arias or dances or choruses so as to raise it nearer to full musical autonomy. To the recitative he gave, first of all, a more varied accompaniment than most composers had given it, though Monteverdi had experimented with, and Schütz had made considerable use of, *recitativo stromentato* (instrumented) or *accompagnato* (accompanied). Lully paid the most careful attention to French prosody, fitting musical accents and rhythms to the native shape of the language, often altering the musical meter several times within a brief space. His arias and passages in *arioso* were successfully written not only to be expressive, but also to be concise, orderly, and neat in ways still thought of as peculiarly French.

Because of Lully's strong feeling for proportion, he lent grace to everything he attempted. Equally admirable was his sense of timing, which taught him to introduce shifts from *recitativo stromentato* to *arioso,* from singing to dancing, from solo to duet or chorus, which saved his operas from the monotony that might otherwise have blanketed musico-dramatic works in which musical patterns were so few and so often repeated, and in which the use of chordal harmony was nearly always unadventurous and stiff.

When the earliest operas had had any introduction, it had usually been either an extended instrumental flourish—a sort of attention-gathering fanfare—or a musically accompanied stage scene called a prologue. This latter served the double purpose of pointing out the meaning and symbolic significance of the action to follow and of dedicating the performance and the work, usually in the most florid language, to a king, prince, or noble patron. Soon, however, instrumental overtures became customary, often before each act. Occurring in various patterns and under a multitude of designations, these gradually adapted two distinct forms. One, the "Italian" overture favored by Alessandro Scarlatti, typically consisted of three sections or movements—fast, slow, fast. Many Venetian composers of opera favored the *"canzona*-overture,"* formally allied to the *sonata da chiesa,* and often labeled "sonata." This was likely to consist of a slow section in duple rhythm and a contrasting faster section in triple rhythm. This was the pattern that Lully enlarged into the "French" overture, the earliest known example of which led off, in 1658, his *ballet de cour* called *Alcidiane.*

As an overture pattern, the Lullyan prologue most often began with a slow section designed to evoke grandeur. Often repeated, this was typically followed by a rapid section in which a brief melodic subject was treated in semi-fugal manner. This two-part pattern evidenced vitality and utility for a long time, at the end of which it was elongated by the addition of a very broad slow close, thus in effect becoming slow-fast-slow, the exact reverse of the "Italian" fast-slow-fast pattern. The Lullyan overture did not

have to bear a close relation to the opera it preceded; it was therefore easily detached, easily composed for its own sake as autonomous music. As such, the "French" overture soon existed outside
the opera house, having become a useful pattern of instrumental
music *per se,* one that would yield precedence only, in the mid-
eighteenth century, to the classic sonata and symphony.

The seventeenth century established the custom of performing
(or, at least, of publishing) groups of instrumental dance movements. Lully appears to have arrived at this practice somewhat independently, so that his concept of the suite was individual. Skele-
ton performances of some of his ballets and operas were given by
entirely instrumental forces, the music played consisting of the
overture and a selection of the dance sections. But neither Lully
nor other composers of his time in France took advantage of the
resulting suite-pattern as inviting composition for its own sake.
German composers, one of the earliest of them Johann Sigismund
Kusser (or Cousser, 1660-1727), took it over. With the suite itself
sometimes headed *Ouverture,* these constellations of brief dances,
preceded by a "French" overture, were composed by Johann Sebastian Bach, his immediate forerunners, and his immediate successors. During the second half of the eighteenth century, however,
this type of suite was largely abandoned, like the "French" overture itself, as a separate composition. In later musical eras the
suite has tended to become again what it originally was, a group
of selections from a long work. Such are the suites from Grieg's
incidental music for *Peer Gynt* and that from Tchaikovsky's *The
Nutcracker.* Occasionally a modern composer will write a suite
as independent music: examples are Darius Milhaud's *Suite prov-
ençale* and *Suite française.*

Lully's life and creative mentality lay wholly within the heyday
of the baroque, which in music may be said to have begun in Italy
about 1575 and to have closed on the death of Handel in 1759.
But François Couperin lived, physically and intellectually, as long
in the eighteenth century as in the seventeenth. He was for forty-
eight years a contemporary of Bach, Handel, and Domenico Scarlatti. And though the actual dates of his life (1668-1733) fall within

the baroque period, he himself announced another musical age, the so-called rococo.[3]

The baroque in music may be defined as an exuberant evolution of means capable of carrying drama, pathos, and passion; the rococo may be described as a shifting within and away from the baroque, from expression to elegance, from the bodying-forth of majesty to its elaborate decoration, from large gestures to small gestures fine in detail. The rococo was first a French outgrowth of the baroque. It manifested itself in architecture, in interior decoration, in literature, music, and painting—in which last its first great practitioner was Watteau (1684-1721). It claimed less territory than the baroque had yearned for, and was content with scintillating achievements small in scale but perfect in proportion. The rococo dallied with the frivolous and the amorous, for its hope was to make aristocratic living not only more sumptuous, but also more entertaining. It is fair to say that while, in music, the baroque examined, extended, and expressed life, the rococo commented on, decorated, and stylized it. To denigrate the baroque as overladen or stylistically corrupt, the rococo as trivial and passionless, is to fail in historic comprehension and to deny by implication the very central meaning of style.

Couperin was the first musical master of the rococo. Although a notable organist, he survives chiefly through his four volumes of *pièces pour le clavecin, i.e.,* for the harpsichord. In these he crowned the school of French harpsichord composers which had been founded by Jacques Champion de Chambonnières (1602-1672?). The several members of this school had also composed suites of pieces—suites not in the Lullyan sense, but simply groups of brief pieces all in one key. These harpsichord suites neither developed a true formal character nor settled upon usual successions or varieties of dance forms for inclusion. Couperin, indeed, tended to drop dance forms altogether, constructing his *ordres,* as he called the suites, from pieces wholly original as to pattern and

[3] The word "baroque" is derived from a Portuguese word meaning a pearl of irregular shape. "Rococo," derived from a French word for rock, indicated originally types of artificial rockwork and pierced shellwork.

form, sections having flowery rococo titles like *Les Vergers fleuris,*
Soeur Monique, and *Les Barricades mystérieuses.*

Remote from music intended to praise or placate God or to
exalt His representative at Versailles, Couperin's *ordres* were
meant to entertain by purely musical means. The music often
seems to lay claim to nothing more than parity with jewelry or
stucco scrollwork; yet it asserts the self-sufficiency of music in a
new way. Despite their often descriptive titles and amusing mim-
icry of non-musical sounds, Couperin's finest pieces are music for
its own sake, unallied to religion, drama, or other non-musical
activity. By this mild assertion of his art's independence, Couperin
helped make possible the great classic period beginning with Boccherini and Haydn.

To accuse Couperin's perfectly proportioned and delightful
ordres of heartlessness is to look for Gothic splendor at Le Petit
Trianon. They are neither searching dramatic symbols nor profound emotional equivalents. Despite their titles they are not
"program music." Despite their many touches of naturalistic imitation—of the clucking of hens, the clicking of heels—they are invited to do more than they can or were intended to do when they
are listened to for more than their formal grace, their mellifluous
progressions and lively figuration, their sweet artificial atmosphere
of courtly gallantry. Cecil Gray, writing in *The History of Music*
that Couperin had been unduly praised by such modern French
musicians as Debussy and Ravel, added suggestively that his harpsichord pieces recall "china shepherdesses and similar antiques of
the period." If nicely interpreted, this phrase suggests not only
the exact nature of Couperin's musical originality, but also a sensible manner of listening to his delicate and charming *ordres.* It
also makes certain that they must be played and heard, not on the
piano, but on the harpsichord.

Charles II, returning from the court of Louis XIV, where he
almost certainly became familiar with the music of Lully, carried
to London the setting and the demand for a new musical style.
England, not so devoid of good composers as many historians of
the nineteenth century have made her appear, had nonetheless
fallen upon musically evil days, poor in nurture and formal sup-

port for a maturing composer, and the short career of Henry Purcell (1658?-1695), for all the beauty it produced, unquestionably suffered from its artistic surroundings. And that was an English tragedy, for Purcell's failure to establish a tradition that could be adapted by eighteenth-century Englishmen led to Italian and German supremacy in England. For two centuries after Purcell's death no Englishman could find about him or in his own person develop the musical sustenance necessary to firm style. Only toward the end of the nineteenth century and in our own time has truly English music been composed which requires mention in company with that of Byrd, the madrigalists, John Blow (1649-1708), and Purcell.

Purcell is remarkable both for his fresh spontaneity and for his Mozartean versatility. In *Dido and Aeneas* (1689), his only true opera (and that first given an amateur performance, there being as yet no large English public for opera), he managed, in the face of Nahum Tate's legendarily silly libretto, to create a formally unflawed small work taking advantage of the best practices of the Italians. To methods he held in common with such an Italian as Pietro Francesco Cavalli (1602-1676), Purcell added an evocative sincerity and depth of feeling all his own.[4]

To *Dido and Aeneas* and to his numerous not-quite-operatic scores for plays, Purcell also brought hints taken from such of his predecessors as had composed masques, those English counterparts of the French *ballets de cour:* the poet-composer Thomas Campion (1567-1620), Henry Lawes (1596-1662)—who wrote the music for that most renowned masque, Milton's *Comus*—Matthew Locke (1630?-1677), and Christopher Gibbons (1615-1676), a son of Orlando Gibbons. And Purcell's use of balletic interludes such as the "Triumphing Dance" and "Dance of Witches and Sailors" in *Dido and Aeneas* possibly indicates familiarity with the scores of Lully.

In choral music, both religious and secular, Purcell likewise towered above his English contemporaries and matched the Continental creations of the period. He long served in several capacities in the Chapel Royal. His *Ode on St. Cecilia's Day* (1692, the

---

[4] See pages 94-95 for a discussion of Dido's Lament from this opera.

finest of several he composed) and *Te Deum and Jubilate* (1694)
are wonderfully realized combinations of choral composition and
full instrumental accompaniment in a truly orchestral style. The
texture is his own combination of polyphony and monody. In his
purely instrumental music—sonatas (those of 1683 were so called
for almost the first time in England) for two violins, violoncello
or *viola da gamba,* and *continuo* (organ or harpsichord); fantazias
(so spelled) for three, four, and five instruments; and harpsichord
suites of short movements—he revealed the era's developing mastery of manners native to non-vocal music. In them, too, he revealed the acute discomfort that seventeenth-century composers
increasingly felt within the narrow limits of the few keys that both
the tuning and limitations of their instruments forced them to
accept, at least within entire sections or movements. In each of
his suites Purcell confined himself to a single tonic key, each of
the short sections to a simple binary form, in which each section
is to be played twice in succession.

Simple binary form in which the first section is in the tonic key,
the second in the key based on the dominant (fifth step) of that
tonic, but moving back to the tonic for the ending, was certain to
lose its popularity with composers when freer movement from one
key to another (modulation) became possible, encouraging the
emergence of larger, more complex forms (often binary too). To
Purcell, simple ternary form was easily available only in repeating
a first section after the second, and he made use of even that almost
exclusively in the *aria da capo.* In the sense that the patterns and
forms available to him failed to evoke and display to best advantage all the inclinations of his musical imagination, and as he himself remained an adapter and improver of forms already existing,
it is fair to say of him, as Harvey Grace wrote in *The International
Cyclopedia of Music and Musicians,* that "he was a frustrated genius, born in a transition period, a century too soon (or perhaps
too late: with his skill and invention what a figure he would have
been among the Elizabethans!)."

Of most artists this sort of speculative criticism, any criticism
of what they are not rather than of what they are, is footless. But
of Purcell it is relevant. *Dido and Aeneas,* the *Te Deum and Jubi-*

late, the *Ode on St. Cecilia's Day,* and some of the sonatas, fantazias, and suites were the last major creations of the transitional, "becoming" period that just preceded the era of free modulation and expanded instrumental forms. But the general suggestion of Purcell's music as a whole is, if not quite of frustration, at least of a harvest incomplete. Certain musical tools that he needed but did not live long enough to obtain lay ahead, just past his reach, in Bach's *The Well-Tempered Clavier,* Handel's oratorios, and both the music and the intellectual formulations of Jean-Philippe Rameau.

Eight

TUNING · HARMONY · TONALITY
MODULATION · MAJOR AND MINOR MODES

On a modern piano in proper tune, any octave is an interval bounded by two tones of which one vibrates exactly twice as rapidly as the other. On that same piano, however—and on any present-day instrument of fixed pitch—any perfect fifth is an interval bounded by two tones of which one vibrates *very slightly less* than one and one-half times as rapidly as the other, while any major third shows a further narrowing of distance between its outside tones as compared with that between those of an "overtone" third.

This discrepancy between pure intervals—those existing in unchanging mathematical relationships between the overtones or partials that sound (audibly or inaudibly) when any single musical tone is struck—and those tuned on our instruments of fixed pitch is a time-honored compromise between nature and art. It was necessitated by the arbitrary, artistically evolved, unnatural division of each octave into twelve equal semitones. This division was forced on music by the gradual accretion of additional semitones to its fundamental alphabet—semitones represented in notation by sharps, flats, and sometimes naturals. The incidence of keys containing several sharps or flats resulted in the possibility, almost the necessity, of shifting from one key to another within a composition or musical section. This modulation was possible in rudimentary, limited ways in some of the systems of tuning employed before the adoption of the present system of equal temperament (temperament meaning tuning), but it became difficult or impossible in those systems when music began to be composed in keys using numerous accidentals.[1]

Before equal temperament was formulated and accepted, various systems of tuning were tried. A large part of Western European music composed between 1500 and 1700, and an appreciable portion of that composed in the Germanies up to 1800 and in England and France up to 1850, was conceived for performance on instruments tuned (or played, in the case of some not of fixed pitch) in the meantone system, which used a fifth very slightly narrower than the pure perfect fifth. All such music is somewhat misrepresented as performed now on instruments tuned or played in equal temperament. Yet the theoretical difference is far greater than the actually audible difference: the ear will make almost any small adjustment rapidly and with satisfaction.[2]

Required for complex modulations and for keys marked by more than two sharps or flats was a system of tuning that would not, to quote the *Harvard Dictionary of Music,* be "perfect in the simple keys and intolerably wrong in the others," but would "spread the inevitable inaccuracy over all the tones and keys." This method, in use throughout Western civilization since 1850, came to be called equal temperament because it solved the problems by arbitrarily dividing the octave into twelve equal semitones. The application of this unnatural mathematics has enabled us to use the tone next higher than any C as either C♯ or D♭; to use C itself as B♯ when we wish; to use one tone as both G♯ and A♭, and so on.

The practically necessary deviation from purity has been spread evenly over the octave, and thus over the keyboard. Except for the octaves, the intervals produced on our instruments of fixed pitch do not usually coincide with the overtone intervals produced by

[1] With the human voice and on instruments not of fixed pitch, unlimited modulation has always been possible theoretically.

[2] Broadwood, the renowned English piano manufacturer, did not design pianos for—or tune them in—equal temperament until 1846. Percy A. Scholes pointed out, in *The Oxford Companion to Music,* that a Broadwood piano built and tuned earlier than 1846 theoretically would have been unsuited to playing either Beethoven or Chopin! •

each individual tone, and we are therefore constantly creating a peculiarly mixed sort of misty dissonance not audible enough to upset any but the most phenomenally sensitive ears. In fact, this misty dissonance has become an integral element in the sonorous material of music, and we might sense its absence with considerable discomfort if we were suddenly to hear that instrumental chimera, a piano or other fixed-pitch instrument on which all the intervals were pure.

With equal temperament we can be generous in our use of sharps and flats; we can modulate with ease from one key to another. The price we have paid for this ability is the conventional falsification of every interval but the octave. As a completely, unthinkingly accepted convention, this distortion may be compared in some ways with that other by which perspective in painting was achieved.

Overgenerously, several individuals have been credited with the "invention" of equal temperament. One of them, Andreas Werckmeister (1645-1706), was an organist who studied and wrote extensively about all the complex problems involved in tuning both organs and keyboard stringed instruments. Werckmeister was working toward a system very like equal temperament, but he was not the first to do so—and he never formulated it as it is now used. Another "inventor" of equal temperament was Johann Sebastian Bach (1685-1750), long assigned this honor because in 1722 he composed *The Well-Tempered Clavier (Das wohltemperirte Clavier)*. This volume contained a prelude and a fugue in each of the twenty-four major and minor keys, and this fact was taken as indicating an instrument tuned so as to be much nearer our equal temperament than to the meantone temperament then in general use. But there is no proof whatever that Bach's own keyboard instruments were in equal temperament as we know it, and it is at least possible that he expected an instrument to be retuned between pairs of pieces. It was easy to retune a harpsichord, and Bach's "well-tempering" can be produced by tuning major thirds a little wide, perfect fifths a little narrow within the given key, the result being a temperament somewhere between meantone and equal.

Aristoxenus, a pupil of Aristotle, who wrote some of the earliest known theoretical treatises on music, is said to have advocated a tuning system (it was in reality a performing system) with many elements of equal temperament. Certainly Bartolomé Ramos de Pareja (1440?-1521?), an erudite Spanish musician, issued in Bologna in 1482 a book in which something close to equal temperament was derived from the circumstance that on the necks of guitarlike instruments the frets to indicate finger-placement—showing, that is, where the left-hand fingers should be pressed down to divide the strings—were placed equal semitones apart, inevitably resulting in a scale of equal semitones. During the sixteenth century the need for something resembling equal temperament was clearly sensed. One proposed system would have split the octave into twelve semitones, of which two would have been slightly narrower than the other ten. Adrian Willaert asked for the acceptance of a system that would, had it been put into use, have been equal temperament. Vincenzo Galilei (1533?-1591), a member of the Bardi *camerata* (and also father of the great astronomer), proposed the adoption of a semitone narrower than that of equal temperament by less than one twelve-hundredth the width of an octave. Gioseffe Zarlino (1517-1590), choirmaster of St. Mark's at Venice, wrote passages on lute-fingering which are equivalent to asking that the lute be fingered like the *vihuela,* a viol-like ancestor of the guitar—which amounted to equal temperament.

The seventeenth century became still more urgent in its drive toward equal semitones. Certain of the English virginalists—John Bull is a notable example—composed music of which the modulation complexity is so great as to call for instruments tuned somewhere near equal temperament. Marin Mersenne (1588-1648), a French savant, delineated the equal-semitone theory in full. Johann Caspar von Kerll (1627-1693), a leading German composer of the period just before Handel and Bach, composed one piece that modulates through every key. Johann Caspar Ferdinand Fischer (1665?-1738) published in 1702 a set of preludes and fugues for organ pedagogy in which nineteen of the twenty-four major and minor keys are represented. Handel's friend Johann Mattheson (1681-1764) issued in 1719 an *Exemplarische Organisten Probe* in which all twenty-four are represented. Bach's *Well-Tempered Clavier* [3] followed in 1722. Others of Bach's compositions, as well as many of Handel's, imply by their harmonic texture that they were written by men who envisaged instruments tuned near equal temperament.

What had been making equal temperament desirable, and finally essential, was the increasingly rapid trend toward classic harmony, the emergence of sharply defined sensations of key or tonality, and the consequent importance of modulation as one of the grammatical processes of music.

By the time of Bach and Handel and their contemporaries, music had become an enormously complex, greatly various, self-confident art. The formal patterns at its disposition were supple and satisfactory. Monody had set its melodic sense free in new regions, and it had learned that monody and polyphony need not be mutually exclusive. The gradual approach to equal temperament was adding free modulation to the art's means. The development of the pianoforte was about to supply it with its most useful single instrument after the organ and the violin. Its right to autonomy, its creators' free choice as to whether they would compose music to a text or music for its own sake, was unquestioned. All that was required for the unfolding of a musical era as fruitful as the most fertile periods of the past was composers emotionally and mentally equipped to seize upon and organize this wealth of means.

Whether the means evoked the men or the men chanced to be able to employ the means, the most important period in musical history after that of the vocal polyphonists may be dated, in one way, by the births of Rameau in 1683, Bach and Handel in 1685, Gluck in 1714, Haydn in 1732, Mozart in 1756, and Beethoven in 1770—all within a span of eighty-seven years. The music of these

[3] Only the first volume was so entitled by Bach, though the second volume—adding twenty-four more preludes and fugues, to make up the so-called "forty-eight"—follows the same scheme.

master composers should never have been allowed (as it has) to cast into shadow the music of their predecessors and successors, or to make us undervalue that of many of their less impressive, less technically important contemporaries. But it is true that between Rameau's birth in 1683 and Beethoven's death in 1827 music summed up its past in one magnificent composition after another and then advanced confidently into three or four remarkable futures.

Genius may either be accepted without question or discussed in terms of biographical or psychological analysis. Recognizing genius as a term, albeit vague, for qualities that cannot be described better, I deal with it here only in examining the specific actions of indicative geniuses as they applied and enriched music's vocabulary, asserting and proving its cohesiveness and probity as expressive creation. To explore the 1683-1827 period it is essential to look inquiringly at harmony, at the continuing evolution of formal patterns, at the flowering of the cantata, Passion, and oratorio, and at the evolution of the orchestra and the piano—as well as to examine the most significant of those periodic crises which have marked the career of opera. The first stages of these inquiries lie everywhere in the preceding pages; we must now isolate some relevant developments in harmony.

The word harmony is derived from a Greek word, *harmos,* meaning a fitting together. In its barest musical use, harmony means no more than the simultaneous sounding of two or more tones. This meaning has been transferred by later usage to the word chord. Webster indicates this by first defining harmony as "musical consonance" and suggesting that it refers only to "pleasant" simultaneities, *i.e.,* combinations of tones whose simultaneity is widely accepted as consonant or proper. This application of the word remains valuable in reference to much music of the seventeenth, eighteenth, and nineteenth centuries, but from our site in history its value diminishes with reference to music composed before 1600 and in our own time.

In its widest and most useful application to music, harmony refers to the unfolding structure defined by the make-up, orderly progression, and interrelationship of chords. In this usage the word is distinguished not only (as Webster states) from those other important terms, melody and rhythm, but also from polyphony. Harmony is the forward movement of vertical units (chords), polyphony or counterpoint that of horizontal units (melodies). Music began as melody; chords were at first one thing that happened to melodies when two or more of them were sounded simultaneously and human ears began to take an interest in the implications and significances of the combinations of tones sounded together. In that sense, harmony is what happens to both melodies and chords when chords succeed one another and our ears recognize relationships among them.

The briefest consideration of polyphony convinces us that all music except that consisting of one melody and nothing else, and even that as we are likely to hear it now, is harmonic by the terms of our evolving definition. But it was not until the half-century leading up to the appearance of opera and the assertion of *le nuove musiche* (1550-1600) that composers and listeners placed important emphasis on harmonic relationships as constituent materials of the musical art. The pressure of this importance constantly grew, itself helping to hasten the adoption of equal temperament, strengthening the sense of tonality or key, and finally bringing about the system herein referred to as "classic harmony." During the first quarter of the eighteenth century, several theorists interested in explaining actual musical occurrences and in attempting to legislate both present and past proprieties insisted upon harmony as a foremost analytical and constructive principle. Specially and enduringly important among them were Johann Joseph Fux (1660-1741) and Rameau.

In view of the fact that many musical practices of earlier periods are discussed in harmonic *terms*, the actual arrangement of harmonic *knowledge* has appeared to many to have occurred late in music's history. But the data of that knowledge, the very logics with which it deals, were impossible and devoid of meaning before the realization of the classic system of keys, of tonality. And that system was impossible under the musical philosophy of the ecclesiastical modes or any of their variations and extensions short of the twenty-four diatonic major and minor scales or keys, out of the relations within which and among which the system itself was evolved.

Of almost every musical work in existence it may be said that it exists in relationships between one principal tone—its tonic—and all of the other tones it employs. Gregorian Chant recognized in each of its melodies the primacy of one tone. The domination of one tone, the existence of a tonic, that is, appears to be a first law of music. In this sense, all music was tonal until some of it became consciously atonal. The constant presence in a composition or musical section of one tonic (or several successive tonics) is the basic premise of any system of tonal harmony.

The concepts of key (tonality) and modulation share a basic assumption: that chords have functions, bear aesthetic-psychological relationships to one another and tend to invite the subsequent appearance of certain other chords. Thus, if a composition mostly in C major arrives, after a time, back at the tonic triad C-E-G in any position, and whether "close" or with its constituent tones spread out to cover more than one octave, the composer has arrived at a strategic point for modulating smoothly into one of several other keys. He may decide to regard C-E-G at this point, for example, as the subdominant triad of G major and to modulate temporarily into that key by so treating it. Or he may regard C-E-G as the triad on the seventh degree of D minor. In this procedure the chord treated as belonging simultaneously to two keys is called a pivot-chord; it supplies the most often used modulatory device.

Another sort of modulation is prepared by some insistence upon one tone common to the key in hand and to a chord pre-selected to provide entrance into a new key. After the tone is sufficiently established, the composer announces the new chord of which it is a constituent. A third method of modulation, enharmonic, can be simply, if somewhat inaccurately, described as that of considering what has been, let us say, G♯ as having become A♭—in equal temperament the same tone, but viewed in a given context as having different functions and implications. After the eighteenth century some composers began to feel it possible to move from one key to another without modulating—by simply ceasing to compose in one key and starting at once to compose in another. This action can be called "modulation" only by a distention of that term.

Modulation has supplied music with one of its psychologically forceful ways to achieve variety. It not only presents the means of showing melodies, chords, and comments on them in different pitches, but also alters the functions and importances of individual tones. In C major, for example, C is the tonic, and tends to be present in chords at points of rest or finality; if the composer modulates to G major, however, C becomes the subdominant, and is seen in a new light, while G (formerly the dominant of C major) becomes the more settled tonic. Modulation, that is to say, supplies perspective, shiftings, ambiguities, and resolutions unavailable to music remaining in one key.

Similarly, the differences between major and minor, once well established, supplied musicians with a tool without which most compositions of the centuries immediately past are inconceivable. Listeners and composers have, in general, agreed that major scales and major keys are brighter, "happier," than the more somber, more easily lugubrious minor scales and keys, but very many instances can be cited of "sad" music in major keys and "gay" music in minor keys. The real significance of the major-minor relationships is far subtler: it supplies a further enrichment of perspective, of possibilities for modulation. To move from a major key to a minor one or vice versa is a more appreciable midstream shifting of values than motion from one major key to another or one minor key to another. Further, it is always interestingly possible to modulate, say, from C major to C minor, two keys having the same tonic, dominant, and subdominant (C, G, F), but differing greatly in internal relationships.

Why does a composer choose to write a given composition or passage in one major key rather than another, one minor key rather than another? (His original choice between a major key and a minor key is easier to understand.) Partly for the ease and naturalness with which, in the key chosen, his tones and chords can be played on the instrument or instruments he is using. In unaccompanied vocal music, his reason might be the pitch of the desired human voice, any major or minor key being higher or lower than any other major or minor key in over-all pitch; this consideration may play some part, too, in choosing keys for instrumental music.

In the meantone temperament—and, in fact, in any system of tuning other than equal temperament—there was some actual difference of interval arrangement between one key and another. But in equal temperament the arrangement of intervals between the scale tones of one major key and another, or one minor key and another, is identical. In composing for equal temperament, the choice of key is made partly for the reasons cited above, and partly for subjective psychological reasons that defy analysis, though their intense reality in composers' minds cannot be denied. Some composers favor certain keys, appear to connect certain keys with certain moods or atmospheres. But except for questions of pitch—which, by affecting the semi-audibility of overtones, clearly affect timbre—and questions of performing ease, and except in relation to other keys, one major key is exactly like another major key, one minor like another. Except as influenced by the practical considerations mentioned, conscious or unconscious, then, a preference for one key above another is either subjective or mystical, and properly speaking lies beyond or outside the possibility of logical explanation.

CANTATA · PASSION · ORATORIO · BACH · HANDEL
HAYDN · LATER ORATORIOS

———————

Evolving with the monodic innovations at the opening of the seventeenth century in Italy, opera and oratorio were paralleled by
the cantata, a smaller vocal-instrumental form. The earliest
known examples of cantata belong to the type later called *cantata
da camera* (chamber cantata) as distinguished from the *cantata da
chiesa* (church cantata). As early as 1610 both Caccini and Peri,
the very men who ushered opera into its career as a distinct form
of stage music, had composed pieces somewhere between the aria
and the cantata. These were extended vocal pieces in which a
form of the variation principle was employed: the same instrumental accompaniment was used for numerous stanzas or stro-
phes, each of which had a different vocal melody. The word
"cantata" was first applied to compositions of this nature in 1620,
in the *Cantade et arie a voce sola* (Cantatas and arias for solo
voice) of Alessandro Grandi (?-1630?). From the cantata's earliest
days it bred elaborate examples in which sections of aria were
contrasted with recitative and *arioso,* and even with purely instrumental *ritornelli.* By the days of Luigi Rossi, Marc' Antonio
Cesti, and Giacomo Carissimi, the cantata had become a mixed
form tending toward standardization, a vocal-instrumental equivalent of the *canzona da sonare.*

Standardization of the cantata gave it the pattern aAbB, two recitatives (small letters) introducing two contrasted arias—again parallel to similar patterns in the purely instrumental *canzona,* which, in turn, it helped toward the *sonata da camera* and *sonata da chiesa.* Alessandro Scarlatti composed between six hundred and seven hundred cantatas planned this way. Such immediate successors of Scarlatti as Leonardo Vinci, Niccolò Jommelli, and Leonardo Leo varied the pattern somewhat, but used the cantata predominantly for the secular purpose of expressing amorous and other sentiments through virtuoso singers.

Handel, who seems to have begun composing cantatas in Italy, remained largely content to follow the Scarlattian way. About eighty of his Italian cantatas are known, and nearly all of them are pastoral or amorous operas-in-miniature for one or two voices and instruments. Handel also composed numerous vocal duets with *continuo* to Italian texts, and there are even two similar vocal trios. All of these cantatas and cantata-like pieces are highly decorative and conventional, full of notably Italianate melody. Perhaps the best-known of the Handel cantatas are *Nel dolce dell' obblio, Fillide ed Aminta,* and *Apollo e Dafne.*

The Italian cantata soon spread to Germany, but there, the influence of the Evangelical Church being pervasive, it was chiefly the *cantata da chiesa.* Heinrich Schütz made use of the pattern, but did not adopt the name. The similar pieces of Dietrich Buxtehude elaborated the form, giving important roles to both chorus and instrumental ensembles. The German cantatas of the seventeenth century were usually more solemn, more dramatically emotional than the Italian. They show a typically Teutonic emphasis on elaboration of texture, as against the Italian care for song. In Germany the use of either the music or the text, or both, of the chorales—those endlessly pliable German Protestant hymns —gave rise to the chorale cantata, much favored by Johann Sebastian Bach. In the main, the early chorale cantatas differed from the more Italianate cantatas of Buxtehude chiefly in that they made use of the chorale melodies and texts instead of being built entirely of freely composed melody and of texts adapted from the Bible or especially written for the purpose.

Of the most signal importance to the whole future of music

in Germany, especially because of its influence on Bach, was the struggle between the Pietists—followers of Philipp Jakob Spener (1635-1705) and August Hermann Francke (1663-1727)—and the less narrowly religious, more worldly generality of Evangelical Lutherans. The Pietists actively preached the necessity for expiating sin by repentance, the superiority of heartfelt devotion over intellectual conviction, and the desirability of experiencing as facts both regeneration and sanctification. They disapproved of the secularizing of music in the German churches, attacking it violently. They correctly saw that the old chorales were losing their central position in the music of the churches, and were being replaced by musical styles borrowed from secular sources, opera in particular. Objects of their attacks included Johann Kuhnau and Handel's teacher, Friedrich Wilhelm Zachau (1663-1712), both of whom composed numerous cantatas in the newer, freer manner.

In defense of the new church music arose Erdmann Neumeister (1671-1756), a pastor with literary talent. Deliberately challenging the Pietistic demand that cantata texts be simplified and confined largely to Biblical quotation and chorale texts, Neumeister rearranged many of his own sermons in poetic form and published them avowedly for the use of composers. He developed a type of text which quoted verbatim from both the Bible and the chorales, but also included poetry of his own, parts of it often so planned as to require setting in the *aria da capo* form, surely "operatic" from the Pietists' point of view. Numerous composers, among them the terribly prolific Georg Philipp Telemann (1681-1767) and Bach, responded by setting Neumeister's texts and those of his disciples and imitators such as Picander (pseudonym of Christian Friedrich Henrici, 1700-1764) and Salomo Franck (1659-1725). It was all but impossible to set a text by Neumeister, Picander, or Franck above a choral *cantus firmus;* the result was a remarkable and sudden liberation of German composers' imaginations.

Some two hundred and thirty of Bach's cantatas survive, mostly religious, but some secular. These vary greatly in style, manner, pattern, length, and forces employed. An average Bach cantata

opens with a chorus, then alternates recitative and arias (sometimes duets) for up to three soloists, and ends on a freely har-
monized chorale melody. The choruses in Bach's cantatas are
largely fugal, but the monodic origins of cantata can be seen in
the solos. The finest of Bach's cantatas—lyrico-dramatic masterpieces of constantly unfolding baroque luxuriousness—contain
some of the most sincere, expressive religious music ever conceived. ·

The forces that molded the German cantatas similarly effected
German settings of the Passion of Christ, with text from Matthew, Mark, Luke, or John, and therefore originally sung respectively on Palm Sunday, the succeeding Tuesday and Wednes-
day, and Good Friday. Passions had been composed as early as the
twelfth century, if not before. In Italy they were couched successively in the motet manner of the great era of polyphony and in
the monodic oratorio style of the early seventeenth century.
Finally, in Germany, they were composed homophonically to
texts in the vernacular. The baroque composers brought to their
settings of one or the other aspect of the Passion all the resources
of instrumentation, chorale, aria, and recitative. Thus the Passion
approached very close to oratorio. As already mentioned, Schütz
composed Passions of extraordinary beauty. At the beginning of
the eighteenth century the verbatim use of Biblical quotation
was dropped altogether from Passion texts, being replaced by specially written texts using dramatic or allegorical paraphrases of
sections of that great tragic story. Popular texts of this sort were
written by Barthold Heinrich Brockes (1680-1747) and Picander.
Brockes's *Der für die Sünden der Welt gemarterte und sterbende
Jesus* (Jesus Martyred and Dying for the Sins of the World) was
set by many composers, including Reinhard Keiser, Telemann,
and Handel.

Bach's *St. Matthew Passion,* composed in 1729 to a Picander
text, is wonderfully pathetic music that may be likened to a chain
of cantatas. Each of its cantata-like sections culminates in a chorale. The voice of Christ is accompanied by a quartet of stringed
instruments, giving it a luminous contrast to the other, more
fully accompanied voices. Every sort of available dramatic, realis-

tic, and imitative effect is here brought to bear in a series of choruses, recitatives, and arias, profoundly pious, but not Pietistic. Somewhat less satisfactory as a stylistic unit is Bach's only other surviving Passion,[1] the *St. John Passion* (1723), which contains *"Es ist vollbracht"* (It is consummated), an alto aria that is perhaps superior in tragic utterance to anything in the *St. Matthew Passion*.

Coincident with the emergence of monody, though not certainly caused by it, was a decline in both the quantity and the general quality of musical settings of the Roman Catholic Mass. After the great sixteenth-century Orlando di Lasso and Palestrina, their first equal in both religious and musical grandeur was the most magnificent of all musical compositions, Bach's Mass in B minor, over which he labored intermittently from 1733 to 1738. A composition of then unexampled length and aesthetic loftiness, the Mass differs little from Bach's Passions in musical usages, widely from them in spirit. In effect it is a liturgical oratorio, the text of which is the Latin of both the Proper and the Ordinary of the Mass. In spirit it reflects Bach's inwardness and piety as surely as the later Masses of Haydn and Mozart reflect more strictly musical attitudes. For grave and profoundly moving magnificence the Mass in B minor was most nearly matched by the *Missa solemnis* that Beethoven composed as his opus 123 (1819-23).

The oratorio, meanwhile, still revealed its descent from the mysteries, those episodes from the Bible and the lives of saints, and its relation to the secular theatrical entertainments of the 1500's and 1600's. Carissimi's important contributions to the evolution of the form have already been discussed. Like its smaller relative, the cantata, the oratorio rapidly increased the participation of the chorus. By the 1730's, when Handel tired of the London public's fluctuating reception of his Italian operas and turned his full attention to oratorio, the form was ripe for his mastery. He thought of it as a musical giant capable of accepting his mightiest choral outbursts, a large ensemble of instruments,

---

[1] Bach is believed to have composed five Passions, but three of them have been lost. A *St. Luke Passion* once held to have been his is now known to be spurious.

and the most baroque-operatic manner of singing. The chorus in a Handelian oratorio revives a basic feature of the Greek drama in a way that Caccini and Peri had neglected: its role is that of commentator on the chief elements of the story.

Setting English words, Handel in the most successful of his many oratorios expressed for the people of England their sense of imperial expansion. His rolling choruses, his celebrations of heroes (Biblical mostly, but easily thought of as English), the sweet melodic streams of his love songs and arias of pathos—these guaranteed his oratorios an enduring reception from large audiences, many of their constituent members not seriously musical. It is scarcely too confining to say that the crowning masterpieces of the musical baroque were Bach's *St. Matthew Passion* and *B Minor Mass* and such of Handel's oratorios as *Israel in Egypt* and *Messiah*.

After Handel's masterworks, oratorio passed the zenith of its usefulness, partly because that sort of drama was replaced to a large extent by purely instrumental music in versions of the sonata manner that is in itself a drama of musical ideas. The subsequent history of oratorio is a tally of occasional lonely accomplishments towering noticeably above surrounding plains. Carl Philipp Emanuel Bach composed several oratorios containing individual numbers of considerable power and attraction, but in them we can read that the baroque era—the very cause and home of the form—had ended somewhat before the birth of a new era of equal artistic fertility. The C. P. E. Bach oratorios—of which possibly the best is *Die Auferstehung und Himmelfahrt Jesu* (*The Resurrection and Ascension of Jesus,* 1787)—can only strike modern listeners as indecisive mixtures of the grand baroque manner of the composer's father and the style of Haydn.

Haydn in old age presented the end of the eighteenth century with the greatest of its religious oratorios—*The Creation* (1797)—and at the age of sixty-nine completed the greatest secular oratorio of the succeeding century, *The Seasons* (1801), the latter making use of a German translation of James Thomson's *The Seasons.* Into the formation of these sure and artistically mature works went Haydn's knowledge of Handel; much of what he had learned during a lifetime of untiring composition; instrumental music in derived sonata manner; his enduring affection for the life of field, farm, and sky; hints from Mozart's handling of *Singspiel* and opera; and Haydn's own striking genius for absorbing these—and many more—influences without submerging his own stanch, forthright, and winning personality. Of the baroque majesty that Handel had harnessed sixty years earlier there remains in Haydn's masterpieces only what was still viable: they are classical works making full and relevant use of the classical orchestra and of the ripened system of classical harmony.

After Haydn there was a sharp decline in the quality of newly composed oratorios. Mendelssohn's *St. Paul* (1836) and *Elijah* (1846), though once looked upon, particularly in England, as of Handelian quality, have lost much of their strength. Their belated assumption of the baroque manners of Handel and Bach has failed to stay well mixed with Mendelssohn's essentially romantic, lyric, undramatic idiom. In the second half of the nineteenth century, however, three quasi-oratorios demonstrated that a composer could still employ chorus, soloists, and orchestra to create non-Handelian works of power and beauty. Hector Berlioz (1803-1869) composed *L'Enfance du Christ* (*The Infant Christ*) and *La Damnation de Faust;* Johannes Brahms (1833-1897) wrote *Ein deutsches Requiem.*[2] The first is a gravely simple, lyrical retelling of the events immediately following the birth of Jesus, the second a "dramatic legend" that Berlioz at first called a "concert opera," the last an extended funeral lament marked by Brahms's tremendous grasp of classical musical techniques and his romantic musical character.

Such modern composers as Stravinsky, Hindemith, William Walton, and Arthur Honegger have composed large works classifiable as oratorios, oratorios-with-ballet, oratorio-operas, and other mixed genres, but neither sacred nor secular oratorio is any longer so dominant a factor in musical creation as, for example, ballet

---

[2] Although entitled *A German Requiem,* this is not a Requiem Mass, for the text is Brahms's own selection of passages from the German Bible rather than the specific Roman Catholic liturgical text. It is therefore a religious oratorio rather than a Mass.

became in the twentieth century. Far too often the musical public's knowledge of oratorio is now gained wholly from amateur or semi-professional performance of that wonderful but difficult and uncharacteristic masterwork of 1741, Handel's *Messiah*. In truth, we have lost many of the techniques of baroque oratorio performance, not least among them the *bel canto* that Handel required from the singers of *Israel in Egypt, Messiah,* and *Jephtha* as much as from the demigods and amorous mythological heroes and heroines of his florid Italian operas. Under the conditions of the modern musical world, oratorio appears to be becoming museum music in performance and a dead form in practice.

(Ten)

INSTRUMENTAL ENSEMBLES · RAMEAU · BACH
THE MANNHEIM ORCHESTRA · INSTRUMENTAL FORMS
SONATA · SYMPHONY · SONATA-FORM
CHAMBER MUSIC · CONCERTO

Such composers of the Renaissance as had made autonomous use of instrumental ensembles had usually favored wind instruments, keeping stringed instruments in subordinate positions. And though seventeenth-century composers increased the use of strings, the practice of writing down only the melody and the *basso continuo,* particularly where it posited the participation of instruments whose parts were not written out, proves that orchestration or instrumentation was not yet of prime importance to composers. It also leaves performers of later periods unable to determine exactly what instruments were really used. Some composers gave attention to the careful combining of instruments—Monteverdi, for example, as noted in connection with his *Orfeo.* In general, however, it is difficult for a modern musician to be certain why a seventeenth-century composer employed one instrument rather than another—or rather than a human voice—so indeterminately is the "orchestration" of that period related to the unique, characteristic abilities, timbres, and other special qualities of the individual instruments used.

The composers of the seventeenth century increased the roles of bowed stringed instruments, notably the various sizes of violins, far better adapted to ensemble use than the recessive viols. They continued, too, to place wind and bowed stringed instruments to-· gether in various proportions. But in the sense in which we now think of "the" orchestra—that nineteenth-century instrument—the seventeenth and early eighteenth centuries had no settled body of instruments and no customary distribution of functions among those used.

On their own initiative and at the prompting of composers and performers, the makers of musical instruments continued to alter, improve, and find new uses for existing instruments and to evolve new ones. Toward the close of the seventeenth century an important addition to the unity and capacity of instrumental ensembles was made when the kettledrums (*timpani*) came to be considered a necessary component. The kettledrums were of the greatest value for rhythmic accents, for laying down a background for other instruments, and—as felt especially by Bach—for representing triumph and joyful demonstration. Bach, Handel, and their contemporaries, however, naturally continued to treat the human voice and the instruments as bearers of contrapuntal strands of melody. Except in specifically "pictorial" or onomatopoeic sections, they did not usually compose music whose character was determined by the special capabilities of grouped instruments. They did not think in terms of a standardized orchestra, but constantly assigned identical melodic lines to several instruments together, wrote for flutes and oboes parts that could as well have been assigned to strings (and vice versa), and used the same distribution of instrumental parts throughout movements and even whole pieces.

It is foolish to pity Bach and Handel for not having enjoyed the advantage of—or not having had the wit to invent—the orchestra of Beethoven's maturity. Their instrumentation, determined by its value in performing contrapuntal music, did exactly what they demanded of it. To "re-orchestrate" the music of the first half of the eighteenth century, to give it the "advantages" of the huge, pliable, greatly various body of instruments which the orchestra later became, is to denature and falsify it. Re-instrumentation of this sort is roughly equivalent to repainting one of

the canvases of the pre-Giotto Italian religious masters to give it
the advantage of later discoveries about perspective. It is equally
silly to listen to, say, the "Brandenburg" Concertos or Orchestral
Suites of Bach or the *concerti grossi* of Handel or Vivaldi as
though they were rudimentarily orchestrated nineteenth-century
music. This music must be listened to as and for what it is, in the
full realization that melodies are not only its essential trait, but
almost its sole reason for existence, however advanced it may be
in harmonic raiment, rhythmic insistence, and occasional splashes
of characteristic instrumental color. It is still far removed from
such a twentieth-century composition as Debussy's *La Mer,* in
which the characteristic effects of finically selected instruments,
both individually and in shifting groups, are as essentially creative and integral a part of the music as its melody, rhythm, and
harmony.

In the instrumental ensemble music of Jean-Philippe Rameau,
contemporary with that of Vivaldi, Bach, and Handel, the manners and conception of instrumentation began to change. Rameau
was what neither of his great German confreres was: an intellectual, an inquirer, explorer, experimenter. He was a leader in the
codification of eighteenth-century harmony. He explored the
natures of several instruments, notably the members of the flute
and oboe families. For these instruments he composed truly orchestral parts that only they could perform, parts growing as much
out of the instruments themselves as out of Rameau's wish to
make audible a certain melodic or supporting line. He began to
inch toward the later concept of coloristic or characteristic orchestration. It is suggestive, though inexact, to say that whereas Bach,
Vivaldi, and Handel were more interested in the music they composed than in the specific timbres through which it reached
listeners, the opposite was often the attitude of Rameau.

Bach's six "Brandenburg" Concertos, today the most familiar
of his purely instrumental ensemble music, demonstrate that his
choice of instruments was still made as much for contrapuntal
clarity as for the emotional effects of timbre. Bach's own instrumentation (still of a *concerto grosso* nature) also shows that no

really settled group of orchestral instruments had yet been
evolved. Here are the forces that he called for:

1ST F MAJOR	2ND F MAJOR	3RD G MAJOR	4TH G MAJOR	5TH D MAJOR	6TH B FLAT MAJOR
2 horns	oboe	strings	2 flutes	flute	2 violas
3 oboes	trumpet	cembalo	à bec†	violin	da
bassoon	flute	continuo	violin	strings	braccio ‡
violin	violin		strings	cembalo	2 violas
piccolo *	strings		cembalo	continuo	da
strings	cembalo		continuo	and solo	gamba §
cembalo	continuo				cello
continuo					cembalo
					continuo

* The violin piccolo was smaller than the regular violin. Its penetrating tone
derived from its being tuned one-third higher than the customary instrument.

† Flutes *à bec,* by which Bach indicated a variety of recorder, had an end mouthpiece, whereas the modern orchestral flute has no mouthpiece, being held in a transverse position and blown through a hole near one end. Technically, the player
blows *across,* rather than *into,* the hole.

‡ The viola da braccio was a viol held against the shoulder when played—as opposed to the viola da gamba, held between (at times on) the knees. Most theorists
regard the viola da braccio as the immediate parent of the second member of the
modern violin family, the viola.

§ The viola da gamba, held between or on the knees, was a bass viol.

The principal body of tone in all six "Brandenburg" Concertos
is supplied by bowed stringed instruments. The Sixth, lacking
both violins and the body of strings, nonetheless calls for five
bowed—and no wind—instruments. In all six, too, there is a
"cembalo continuo," i.e., a figured bass part for harpsichord, used
mostly to outline and support the harmonies, but in the Fifth
broadened into a solo part, giving this concerto some of the nature
of a concerto for soloist and orchestra. Two of the "Brandenburgs"
—the Third and Sixth—are for strings and harpsichord alone;
two—the Fourth and Fifth—are for strings, woodwinds, and harpsichord; in only two—the First and Second—is brass added to
strings, woodwind, and harpsichord: horns in the First, a trumpet
in the Second. Although the modern tendency, in performances
of the "Brandenburg" Concertos, is to substitute the violin for
the violin piccolo, regular transverse flutes for the flutes *à bec,*

members of the violin family for the viols, and a piano for the
harpsichord—changes justified in varying degree by altered circumstances of performance, but all robbing the listener of the
effects Bach intended—it is occasionally possible to hear them as
originally written. In either sort of instrumental clothing their
instrumental texture is far removed from what later men call
"orchestral tone."

The "Brandenburg" Concertos are as disparate in formal design as in instrumentation. The Third consists of only two movements, both rapid. The Second, Fourth, Fifth, and Sixth are each
made up of three movements in the conventional Italian overture
order: fast-slow-fast. The First, however, adds to three movements
in that order a fourth movement compacted of dance themes.
This movement consists of a minuet with a trio,[1] a *polacca,* and
the minuet repeated with a different trio.

All but completely absent from the "Brandenburg" Concertos
and the other instrumental ensemble music of the first half of
the eighteenth century is the principle of contrasting themes
within a single movement, the principle destined to give life to
the classical sonata, symphony, and string quartet. Instead, the
individual movements are, rare exceptions aside, each the expansion or prolongation of one musical idea. Within a movement
the baroque composers fractured one musical idea into its natural
segments and simultaneously added them together, without any
sign of divisions, into free-flowing, continuous musical textures.
The great kinetic power of baroque music lies in the apparently
inexhaustible decorative details by means of which it is continued
for long stretches, repeating the same fundamental idea over and
over, not so much seeing it constantly in new lights (variation) as
constantly seeing it more and more nearly complete. At times the
effect of listening to one movement by Bach or Vivaldi or Handel

---

[1] "Trio" here refers to a contrasting middle section played between the first presentation and the repetition of the principal section of a movement. This use of the
word grew out of the custom of Lully and others—including Bach in the movement
here discussed—of composing this contrasting middle section for three instruments.
(The trio here is for two oboes and bassoon, while the principal minuet, both as
first presented and as repeated after the trio, is for the larger body of instruments.)
Later composers tended to forget the origin of this use of "trio," and to employ the
word to designate the middle section of any movement in ABA form.

may be compared to that of approaching closer and closer to a great baroque building, until at last its totality is discovered to consist of uncounted thousands of small carvings and scrollworks, each in the only right place, and all contributing to the structure's unity.

Not only were long sections of movements, and often entire movements themselves, of one unchanging instrumental-ensemble color in baroque music; they were also largely of one unchanging volume. Dynamics, the entire constructive application of changing loudness and softness, was still preponderantly a question of the number of instruments being sounded. Such absolute essentials of modern orchestral music as sudden increases and decreases of volume, prolonged gradual increases (*crescendos*) and decreases (*decrescendos*) of volume, and sudden silences after a loud climax, though hinted at earlier, played no important part in baroque instrumental music. They began to be used in several widely separated musical centers, Prague and Vienna included, toward the middle of the eighteenth century.

The most productive of these orchestral proving grounds was the famous orchestra of the Elector Palatine Karl Theodor at Mannheim. As conducted by Johann Stamitz (1717-1757) and by such of his successors as his sons Karl (1746-1801) and Anton (1754-1809), and by Christian Cannabich (1731-1798), this was the first modern orchestra. An innovator sometimes called a fanatic, Johann Stamitz fused a more or less permanent body of instrumentalists into an ensemble of virtuoso quality which became renowned throughout Europe.

The Mannheim orchestra and the music composed especially for it by its conductors were increasingly, and at last essentially, non-contrapuntal in emphasis. Homophony was more and more the favored texture, a group of violins being entrusted with most of the leading melodies while other instruments supplied harmonic chordal support. With the temporary decline of counterpoint as the ruling syntax, of course, such tectonic musical means as imitation—fugue included—went temporarily by the boards. When the necessity of maintaining the clarity of separate but simultaneous melodic strands was no longer the primary concern, the speed of performance could be increased. True orchestral prestos resulted.[2] The Mannheim orchestra could and did produce sudden, immediate, very loud (*fortissimo*) and very soft (*pianissimo*) passages; long, graduated crescendos and decrescendos; single loud chords (*sforzato* or *sforzando*) in the midst of softer passages; telling sudden silences of the entire ensemble, often next after a fortissimo climax; string *tremolo* [3]; and very rapid broken [4] chords.

The compositions of the Mannheim conductors, like the works of many stylistic innovators, generally fail to satisfy as artistic wholes, whatever their eighteenth-century charm. But the suppleness, the virtuosic precision, introduced into ensemble performance by the Stamitzes, Cannabich, and Ignaz Holzbauer (1711-1783) affected the whole future of music. Without them or their equivalent, the orchestral compositions of Carl Philipp Emanuel Bach, Boccherini, Haydn, Mozart, and Beethoven—and the entire orchestral repertoire ever since—would have been impossible. With the Mannheim orchestra at its zenith, that is to say, a customary, semi-standardized grouping of instrumental tones had been made as reliable and useful and varied an artistic medium as the organ.

Far from providing a good medium for the performance of baroque music, the Mannheim orchestra would have been as detrimental to that style as is a modern symphony orchestra at full war strength. It had developed in response to a slow shifting in the very nature of the music being composed. Men like Giovanni Battista Sammartini (1701-1775) in Milan and Georg Christoph Wagenseil (1715-1777) and Georg Matthias Monn (1717-1750) in Vienna, occurring in the stream of artistic evolution which had produced Stamitz, were composing music for which the Mannheim orchestra was not only a proper performing medium, but also the best instrument existing.

[2] No Bach, Vivaldi, or Handel movement for instrumental ensemble should be played faster than a well-considered allegro.

[3] *Tremolo* is the rapid repetition of the same tone by quick up-and-down bowing. A drum-roll is also a *tremolo,* to be distinguished from a *vibrato,* the effect of slight, continuous fluctuation of pitch produced by a slight rolling movement of the finger pressing down a bowed string (and also, unhappily, produced by many singers).

[4] A broken chord is one of which the constituent tones are sounded in quick succession rather than all together.

At the heart of this new instrumental-ensemble music lay the first achievements of the classical sonata. This is perhaps the most complex, exception-ridden question in musical history. About the use of its terminology, in whatever language, experts quickly fall to quarreling; no two historians or musicologists exactly agree as to what a sonata is—or was—or how it came to be just that. In broadest outline, however, the essential facts are these:

1. The classical sonata blossomed only when preponderantly homophonic texture was substituted for preponderantly contrapuntal texture. The gradual replacement of the latter by the former can be watched in the brilliant violin sonatas of Corelli and Vivaldi. A further enrichment of homophonic, dramatic ("operatic") treatment of themes (as opposed to continuous contrapuntal presentation of substantially unchanging melodies) can be watched in the works of Sammartini, Stamitz, and C. P. E. Bach. Dramatic contrast, homophony, intense emotional expressivity—these were the elements from which C. P. E. Bach constructed his transitional art. They are also the central elements of the classical sonata.

2. The pattern of the Italian overture (fast-slow-fast) was standardized by Alessandro Scarlatti; Vivaldi adopted it as the pattern of movements in his concertos. Johann Sebastian Bach accepted it without question: he used it, with slight variants, in organ sonatas, the Italian Concerto for solo harpsichord, and four of the "Brandenburg" Concertos. Sonatas for harpsichord written during the late 1700's were also generally in three movements.[5] With Johann Stamitz's invariable practice of composing symphonies and several-movement pieces for chamber ensembles in four movements (often fast-slow-minuet-fast), the symphony and the chamber piece (quartet, quintet, trio, and so forth) began to be more or less set as four-movement sonatas. The sonata for solo instrument and the concerto, however, tended to retain the three-movement pattern. Although exceptions are extremely numerous, the eighteenth cen-

---

[5] Italian harpsichord sonatas from this period also occur in two movements. Domenico Scarlatti (1685-1757), son of the great Alessandro, was long supposed to have formed his sonatas in one movement, but research by Ralph Kirkpatrick has showed that many of his so-called *"sonate"* were built in pairs that have since drifted apart, and were therefore in real two-movement form.

tury increasingly accepted the following significance for these
terms:

(a) *sonata*—a three-movement work for solo instrument, alone
or accompanied;

(b) *symphony*—a four-movement work for large instrumental
ensemble;

(c) *concerto*—a three-movement work for large instrumental ensemble in which one or more solo instruments or a group of
instruments plays a leading role;

(d) *trio, quartet, quintet, sextet,* and so forth—a four-movement
work for three, four, five, or six players.

3. Certain formal patterns came to be associated with, and then
to be required of, certain movements of sonatas, symphonies, concertos, and chamber pieces. Most of the movements in such works,
in both the baroque period and the rococo period were binary:
section A was presented and repeated, then section B was presented
and repeated, giving the two-division pattern AABB. An exception
was the dance form known as the minuet,[6] which characteristically
had a trio, the resulting pattern being ABA. Gradually, however,
the first movements of sonatas for any instrument or group of instruments began to evolve a pattern of their own. Exceedingly
difficult to isolate in pure state, this pattern is confusingly spoken
of by two inappropriate designations: "sonata-form" and "first-
movement form." "Sonata-form" is ambiguous because what it de-
fines is not the form of a sonata, but that of one movement of a
sonata; "first-movement form" is equally misleading because while
the pattern is very often that of first movements, it is also often
used for other movements. Accepting the better of the two mis-
nomers, I shall refer to it as first-movement form, reminding my
readers that it is not at all unusual to find third and fourth movements in "first-movement form."

In general, first-movement form is a three-section pattern, the
comparative lengths and importances of the three sections being
different from composition to composition. The main melodic ma-

[6] Originally, in French, *menuet,* derived from *menu,* small, and referring to the
dance's small steps.

terial is presented in the *exposition,* examined and commented upon in the *development,* and then repeated in variant state in the *recapitulation.* At times a brief formal conclusion known as *coda* (the Italian word for tail) is added as a summation at the end.

(a). *Exposition.* What is exposed or demonstrated in this section of first-movement form is not often a single melody; it is most often several melodies or melodic ideas or constructive melodic fragments, referred to as themes. The exposition customarily ends with a sign (:‖) indicating that it is to be repeated; in many cases, in fact, it is supplied with two differing closes, one that smoothly leads back to the beginning of the movement, another that ends the section with some sense of finality before the *development* begins, at the same time supplying modulation to the next section.

The musical materials presented in the exposition are commonly grouped in two systems, often misleadingly called "first theme" and "second theme," though each "theme" may be composed of several molodies or melodic fragments. Traditionally the first system is vigorous and dramatic, the second somewhat more lyrical or pastoral. The first system is composed in the tonic key of the movement (C major if the key signature of the movement indicates that key; B♭ minor if the key signature of the movement indicates that key); the second system is in the key of the dominant if the movement as a whole is in a major key (G major if the movement is in C major; F♯ major if the movement is in B major) or in the relative major key if the movement as a whole is in a minor key (C major if the movement is in A minor; A♭ major if the movement is in F minor). In a very large number of classical first movements, the final melody or melodic fragment of the second system is strong and prominent, and is referred to as the "closing theme" because it effectively culminates the exposition.

(b). *Development.* This is the dramatic center of first-movement form, that section of a movement in which the relationships among the ideas already exposed are heightened. Just as classic harmony came to full maturity in the sonata for one or more instruments, so the dramatic contest at the heart of the sonata matured in this section. An operatic broadness of thematic drama was considered permissible here, where the melodic hints and rhythmic and harmonic tensions of the materials are revealed, released, or set in motion. In many sonatas of the early classic period the development section of the first movement used no materials not presented in the exposition; in later sonatas composers freely introduced new materials for contrast or for intensifying dramatic effect.

In the development section of first-movement form, the composer may dissect some or all of his melodies or thematic fragments, presenting them in fragments so as to learn what can be evoked from them. He may modulate slowly into and out of several keys, usually avoiding those keys which he has used in the exposition; he may modulate with rainbow brilliance and swiftness; he may treat one of his thematic elements—and not necessarily the most imposing one—in imitation or combine it fugally with another element (for fugal passages had become common in predominantly homophonic music); he may present one or more of his ideas with the length of the notes doubled ("in augmentation") or halved ("in diminution"); he may turn one melody upside down ("inversion") note for note or present it backwards ("*cancrizans*," *i.e.*, crablike) note for note; he may employ erudite scholastic clevernesses from the polyphonic past, showing how one of his fragments or melodies can be simultaneously inverted, played backwards, and made into a brief canon. The almost unlimited possibilities of manipulation are wasted, however, if they do not make the listener feel that the materials he encountered for the first time in the exposition have become vitally involved in new activity.

Any composer with a gift for melody can produce relatively satisfying expositions, but it requires one with firm and searching intellectual command of the techniques of composition to produce satisfying developments. However exquisite the materials exposed, for example, in a Schubert exposition, however much more melodically compelling *per se* they may be than corresponding materials in a Beethoven exposition, Schubert's neglect or inability to think with Beethoven's concentrated power often results in developments that are dull, overlong, loose-textured, or otherwise greatly inferior to Beethoven's. This does not necessarily mean that Schubert had not mastered the concepts of first-movement form; what it certainly means is that the materials spontaneously occurring to him (there are very few traces of such spontaneity in Beethoven) were not often well suited to classic compositional techniques.

Because the development is dramatic rather than expository, it is naturally not repeated entire, as the exposition usually is.

(c). *Recapitulation.* In a majority of classical examples of first-movement form, the recapitulation presents again all the thematic materials first heard in the exposition, though most often with changes in connective tissue (sometimes referred to as "bridge passages," "intermediate groups," or "connecting groups"), and with the second melodic system of the exposition given in the tonic key rather than (as in the exposition) in the dominant, it being aesthetically essential to end the movement in the tonic if the sense of enclosure or finality is to be provided. In many cases the recapitulation is shorter than the exposition.

This, then—exposition, development, recapitulation—is the general ground-plan of classical first-movement form, "sonata-form," or "sonata-allegro form," a pattern almost never to be encountered without variants dictated by genius or whim. The pattern may be used with the most moribund results by a composer who lacks taste or does not evolve materials fit for this sort of manipulation. It was very often the vehicle of the loftiest musical imaginings and compositional adventures of Haydn, Mozart, and Beethoven. It was never a formula for the creation of good music. Several other patterns found equally good uses. It was nonetheless one of the most important means by which the composers of the classical period contained, delineated, and balanced some of their finest music.

Not all sonatas, symphonies, concertos, and sonata-like chamber pieces of the classical period were given first movements in some variant of this pattern. Mozart's Sonata in A Major, K.331 (1778), begins with a movement made up of a theme and six variations. Beethoven employed the theme-and-variation form for the opening movement of his A♭ Major Sonata, Opus 26, while in the "Moonlight" Sonata, in C♯ Minor, Opus 27, No. 2, he began with a movement evolved from an unchanging rhythmic figure; this is not in first-movement form, for which reason, among others, he carefully designated it a *"sonata quasi una fantasia"* (sonata like a fantasia). Several other patterns were used. But it remains generally true that first-movement form was favored by Haydn, Mozart, Beethoven, and Schubert as the best pattern for first movements, that during their era other first-movement patterns were deviations from the customary. They also employed first-movement form for slow second movements and for final movements. The pattern was at first, and long remained, the distinguishing formal mark of the sonata for one or more instruments.

Second movements of classical sonatas were nearly always slow movements, in necessary contrast to the traditionally rapid opening movements in first-movement form. If a second movement, too, was not cast in first-movement form, it was likely to be composed in some variety of binary or ternary form, though it too occasionally turns up as a theme with variations.

At first glance, such a binary pattern as that of first-movement form—say AABA—looks much like the ternary pattern of the *aria da capo,* ABA. Some musicologists, in fact, have called first-movement form ternary. The difference lies primarily in the fact that in first-movement form the B section is derived from the A, while in the *aria da capo* the whole *raison d'être* of the B is its utter difference from the A. Like such simpler binary patterns as AB and AABB, however, the first-movement AABA pattern consists of two counterbalancing parts of approximately equal importance, though often varying in length. In classical sonata usage, too, A-as-leading-to-B and B-as-first-presented bear a mirror relation to each other with respect to key. Section A, that is, most often starts in the tonic key of the movement and moves to its dominant—or, if its tonic is a minor, to the relative major. The B section then reverses this modulatory movement, returning to the tonic.

In ternary form as used in the classical sonata—ABA—section A most often begins *and* ends in the tonic key of the movement; section B is usually composed in the dominant key of that tonic, its relative major or minor, or its parallel [7] key—and likewise begins

---

[7] A "parallel" key has the same tonic tone as the key to which it is parallel, but is major if that key is minor, minor if that key is major. Thus the parallel key to C major is C minor, whereas the key of the dominant of C major is G major, and its relative minor is A minor.

and ends in the same key. While the A and B of binary form as used in the first movement of the classical sonata have usually, harmonically speaking, a mirror relationship, forming a continuous whole with a peak of connecting modulation where they join, the A, B, A of ternary form must achieve unity in more subtle ways, being made up, harmonically speaking, of self-enclosed sections.

Whereas the second movement of a classical sonata may be in first-movement form, theme-and-variation form, or some variety of either binary or ternary pattern, the third movement (appearing only in symphonies and chamber pieces, for the solo sonata and the concerto usually omit this movement) is nearly always a minuet (early in the period) or a scherzo (Beethoven and later). This is a special sort of ABA ternary form, in which each of the sections will betray its origin in a dance form and itself be in binary pattern. Because both the minuet and the scherzo are relatively rapid movements in triple time employing a ternary pattern, the difference between them is easy to define only in examples widely separated as to time of composition. A typical early Haydn minuet is courtly and polished; a typical Beethoven scherzo is brusque, often humorously rough, and sometimes fantastic. But early Beethoven scherzos are very like Haydn or Mozart minuets in everything but the stigmata of the composer's most individual speech and gesture.

It may well be asked: what differentiates the ABA of first-movement form from the ABA of minuet-trio-minuet or scherzo-trio-scherzo? The answer is that some minuets or scherzos can be analyzed as perfect examples of binary first-movement form, but that they usually lack the essential key-relationships and are ternary, and that they most often appear without the essential development activity in the B section.

The fourth movement (or, in solo sonata and concerto, the third, final movement) is most often a very rapid movement in first-movement form, rondo-form, or theme-and-variation form. Rondo-form evolved from the rondeau, a pattern favored by such French harpsichord composers as Chambonnières, Couperin *le grand*, and Rameau. In their interpretation the rondeau was a refrain form, *i.e.*, one in which a short thematic idea is repeated with contrasting ma-

terials between each two of its appearances. Such a pattern is
ABACADAEA. In many French harpsichord pieces, too, the key
relationships among the sections were delicately elaborated. Section A, known as the refrain, would always be repeated in its original key, but section B (the alternating sections were referred to as
couplets) would be in that same tonic key, while section C would
appear in the dominant, D in the relative major or minor, and E
in the parallel key. In the rondo-form of classical sonata use, the
couplets came to be limited to three, the form thus crystallizing as
ABACADA, or—rather—ABACABA, for the third couplet commonly repeated the first. In classical terminology, the A came to be
known as the rondo, while the couplets were called diversions or
episodes.

All sonata movements may be preceded by several sorts of intro-
ductions and followed by several sorts of codas. Either the introduction or the coda may take on large proportions, so large in
some codas that they can only be interpreted as sections of additional development. Even when this is true, however, the essential
AABA form is often preserved intact and visible in movements
partaking of first-movement form.

The over-all pattern of the classical sonata, then, though often
spoken of stupidly as though it had been a straitjacket restraining
the originality and creativity of its users, was in actuality an endlessly variable group of ground-plan suggestions rather than a collection of accurate maps. Each movement could be one of a number of things, each thing occurring in a wide variety of possible
shapes. Yet a sonata—a classical sonata, at least—is unmistakably
different from a fantasia or a set of variations or a rhapsodic composition in one movement. At its heart is the concept of a several-
movement composition in the fast-slow-fast succession (for the solo
sonata and the concerto) and the fast-slow-minuet (scherzo)-fast
order for the symphony and chamber piece. Its dynamism was derived from drama and contrast, the contrasts being of speed, of key,
and of melodic temper and disposition. The classical sonata exploited fully the delicate, powerful principle of unity through di-
versity.

What differentiates the form of a classical solo sonata from that of a symphony, the classical sonata for orchestra? Substantially they are alike, if pattern alone is considered, though the symphony very often begins with an introduction leading to that point within the form at which the solo sonata usually begins. The important differences between the classical solo sonata and the classical symphony tended more and more to be of treatment and expansiveness, though Beethoven and Schubert, both late in their creative lives, composed solo sonatas that might justly be called symphonic in scope. In general, a classical symphony is quite simply an extended four-movement sonata for orchestra.

What about the difference between a classical solo sonata and a classical string trio, piano trio, string quartet, clarinet quintet, or string sextet? Substantially they are alike in pattern, though in early classical chamber music for strings alone the patterns were manipulated so as to give the leading ("first") violin a stellar role, and in such later works as posed a wind instrument or piano against strings the same kind of manipulation is repeated. But in general a classical chamber piece in sonata form is quite simply an extended four-movement sonata for several instruments.

What is the difference between the form of a classical solo sonata and that of a classical concerto for one or more solo instruments and orchestra? The concerto is almost always, like the solo sonata, in only three movements.[8] The scherzo never became as native to the concerto as to the symphony and the chamber piece. Making almost invariable application of first-movement form in its opening movement, the concerto modified it. The exposition is most often played complete by the orchestra. Then it is repeated for orchestra and soloist, again in the tonic key, but leading to a second ending that modulates to the dominant. Midway in the recapitulation, but nearer its close than its beginning, the orchestra pauses on a well-defined six-four chord,[9] whereupon the

[8] The enormous Brahms Concerto for piano and orchestra in B♭ major, Opus 83, is uncharacteristically in four movements, but it is questionable on other grounds that it is rightly to be called a classical concerto.

[9] A six-four chord is the second inversion of a triad. In C major, the tonic triad being CEG, the first inversion would be EGC, the second GCE. If GCE were the six-four chord on which the orchestra were to pause at the juncture under discussion, it is likely that the deeper instruments would insist on the G in order to fortify in the

soloist enters alone with his *cadenza,* his big opportunity to show technical agility in a longish section given over entirely to him. The cadenza is apparently or actually improvisatory in mood, though it makes prominent use of one or more melodies or fragments from the preceding exposition and development. When composers were likely to be their own performers, cadenzas were rarely written out, it being taken for granted that they would be improvised. Mozart wrote out cadenzas for only a few of his concertos. Beethoven, however, composed cadenzas for all his concertos, himself printing one in his fifth Concerto for piano and orchestra, in E♭ major, Opus 79 (the "Emperor"). Later composers, aware of the horrors that pianists given over to virtuosity had composed for insertion at the drop of a six-four chord, almost invariably wrote out in full the cadenzas to which they had devoted all the care they gave to any other musical element of the concerto.

The typical classical-concerto cadenza closed on the dominant key of the movement, thus allowing the harmonic motion back to the tonic to lend a satisfying atmosphere of finality to the close of the movement.

A last movement in rondo-form became so usual in solo concertos as to become an almost integral part of the concerto concept.

With these variants, then, and with composers feeling free to insert brief, cadenza-like passages elsewhere than in the first movement, the concerto was in general simply an extended three-movement sonata for the display of those contending colleagues, the one or more soloists and the members of the orchestra. Piano concertos and violin concertos were composed in staggering numbers, but there were also soon concertos for almost every conceivable instrument (flute, oboe, English horn, French horn, trumpet, trombone, bassoon, harp, and so forth); double concertos for flute and harp, two pianos, violin and viola, and other combinations; and triple concertos like Beethoven's Opus 56, in C major, for violin, cello, and piano. It is usually safe to assume

listener's mind its necessary position as the bottom, root, or principal note of the six-four chord.

that any concerto-like piece whose instrumentation calls for more than three solo instruments will turn out, upon being heard, to be closer in style to the baroque *concerto grosso* than to the classical solo concerto, even though its movement-patterns follow those of the classical sonata.

Eleven

CLAVICHORD · HARPSICHORD · PIANO

ORNAMENTATION

While new ideas about harmony, temperament, instrumental ensemble, and musical forms were evolving, events of enormous importance were occurring among the makers and players of the clavichord, the harpsichord, and their younger relation, the pianoforte—sometimes then called the forte-piano, *i.e.*, "loud-soft" instead of the now accepted name, literally "soft-loud." These events influenced both composers and the nature of music.

One of the most ancient stringed instruments is the psaltery, a name familiar to the men who made the King James translation of the Bible, who used it to designate instruments that may or may not have been what we now call psalteries. All during the 1300's and 1400's, in fact, the psaltery was played throughout Europe, where it was often mentioned by poets and other writers and represented in both painting and sculpture. It then had a small flat surface with raised edges; it was in effect a box with an open top. Between its raised edges extended strings that the player plucked either with his fingers or by means of a small pick called a plectrum. Whether the psaltery be classified as a variety of harp to which a resonating box has been added or as a rudimentary form of that typically Tyrolean instrument, the zither, it was an ancestor of the harpsichord, which differs from the psaltery mostly in that its strings are set vibrating by plectra activated from a keyboard rather than by the direct contact of fingers or hand-held plectra.

Related closely in basic design to the psaltery was an instrument whose strings were struck by small hammers, usually of wood, held in the hands. Of great antiquity also, the dulcimer (mentioned by Coleridge in "Kubla Khan" because of the evocative sound of its name) endured in Western Europe through the seventeenth century, after which it became less familiar there, though as the cimbalom (variously spelled) it survives today among the gypsies of southeastern Europe.[1] In basic principle the dulcimer is to the pianoforte what the psaltery is to the harpsichord: the most important mechanical difference between the dulcimer and the pianoforte being that the latter's hammers are activated from a keyboard rather than being held in the player's hands.

Although the descent cannot be documented in equal steps, it is all but certain that the dulcimer led to the clavichord—in which the strings are also struck by hammers activated from a keyboard instead of being held in the player's hands. In turn, the clavichord led to the idea of the pianoforte. Confusion entered the history of these interrelated instruments when early makers and players of the pianoforte spoke and wrote about it as though it were an "improvement" on the harpsichord—which it clearly was not—rather than as what it was: an expanded, much more powerful, and far more flexible "improvement" of the clavichord. The qualities at which these men were aiming as they experimented with the new instrument actually derived from both clavichord and harpsichord. What they desired was an instrument that could be heard at least as easily and as far as the harpsichord—the clavichord emits a faint sound that must be listened for carefully even in a small room. From the qualities of the clavichord they wished to save the possibility of sustaining tone and of increasing and decreasing volume at will—the harpsichord could sustain tone scarcely at all, and its only shadings in volume depended upon the player's shifting hand-stops (later pedals) or, on larger examples of the instrument, moving his hands from one bank of keys to another and using coupling

[1] The cimbalom was employed tellingly by Igor Stravinsky in the chamber orchestra of his "burlesque tale," *Renard* (1916-17).

devices permitting more than one string to be plucked by the depressing of one key.

During the seventeenth century, and perhaps earlier, various instrument manufacturers had considered the project of applying the clavichord principle of hammer-struck strings to a larger, more powerful instrument. Not until early in the eighteenth century, however, did a harpsichord maker of Padua (later of Florence) make four *"gravicembali col piano e forte"* ("harpsichords with loud and soft") that historians have accepted as the first pianofortes. These four instruments made by Bartolommeo Cristofori (1655-1731) were modern pianos in all fundamental respects except that they had no pedals. They included an escapement mechanism due to which the individual hammer, having struck its corresponding string, immediately returned to inactive position, thus leaving the string free to vibrate slowly into silence. They also included separate dampers that came into contact with the strings when the keys were released, thus allowing the player to cut off the vibrations at will. By holding down a given key, that is, the player could keep a desired string vibrating; by releasing the key he could silence the string at once. At least two pianofortes made by Cristofori survived into the twentieth century. One is—or was—at Leipzig; the other, dated 1720, is in the Metropolitan Museum of Art in New York.

About 1725 Gottfried Silbermann (1683-1753), a renowned builder of organs and clavichords then living at Dresden, having studied Cristofori's principles of pianoforte construction, imitated the Italian instruments with superb craftsmanship. Sometime after 1726 Silbermann invited Johann Sebastian Bach, well known as an authority on organ construction, to try critically two of his instruments. Bach played on them and said bluntly that they had a heavy touch and that their higher notes were too weak. This seems to have discouraged Silbermann temporarily, but he lived to learn that Bach, visiting Frederick the Great at Potsdam in 1747, played on at least one of the King's three later Silbermann pianofortes and found it good.

Neither Cristofori's nor Silbermann's pianofortes had any of the three pedals to be seen on modern grand pianos. They were constructed in the harpsichord shape, the one still used for the grand piano. In England about 1760 the first "square" piano—which is not square, being an oblong with the keyboard along one of its longer sides—was built. London became the greatest center of piano construction during the heyday of John Broadwood (1732-1812). English pianos were mostly of the square type. The only other basic shape of piano, the upright, did not occur until the nineteenth century. Occupying less floor-space, the upright soon exceeded the square piano in popularity, but the fact that its dampers must be activated by springs (because the strings run vertically) rather than, as in the grand and square pianos, by gravity has kept it a less satisfactory form. Today, as in the experiments of Cristofori and Silbermann, the best pianos retain the harpsichord shape.

Other important landmarks in the evolution of the modern grand piano and its repertoire were (1) the so-called Viennese action, (2) the American development of the all-metal frame, and (3) the addition of pedals. Other alterations have been numerous: there have been changes in the strings, hammers, sound-boards, and key mechanisms.[2] But these three landmarks are of sufficient importance to ask for brief explanation, particularly as they influenced the music composed for the instrument.

1. In Vienna, Johann Andreas Stein (1728-1792) and his son-in-law Johann Andreas Streicher (1761-1833) developed a pianoforte notable for the ease with which its keys could be depressed (a "light touch") and the elegance—some called it thinness—of its tone, especially in contrast to the somewhat stiffer, more sonorous Broadwoods. So different were the Viennese pianos from their English contemporaries (which last were widely used as models in France and the Germanies) that they required distinct playing techniques. This difference, in turn, had an appreciable effect on the nature and style of the music composed for the instruments. Both Haydn and Mozart were influenced by the light Viennese action, whereas German and British composers almost invariably produced a somewhat "heavier" sort of piano music, influenced to

[2] Additionally, there have been attempts to produce pianos with more than one keyboard, capable of quarter-tone intervals. To date these efforts, mechanically successful, are musically sterile.

some extent by the Broadwood action and its requisite playing technique.

2. Whereas earlier pianoforte frames had been wood, upright pianos made in Philadelphia early in the nineteenth century had an interior frame of iron. Not until 1856 did Steinway and Sons make the first grand piano with an all-iron frame. This stronger, more solid framework allowed the rapid evolution of the huge modern concert grand piano, able to produce auditorium-filling tones because its metal frame will withstand a pull (by the bass strings) of as much as thirty tons. As the size and volume of the piano grew, the thickness of the strings—now also, of course, entirely of metal—naturally increased too. Anyone who attempts to move or lift a concert grand will retain a clear idea of its massiveness and enormous weight.

3. (a) In 1783 Broadwood patented the so-called "damper" or "sustaining" pedal. This applied to the instrument a principle that earlier had been applied rather tentatively in the form of a board moved from side to side by the player's knee. That principle is the removal all at once of all dampers from the strings, with the result that no damper cuts off the vibration of a string when the player removes his finger from its corresponding key. It has the further result that all the strings are left "open" to sympathetic vibration.[3]

(b) The second pedal, called "soft," formerly operated one way in grand pianos, another in uprights. The modern piano has one, two, or three separate strings for each tone, depending upon pitch —the lowest tones requiring one long, thick string (now usually coiled about with thin wire); the middle tones two shorter, thinner strings; the highest tones three very short, very thin strings. In the grand piano the soft pedal formerly moved all the hammers slightly to one side, with the result that only one string would be struck for every tone, the unstruck strings being left free to vibrate sympathetically, the tonal result being a diminution of volume and an alteration of timbre.[4] But in almost all modern pianos the soft

[3] An open string will vibrate as the overtone of another sounding tone. See page 57.

[4] This explains the directions in piano music: "*una corda*" (one string) for soft, "*tre corde*" (three strings) for loud.

pedal simply moves the hammers nearer to the strings, making it impossible for the player to strike the strings with the usual force. This method of reducing volume has lost the alteration in tone-quality inherent in the older mechanism.

(c) A third, middle pedal has been added to many American pianos since Steinway and Sons introduced it in 1874. This so-called "sostenuto" pedal—apparently invented in France in the 1850's—activates a mechanism that takes hold of any single damper at the instant it is raised by the depression of a key, holds it away from the corresponding string or strings, and releases it again only when the pedal (rather than the key) is released. This complex device makes it possible for the player to keep one tone or group of tones vibrating by themselves while he goes on to play other tones unaffected (except sympathetically) by the tones thus left vibrating. Some twentieth-century composers have evoked magical effects by the use of this pedal, but it has never won world-wide acceptance.

The earliest pianofortes had a compass of four octaves or four and one-half octaves. This has increased gradually to the modern standard of eighty-eight notes, seven and one-quarter octaves. In Mozart's day it was five octaves. The compositions of Chopin and Schumann were conceived for instruments not wider in compass than six and one-quarter octaves. Nothing in their music gives any evidence that they considered this compass cramping. The impatient Beethoven, however, was driven to altering the very contours of certain melodic passages repeated in various pitches by the fact that he wanted—but could not command—notes higher than any existing on the pianos of his day. It was precisely such urgent demands by composers which forced piano manufacturers to add more and more notes to their instruments.

Purcell and Handel in England; Johann Sebastian Bach in Germany; Couperin and Rameau in France; Domenico Scarlatti in Italy and Spain—these men and their contemporaries had composed for the harpsichord and, in some cases, for the clavichord. But beginning with C. P. E. Bach, Johann Christian Bach, Haydn, and Mozart, the men who evolved the classical sonata and concerto forms conceived keyboard music more and more for the pianoforte.

By the Schubert-Beethoven era, composers had begun to think in pianoforte terms inapplicable to performance on the earlier instruments. Mendelssohn, Chopin, Schumann, and Liszt at times drew the very texture and profile of their keyboard music from the piano's evolving capabilities. Debussy and Ravel intensified this tendency until much of their keyboard music—Debussy's in particular—appears to have been produced almost as much by the character of the piano itself as by the composing mind. Still another tendency, that of treating the modern concert grand piano as a percussion instrument—which in one sense it certainly is—became noticeable in the music of many later composers: Prokofiev, Bartók, and Aaron Copland in particular. These men have removed the style of keyboard music as far as it is now possible to imagine from the flowery traceries and tripping graces of a Couperin.

Compositions for both harpsichord and clavichord had been strewn with ornamental figurations of many sorts—so many sorts that the mere accurate reading of much of this music sometimes parallels the solution of puzzles. These ornaments were not commonly written out as groups of notes, but were either left to the performer's discretion or were indicated by conventional signs. Either of these latter procedures had the advantage, on the engraved page, of leaving the chief harmonic and melodic outlines clear. The notes included in such ornaments as turns, *appoggiature,* mordents, and trills—there were dozens of others—were thus correctly indicated as extra tones, decorations of the basic music.[5]

The frequency of ornaments in harpsichord music was in part composers' response to the instrument's inability to sustain tone. Composers and harpsichordists had a feeling that they must fill in the otherwise inescapable silences between tones without hurrying the tempo of the music. They accomplished this in part by filling the interstices with ornamental notes. This necessity was

[5] A turn is basically a group of four or five notes in some such order as principal note-note above principal-principal-note below principal-principal. For *appoggiatura,* see page 59. A mordent is basically a group of three notes: principal-note below principal-principal. A trill is a group of notes, varying in number, consisting of principal note and note above principal, the two rapidly alternated.

still felt with respect to the relatively weak early pianofortes, but it grew less demanding as later instruments expanded in sonority and became more and more capable of sustaining tone. The keyboard music of the sixteenth and seventeenth centuries (except that for the organ, *par excellence* the sustaining instrument) remains dead when it is played without wisely chosen ornamentation. Early eighteenth-century pianoforte music is scarcely different in this respect, though the performer is assisted by the increased tendency to indicate ornaments by conventional signs. But late eighteenth-century pianoforte music has begun to shed ornaments, which have by then come to be used sparingly and largely for melodic reasons rather than for keeping the instrument sounding.

Another reason for the profusion of ornaments in harpsichord music was that, when played before important melodic notes, they made a kind of accentuation possible on an instrument on which otherwise what we now understand by accentuation—the playing of a note or chord more forcefully than surrounding notes or chords—was impossible. The disappearance of this reason likewise diminished the frequent use of ornaments.

Several kinds of music were unsatisfactory, except in a relative sense, on the harpsichord. Undecorated slow or stately music, for example, came from the harpsichord as a series of widely separated notes or chords. Grand or thunderous effects of volume were beyond its strength, except—again—relatively. The style of keyboard playing known as *legato* (literally, bound), in which there is no perceptible silence between one note or chord and the next, became fully possible only on the pianoforte, making available to composers and pianists effects of slow or stately music without ornamentation. In fact, the pianoforte opened up to composers a universe of keyboard-produced sound approximating that previously available only on the organ.

Certain abilities of the harpsichord were lost to the pianoforte. You cannot on a piano play more than one note by striking a single key. Nor can you select one of several different timbres by shifting pedals or play interlacing melodies in two distinct, simultaneous timbres. These advantages went with the older instrument. The

twentieth century has had the great musical advantage of hearing
the restoration of the harpsichord, after too long an absence, to
the company of living instruments. Largely, this restoration has
been the determined labor of Wanda Landowska. It must be said,
however, that the metal harpsichord on which Madame Landowska commonly performs in public is a much more powerful instrument than the harpsichord in use when the pianoforte was
invented. To hear her play Bach, Rameau, Couperin, or Scarlatti
is a surpassing musical experience, but it would be proliferating
error to suppose that what is heard at one of her recitals is the
exact equivalent of what those composers conceived for smaller
rooms and far less sonorous instruments without pedals. In this
sense, Madame Landowska's performances are far more historically exact when she plays music composed for harpsichord
(largely for her) by twentieth-century composers.

Haydn wrote a large amount of charming music for the piano,
but his most profound creations by far were in orchestral music,
chamber music, and oratorio. With Mozart, however, the piano
assisted the birth of some of the greatest music ever composed, a
series of concertos for piano and orchestra into which he poured
a wealth of his richest musical ideas and structural conceptions.
Many critics rank Mozart's numerous piano concertos above all
but the very greatest of his symphonies, as they are certainly superior to his violin concertos and his sonatas for solo piano. Only he,
up to the time of his death (1791), had composed music for piano
that no one would hesitate to consider alongside his best chamber
music and surpassing operas.

Beethoven was not so prolific of piano concertos as Mozart had
been, but three or four of those which he composed are music on
the very highest level. More important than Beethoven's piano
concertos to the historic evolution of music—equal in interest to
his chamber music and symphonies—are his thirty-two sonatas for
solo piano. In them, at last, he may be said to have forced the
piano to do more than it can do. Some of his famous thirty-two
are among the most popular serious music ever created; scarcely
one of them is less than a masterwork. In Beethoven's strong
hands, as in Mozart's infinitely dexterous ones, the instrument in-

vented so short a time before had become the expressive equal of the organ, the chamber ensemble, and the orchestra.

The most fruitful and enduring technical achievements of the period stretching from the birth of Rameau in 1683 to the death of Beethoven in 1827 were equal temperament, the symphony orchestra, the sonata concept in all its variations, and the invention and rapid development of the piano. Other achievements were of equal artistic importance, but these four made possible most of the music we listen to frequently today.

No other instrument since the era when the organ reigned supreme has attracted so many composers so strongly or has had so enduring an effect on the style, the very nature, of music itself, as the pianoforte. The pipe organ was once properly called the king of instruments. But whatever its powers and unique abilities, it has been no ruling monarch for more than a century. No instrument, of course, truly "rules" music. But there is no doubt possible that the piano became—and to this day remains—the single most important musical instrument of Western civilization.

Twelve

CHAMBER MUSIC · ORCHESTRAL MUSIC

BACH · HANDEL · HAYDN

Almost from the time when musical instruments other than the organ came into being—and certainly from the hour when they began to be played independently, apart from their role as support for, or accompaniment to, the human voice—they must have been played together. Perhaps—there is no documentary proof—they were joined first in twos, then in threes, and then in increasingly large numbers. Music for instrumental groups became a recognized form during the Middle Ages. It was composed by such musicians as Obrecht, Isaak, and Paulus von Hofhaimer (1459-1539) in the fifteenth century; by Adrian Willaert and others in the sixteenth; and by very numerous men in the seventeenth. The instrumental *canzona* was, as some of these composers handled it, an ancestral version of what we now call chamber music.

During the baroque era the *sonata da chiesa* and *sonata da camera,* the two principal forms of the trio sonata, were further ancestors of modern chamber music, though they led along diverging paths to two sorts of music between which musicians since the eighteenth century have tended to distinguish sharply: orchestral music and music for chamber ensembles. With the arrival on the musical scene of such composers as Boccherini, Haydn, and Mozart, it becomes essential to make this distinction in terminology.

1. *Chamber music (musica da camera,* literally music to be

played in a room) is, in the modern understanding, for an instrumental group of small size, usually with only one player to each
part. In it, the over-all emphasis is on ensemble activity; except in
certain special cases, individual parts stand out from the general
texture only temporarily and occasionally.

Chamber music for two players is comparatively rare. When it
occurs, it is usually referred to as a sonata or duo, but music for
two instruments (violin and harpsichord or piano, cello and piano,
and so forth) is often in reality solo music with a keyboard-instru-
ment accompaniment, and is therefore not accurately called chamber music. Music for three instruments is called a trio (string trio
if all three instruments are stringed; piano trio if one instrument
is a piano; horn trio if one is a horn, and so forth).

Because four-part (four-voice) harmony has proved especially
and enduringly satisfactory, chamber music for four instruments
has been composed in far greater quantity than any other kind.
The quartet, particularly the quartet for four stringed instruments
(as distinct from the piano quartet—three stringed instruments and
one piano—and other combinations) became in the eighteenth century, and ever since has remained, the central type of chamber
music. Luigi Boccherini (1743-1805) in Italy, France, and Spain
and Haydn in Austria set the form, if not entirely the classic texture, of the string quartet. The standard group of instruments
came to be two violins (first and second), viola, and cello. At the
outset, the first violin tended to dominate this ensemble, so that
violinists often spoke and wrote as though they played quartets
by themselves, but the string quartet came more and more to be
a genre in which the participating instruments played roles of
approximately equal importance.[1]

Chamber-ensemble compositions for more than four players,
came similarly to be known by numerical terms, beginning with
quintet and going through sextet, septet, and octet to nonet. Cham-

---

[1] Purists point out that many early string quartets were at first performed by
more than four players. Parts (voices), that is, were doubled and tripled, the result
being orchestral, rather than chamber, music—if our definitions of the two classes
be applied with ironclad literalness. In the spirit of the definitions, however, it may
be doubted that any music for no more than four unchanging parts or voices is
really orchestral, however many performers take part in playing it.

ber music for more than nine players customarily goes under
such other names as serenade, *divertimento,* chamber symphony,
and rhapsody. Paul Hindemith and some other modern composers
often call it, in complete simplicity, *Kammermusik—i.e.,* chamber
music.

As explained earlier (page 145), the sonata form in several
variants soon invaded chamber music so completely as all but to
banish older patterns from it. Trios, quartets, quintets, all became
sonatas for small ensemble. And though the inception of chamber
music, and of the string quartet in particular, is difficult to date
accurately, it is certain that the genre has maintained its place in
the affections of composers and players (though not always in those
of audiences) without interruption from that inception to this day.
Without as much alteration in its pervading patterns as has modified orchestral, solo instrumental, and vocal music, chamber music
has nevertheless changed styles with the times.

After the classical chamber works of Boccherini, Haydn, Mozart,
and the early Beethoven, it was the later Beethoven himself who
began to expand and alter the genre. Schubert led it toward romanticism, and it was favored by such central romantics as Mendelssohn and Schumann. In the second half of the nineteenth century
it was employed by César Franck, Brahms, Dvořák, and others as
a particularly personal vehicle. Such later composers as Debussy,
Ravel, Schoenberg, Bartók, Milhaud, and Stravinsky have created
notable chamber music; in much of it the idiom differs greatly
from that of Boccherini and Haydn, but the structural patterns,
the movement-by-movement layout or ground-plan, have tended
to change but little. Looked at structurally, the chamber piece has
preserved its original eighteenth-century patterns no matter what
the musical ideas and dialects with which composers have chosen
to erect and fill out those patterns.

Chamber music is often cited and regarded with knowing snob-
bishness as the "purest" variety of music. By this curious adjective
is meant that the string quartet, for example, is made of four melodic parts that can be apprehended distinctly and that it gets along
stoically without the seductions of orchestral color, which the

speakers assume to be used to cover up poverty of honest musical thought. Yet this sort of musical distinction in the void is without meaning. All forms of music are equally "pure" if they are purely used, employed with taste and understanding of what potentialities each possesses. In the works of a sensitive composer the chamber piece often contains sovereign music of the noblest or the most delightful sort. But so, in the hands of a sensitive composer, does music for a solo instrument, for vocal soloist or ensemble, for full symphony orchestra, for all the varied forces of opera—and for various "impure" mixtures of them all. Attempts to enthrone chamber music at the peak of the musical society are in reality mere rationalizations of personal preference. They can be given no more serious consideration than can be given to judgments calling all chamber music dull, dry, "purely" intellectual scraping, striking, and blowing.

By the same token, it is stultifying to listen to a Mozart string quartet, a Beethoven piano trio, a Schumann piano quintet, or a Ravel septet as though it were orchestral music in miniature. Its whole philosophy and psychology, so to speak, differ from those of both orchestral and solo music. It is music whose fullest effect depends upon the audibility of several separate voices—not always in the polyphonic sense of independent melodies, but in a more purely instrumental sense. It is music in which, except to a narrow extent, the special tone-colors of the instruments are not of primary importance; and in which polyphony of one sort or another is likely to play a major constructive role. It cannot depend upon very wide-swinging changes of volume, for the number of decibels available to its performing instruments is limited. It is usually rather soft as compared with orchestral music, and it tends toward the intimate and the directly personal. Best listened to in a small auditorium, chamber music possibly requires more co-operation by the listener—particularly the uninitiate listener—than any other sort of music.

2. *Orchestral music.* Orchestral music is music for a large body of varied instruments in which many of the parts or voices customarily are played in unison by groups of the same instrument or

different instruments.[2] Except in special cases, the orchestra, from the day of the Mannheim ensemble to our own day, has contained more stringed instruments than any other kind. The modern orchestra usually has about half as many wind instruments as strings; the winds are about equally divided between woodwinds (especially members of the clarinet, flute, and oboe families) and brasses (especially horns, trumpets, trombones, and tubas). Somewhat fewer, usually, are the percussion instruments, which may include drums, xylophone, tambourine, cymbals, triangle, gongs, and various noise-makers. A modern symphony orchestra may contain upwards of sixty stringed instruments: violins in two groups known as "first" and "second" violins, the difference between them being in what they are assigned to play rather than in the instruments themselves; violas; violoncellos; doublebasses; and harp.

The modern orchestra may include from ten to fifteen woodwinds: clarinets, English horns, flutes, and oboes; about the same number of brasses: horns, trumpets, trombones, and tubas; and ten or one dozen percussion instruments, including timpani (kettledrums), glockenspiel (a small metal xylophone of bell-like sound), cymbals, triangle, tambourine, celesta (in effect a glockenspiel with keyboard), and piano—though the piano may also be considered a non-orchestral instrument or an orchestral solitary. Every instrument (and the human voice) has at one time or another been included in an orchestra—from the organ to the saxophone, from the bugle to the policeman's whistle—and including such nonmusical instruments as the typewriter, the automobile horn, a paper bag full of sand, and shaken oyster shells. But the instruments fundamental to most orchestras have remained about the same for nearly two centuries, though their number and their relative importance have varied. At full strength, and when playing Berlioz, Wagner, or post-Wagnerian music, a symphony orchestra may consist of more than one hundred players all actively making their instruments sound.

---

[2] The band is a variant of the orchestra. A typical band, and especially a military band, contains no (or very few) stringed instruments, being made chiefly of winds, among which the brasses dominate. The jazz band, however, is very often actually a chamber ensemble in which each part is played by a single instrument.

The orchestra did not begin as so gigantic a machine. Giovanni Gabrieli, who composed what many musicologists consider to have been the earliest truly orchestral music, was content with bassoons, cornetts, trombones, and violins to support the human voices in his *Sacrae symphoniae,* composed near the close of the 1500's. Monteverdi used specifically orchestral group tone-colorings for emotional-musical effect, but did not hit upon the string-dominated orchestra, his ensemble remaining the Renaissance one in which wind instruments supply the foundation, strings being brought in chiefly for pathetic or other specifically emotional effects.

It was the baroque age, culminating musically in Bach and Handel, that produced the string-dominated instrumental ensemble, almost—but not exactly—the classical symphony orchestra. (It is as clear that the sonata-symphony produced the symphonic orchestra as it is that the emergence of the symphonic orchestra hastened the evolution of the classical symphony.) During the seventeenth century, no special importance was placed upon individual instrumental timbres or colorings, as is proved by the widespread practice of thorough-bass, the writing out of parts only for melody and bass, the other parts being filled in more or less *ad libitum.* In such almost-orchestral compositions as many of Bach's and Handel's, nevertheless, a transitional step is visible from the Renaissance ensemble (which was in reality a wind-dominated chamber group) to the modern orchestra divided into "choirs" of instruments. Members of the violin family, gradually besting their viol cousins, made possible domination by the strings. The wind instruments tended toward standardization: flutes, horns, and oboes (clarinets came later) were increasingly basic and normal.

Bach did not carefully assign to each instrument or choir of instruments—all meticulously indicated in the written score—a part that it could play better than any other instrument or choir. When assigning a part to an instrument Bach appears most often to have considered only the instrument's relative audibility and its compass. As a result, no severe damage would be done to many of Bach's instrumental pieces if musical lines now performed by flutes were transferred to violins; to make this change in music by Wagner or Rimsky-Korsakov, Berlioz or Ravel, would be to destroy a significant part of the composer's musical conception. In Bach's instrumentation the parts are very often actually interchangeable. Nor did Bach often alter instrumental colorings midway in a piece or movement by changing instruments, a practice exceedingly common among later composers, many of whom would have felt frozen without it.

Handel, composing operas and dramatic oratorios, displayed more interest than Bach in the notable individualities of ensemble instruments, more awareness of the distinctive possibilities of the timbres of instruments grouped within the larger group. He scored for special instruments briefly for special effects (the contrabassoon, for example, and the harp). He needed to be more constructively aware of the architectural potentialities of contrasted timbres than Bach had reason to be. But it was Jean-Philippi Rameau who, first of the great composers, showed some of that delicate care in selecting instruments for their color and special capabilities as well as their volume and compass which became one of the fruitful constructive principles of symphonic music. Contrasts of timbre attracted Rameau, who not only set in French music a style that was still evident in both Debussy and Ravel, but also helped definitively the formation of the classical symphony orchestra.

The Mannheim orchestra was of lasting historic importance, as we have seen, chiefly for its development of effects and for its conclusive demonstrations of the values of rehearsal and exactness. In the Mannheim ensemble the importance of the stringed instruments was enormously increased, in part because they responded excellently to the desire of Stamitz and his associates for prolonged crescendos and decrescendos, trills, and sudden louds and softs. In the works composed with the Mannheim orchestra in mind, instrumental ensemble music reached, from a technical point of view, an unprecedented complexity, though the compositions of the Stamitzes, Holzbauer, Richter, Cannabich, and the other Mannheimers have proved to be of smaller purely musical value than, on one side, the masterworks of Bach and Handel and, on the other, those of Haydn and Mozart.

The harpsichord was kept in the ensemble in its *continuo* role even in symphonies that Carl Philipp Emanuel Bach composed nearly three decades after the death of his father in 1750. These four interesting works, in which the sonata-symphony was all but born, require the now-standard groups of stringed instruments and a group of eight (sometimes seven) winds: bassoons, flutes, horns, and oboes. It is possible to look closely at most single instrumental lines in a C. P. E. Bach symphony and determine by their contour the instrument for which each was intended. Similar examination of a part in one of his father's works would often produce data only for vague guesswork. The son, that is (his father's inferior in every musical respect), belonged to a later, more nearly orchestral, era. He labored at the very entrance to the age during which Haydn and Mozart would consolidate the orchestra and its primary position.

Experimenting with the orchestra during a long lifetime, Haydn gradually dropped *continuo* and harpsichord from it. Slowly he increased the proportion of strings to winds; brought instruments in or dropped them out in the midst of symphonies or movements; often assigned leading melodies momentarily to a wind instrument chosen for its peculiar timbre; and at last formalized the make-up of the orchestral choirs. In Mozart's last orchestral works and the later among Haydn's more than one hundred symphonies, the orchestra commonly consists of first and second violins, violas, cellos, doublebasses, two bassoons, two clarinets, two flutes, two horns, two oboes, and two kettledrums. With this aggregation, perhaps the first that can be described accurately as a symphonic orchestra, these men created masterworks that were really something new. This orchestra sufficed (though with almost constant changes, subtractions, and additions) for Beethoven and Schubert. Basically it suffices now, though it has expanded, though alterations in the manufacture of several instruments have changed their powers and colors, and though new instruments have occasionally (at times temporarily) been added.

What has happened in less than two centuries to the size of the forces that a composer could feel justified in demanding can be vividly seen in a comparison of a "large" orchestra of Haydn's day [3] and a large orchestra of the twentieth century.

ORCHESTRA OF HAYDN'S "LONDON" SYMPHONY (No. 104, D MINOR-MAJOR), COMPOSED IN 1795	ORCHESTRA OF STRAVINSKY'S *Le Sacre du printemps*, COMPOSED IN 1912-13
	1 bass clarinet
	1 bass trumpet
2 bassoons	4 bassoons (one interchangeable with a second contrabassoon)
2 clarinets	3 clarinets (one interchangeable with a second bass clarinet)
	1 clarinet in E flat
	1 contrabassoon
	1 English horn
2 flutes	2 flutes
	1 flute in G
2 horns	8 horns (two interchangeable with Bayreuth tubas)
2 oboes	4 oboes (one interchangeable with a second English horn)
	2 piccolos
	3 trombones
2 trumpets	4 trumpets
	2 tubas
2 kettledrums	4 kettledrums; small kettledrums; bass drum; tambourine; cymbals; antique cymbals; triangle; tam-tam; rasp or scratcher
strings	strings

Leaving out of consideration the stringed instruments and the percussion, Haydn's orchestra in this case called for ten players, Stravinsky's for thirty-eight. Until he went to London, Haydn considered himself fortunate when, with strings and drums, he commanded any number of players in excess of twenty-four; *Le Sacre*

[3] Great masses of instruments had been assembled on festal occasions during earlier periods. In 1749 the overture to Handel's *Royal Fireworks Music* was performed in London in the open air by twenty-four oboes, twelve bassoons, nine trumpets, nine horns, one contrabassoon, three pairs of kettledrums, and a huge bass cornett known as a serpent. But this was a variety of ceremonial band rather than an orchestra—and it was notable chiefly for its rare monstrousness.

du printemps cannot be performed properly by less than eighty. The point is not that Haydn did so much with so little—or that Stravinsky required huge forces. Supposing Haydn and Stravinsky to be equally in command of the forces at their disposition, any contrast of importance between them cannot be made on the basis of size, but only on that of musical ideas conveyed or elicited by their music. Both, though in wholly different senses of the phrase, are complete orchestral masters.

The important point is that the modern orchestra, starting as an expansion of the chamber group,[4] has developed into the mightiest musical instrument ever devised. At each step of its growth men able to use it creatively at its then standard size have taken advantage of it to convey many of their richest musical conceptions.

[4] Aggregations of instruments smaller in number than the great symphony orchestras often operate under such names as sinfonietta, symphonette, and chamber orchestra. "Chamber orchestra," though superficially self-contradictory, is the most useful term for this very useful ensemble of intermediate size: it is truly an orchestra, but it keeps somewhat to more intimacy of texture and aim than is possible to a group of eighty or ninety musicians performing in a huge auditorium. A considerable repertoire of music exists for which the chamber orchestra is far more appropriate than its larger counterpart; much of this has been composed by modern musicians.

Thirteen

OPERA · LULLY · RAMEAU · HANDEL
THE NEAPOLITAN MANNER · GLUCK · MOZART

Opera, started on its long, colorful history in the dawn of monody by Florentines yearning to revive Greek performances of drama, had first enlisted the services of a great composer when Monteverdi turned his attention to it in *Orfeo* (1607). In his musico-dramatic works Monteverdi exercised his genius on the combining of text, music, and stage presentation. Florence, Rome, and Venice thereafter produced operas and almost-operas in huge supply. Many of these were written by men of cherishable talent. They contained overtures, *sinfonie,* arias, concerted numbers, and choruses. Turning their backs on the dry recitative of the Florentine way-breakers, other composers mixed polyphony with monody, coming to feel that almost any style or technique of music could be drawn upon to furnish operatic structure.

As the seventeenth century wore on, arias and concerted numbers (duets, trios, and quartets) became more and more sharply different in musical texture from the merely reportorial or plot-forwarding recitative. The chorus as employed by such Roman composers as Stefano Landi (1590?-1655?), Luigi Rossi (1598-1653), and Michelangelo Rossi (seventeenth century) played a constantly more dramatic role in the unfolding of the libretto's story. Comic episodes and interludes, both within the operas themselves and as performed between acts, became common, being called for as con-

168

trast to and relief from the prevailingly solemn classic-mythological or Graeco-Roman historical plots. The vocal agility of superbly trained singers—sopranos especially, both female and male (*castrati*)—won public enthusiasm and was catered to by composers. In the Venetian operas of Pietro Francesco Cavalli (1602-1676) and Marc' Antonio Cesti (1618-1669) the grandeurs and complexities of the young art form reached amazing intensity. Involving many singers in tortuous plots, filling well-equipped stages with eye-dazzling pictures, catering to the growing taste for comic interludes, and generally enlarging all the elements involved to a size that would have astonished and displeased Caccini and Peri, the Venetians set styles that have persisted ever since in the Italian presentation of opera. With their works, opera as a theatrical spectacle in the Italian style had been born.

In France, meanwhile, that other Italian, Jean-Baptiste Lully, had begun to suggest the Franco-Italian manners of opera. In Italy itself opera succeeded immediately because it supplied attractive theater to a spectacle-hungry people. In seventeenth-century France, on the contrary, it at first suffered stiff competition from ballet and from the well-entrenched spoken drama of Corneille, Molière, and Racine. Lully simply imported ballet into the capacious precincts of opera and—from the French point of view—naturalized its presence there forever. He paid to the instrumental texture of his operas far more thoughtful attention than was lavished on that musical element by most of his Italian predecessors and contemporaries, Monteverdi being a notable exception. Too, with serious spoken drama alive and popular, he insisted more than most Italians on strength and theatrical credibility in the plot and situations of his librettos. Not for him were the long *scene* (elaborate formal arias, often *da capo*) of an Alessandro Scarlatti, those magnificent musical outbursts that tended to congeal dramatic action and call attention to their own expressiveness. Rather, Lully favored brief, dancelike songs, called *airs*, often built over actual dance rhythms.[1]

The Lullyan opera was carried forward, not materially altered in structure, by Jean-Philippe Rameau. Rameau arrived at opera

[1] For Lully's treatment of the overture and recitative, see pages 104-106.

when he was fifty years old, already a renowned theorist and composer. Although he was immediately attacked in the name of Lully as a defiler of tradition, he actually intensified tendencies clear in Lully's operas. He sacrificed interest in the voice to interest in the orchestra, and was not above suspending story and action for the time required by a good ballet. He wrote magnificent overtures in a manner between the "French" overture and the sonata. He applied his advanced harmonic ideas and resources to opera as to other musical genres. And he sought, in the operatic orchestra as elsewhere, for characteristic instrumental effects, for the touches that each instrument or choir could produce better than any other.

On the operatic scene in Germany there appeared in 1705 a composer greater than Monteverdi or Rameau: it was then, at Hamburg, that *Almira* was sung, the first of nearly forty operas by George Frideric Handel. *Almira* was composed to an Italian text.[2] It was not in any aspect of importance a Germanic opera, though Handel had learned much of what he knew about operatic techniques from another German, the director of the Hamburg Opera, Reinhard Keiser (1674-1739). Keiser, using both German and Italian texts, and Handel, using only Italian, wrote mostly the sort of opera which has come to be called Neapolitan whether composed in Naples, Rome, or Hamburg.

"Neapolitan" opera was, first of all, serious, usually tragic (of Handel's many operas only one—*Xerxes,* which contains the world-famous "Largo"—is comic), what the Italians called *opera seria.* It entertained little tolerance for comic interludes, being closer in purely narrative solemnity to the concepts of the Florentine pioneers of opera. It was most often divided into three longish acts, each divided roughly into two sections: first one devoted to getting on with the story, in recitative, mostly *recitativo secco;* then a section devoted to commenting upon the recent plot events, this mostly in arias. These were singing operas, largely for solo singers, and in them little of importance was assigned to the instruments once the overture had been played—though there were notable

---

[2] The first known opera in German, the *Daphne* of Schütz, had been heard in 1627. Probably the first opera ever sung in Germany, this was—as already said—an adaptation of a translation of Peri's *Dafne.* Unfortunately, this early victim of the insuperable difficulties of translating opera has not survived: the score of *Daphne* was burned in 1760.

exceptions to this generality. Each of the chief singers was given arias of a certain importance at predetermined places in the acts, and battles were fought if these strait traditions were flouted even momentarily. The singer and what she or he sang were all-important. Neapolitan opera seemed more likely than most to develop into an uninterrupted chain of arias.

Wherever composed and wherever sung, Neapolitan opera was the special habitat of the surpassing vocal technique known as *bel canto* (beautiful song). This technique was accused of sacrificing "feeling" (by which the accuser too often meant a tearful vocal quality) and of subordinating to display the "characteristic" vocal colorings demanded by the changing emotions of the libretto. Its prime emphasis was on beauty, accuracy, and brilliance of tone-production. As practiced by the best female sopranos, male sopranos, and—more rarely—other voices of the eighteenth century, it provided vocal displays that can now only be imagined. Later eras have developed other vocal techniques and emotional emphases with other values, but the most important of the reasons why operas of the Neapolitan style are now seldom sung is that few living singers can surmount their difficulties and at the same time sing expressively. An idea of what a singer could be expected to do may be gained from the following measures from the solo vocal line of an aria from *Vespasiano,* an opera by Attilio Ariosti (1666-1740?):

To composers' demands for librettos that would be dramatic and (in their view) sensible, and at the same time would supply each first lady (*prima donna*), first man (*primo uomo*), second lady (*seconda donna*), and so forth with the essential arias at the required times, two literary men of talent responded. The earlier, Apostolo Zeno (1668-1750), served as court poet both in Vienna and in Venice. Pietro Trapassi, known as Metastasio (1698-1782), court poet at Vienna for the last fifty-two years of his long life, excelled Zeno and became librettist to a century. He was so adept at ringing acceptable changes on the narrowly delimited form of Neapolitan libretto that more than one thousand eighteenth-century operas used one or another of his texts. The same Metastasio text was set by ten, twenty, even forty different composers. Johann Adolf Hasse (1699-1783) set one of Metastasio's most popular librettos—*Artaxerxes*—three times; he boasted that he had made operas of all but one of the Italian's operatic texts. Handel, Haydn, Mozart—even so purely nineteenth-century a composer as Giacomo Meyerbeer (1791-1864)—found Metastasio's texts useful. His popularity as a provider of librettos has never been approached by that of any other writer.

Still mostly stories about personages from Greek or Roman mythology or pseudo-history, the finest operas of the Neapolitan style were grave, exquisitely constructed, and prodigal of melody. From a later point of view, they were as static as a hall of statues. Aside from the stage pictures, often of extravagant complexity and notable beauty, they offered the eighteenth-century operagoer supremely supple and accomplished singers performing difficult feats easily, clusters of the most luscious melodies ever imagined, and opportunity to enjoy and contrast the highly conventionalized dexterities of librettists and composers. The public did not object (as why should it have objected, being offered so much?) if what was offered was really a concert in costume before handsome scenery. It did not expect—nor should we expect when listening to eighteenth-century opera—the emotional realism or musical dramatics that the operas of Wagner, Verdi, and Richard Strauss have taught twentieth-century opera-goers to consider the only norms of "good" opera. On its own terms an opera by Handel—

or by such greatly gifted Neapolitans as Tommaso Traëtta (1727-
1779) and Niccolò Jommelli (1714-1774)—is as reasonable, as secure
an artistic fabric, as *musically* expressive, as *Carmen, Aïda, Tristan
und Isolde, Elektra,* or *Tosca.* It is only more strictly musical in
its appeal and—all appearances to the contrary notwithstanding—
far more difficult to sing.

Neapolitan opera, for all its stores of beauty, did not provide a
home for the comic spirit. As mentioned earlier, comic interludes
or episodes made their way very early into Roman opera. Even
Monteverdi's *L'Incoronazione di Poppea* (1642) had room for
comedy. The future Pope Clement IX, when still Giulio, Cardinal
Rospigliosi, wrote comic librettos that were used in the middle
1600's for the earliest known entirely comic operas. One composer,
Marco Marazzoli (?-1662), was involved in two settings of Rospigliosi librettos: in *Che Soffre Speri* (1639) with Virgilio Mazzocchi
(1597-1646), who was primarily a religious; in *Dal Male il Bene*
(1654) with Antonio Maria Abbatini (1595?-1677), who was once
invited by Urban VIII to revise the Hymnal. This Rospigliosi-
Marazzoli-Abbatini collaboration is notable in that it established
the practice of ending comic operas with ensembles in which all
the principal characters sing together.

Zeno and Metastasio genuinely disapproved of the comic spirit
in opera. Their librettos "reformed" opera by removing from it
not only integral comic episodes, but also the possibility of breaking the grave, mostly tragic atmosphere of an opera by playing a
frivolous, often hilarious, brief comic musical play between its
acts. The comic *intermezzo,* responding as it did to an enduring human desire, and having been pushed out of *opera seria,*
gradually evolved by itself into *opera buffa* (comic opera), generally a two-act form. The most renowned *opera buffa* of the
first half of the eighteenth century was *La Serva Padrona* (1733),
composed by Giovanni Battista Pergolesi (1710-1736), and still occasionally staged. Having only three characters, one of them a
mute, *La Serva Padrona* is easy to stage, and it became widely
popular. It is marked by broad farce, music often of the warmest
good humor, and great swiftness of development.

Pergolesi's masterly trifle, as performed in Paris in 1752 by a

company known as Les Bouffons (the comedians), led to a pro-
tracted controversy known as the *guerre des bouffons,* in which the
ever-double nature of opera was clarified forever, but not recon-
ciled to itself. On one side of this peculiarly Parisian "war" stood
Louis XV, Madame de Pompadour, a large section of the upper
nobility, and the wealthiest merchants. This party said (and believed) that it was defending French opera—the French brand of
serious opera as practiced by Lully, Rameau, and their followers—
though in actual fact it was involved in a foredoomed attempt to
keep alive the pure baroque spirit that had given birth to *opera
seria,* and which had begun to die out by 1752. Against the pro-
baroque party stood the Queen, Marie Leczinska, the most learned
and accomplished French musicians, such intellectuals as D'Alem-
bert, Diderot, Baron Grimm, and—most important and vocal of
all—that apostle of the natural, Jean-Jacques Rousseau, a musician
of learning and some talent. This party, whatever its stated motives
and published beliefs, was defending the newborn spirit of the
rococo, destined to replace the baroque.

The actual (as against the literary) *guerre des bouffons* lasted
one day. It was won by the "Queen's party" for the rococo, but
its supporters were not clear as to what they had won. The manager of the theater where *La Serva Padrona* had set off the war
announced an opera called *Les Troqueurs,* which, though composed by an Italian, was to be sung in French. The "Italian composer" was intended to win the "Queen's party," which believed
that it was fighting for Italian opera, while the "sung in French"
was planned to please the King-Pompadour party, which said that
it was aiding opera in the national tongue. *Les Troqueurs* pleased
almost everyone, though it seems to have been indifferent stuff.
Then the daring manager revealed that it was in reality the work
of Antoine d'Auvergne (1713-1797), a Frenchman. In short, it was
opera buffa in French: *opéra bouffe.* Other French composers, Rameau among them, had tried vainly earlier to interest the Paris
public in comic opera. It had taken a Parisian "war" and a delicate
trick to win that public to it. Operatically speaking, the *guerre des
bouffons* ended the exclusive dominance of baroque *opera seria*
in France. On the international scene, it made possible the so-

called "operatic reform" of which the central figures were Christoph Willibald von Gluck (1714-1787) and his librettist and private pamphleteer, Ranieri da Calzabigi (1714-1795), neither of whom had more than a passing interest in comic opera.

For the first two decades of his opera-composing career, Gluck had evidenced little difference from a dozen other non-Italian (or, for that matter, Italian) manufacturers of Neapolitan opera. He was forty-seven years old when he produced the ballet *Don Juan* (1761), from which a clever soothsayer might have made the guess that Gluck was going to compose something different in kind from the twenty-five or so operas and *pasticci* [3] with which his past was starred. Gluck, *Don Juan* demonstrated, was weary of re-using the same conventions over and over.

In Calzabigi, Gluck encountered exactly the mildly revolutionary intellectual refreshment he needed. In their *Orpheus and Eurydice* (1762) the collaborators served preliminary notice that their ideal of opera was severe, restrained, a partial glance back to the ideals of Peri and Caccini. Even though *Orpheus* is half-hearted revolt (it bows to the convention of the obviously contrived happy ending), it was strange enough so that the Viennese did not take it to their hearts. Five years passed, during which Gluck went back to setting Metastasio's librettos. Then he collaborated again with Calzabigi. When their *Alceste* was sung in Vienna in 1767, it seemed that Gluck and Calzabigi were conscientiously mixing Metastasian-Neapolitan usages with their ideals. In place of the accompanied recitative used throughout *Orpheus and Eurydice*, *recitativo secco* had in part returned, and the libretto itself employed some of the least fresh of Metastasio's tricks. But Gluck's music was very far in manner from the bright and charming irrelevancies of many Neapolitan operas. It was, instead, dramatic, strictly related to the classic tragedy it supports in a spare, powerful way. It has often been said that Gluck was a poor harmonist, a charge that is perhaps true and certainly meaningless. For the

---

[3] The *pasticcio* was a commonplace of the period. Literally "pastry," it was either an opera composed in collaboration by two or several men or a medley of operatic excerpts by various composers (sometimes a single composer) strung together on a frail thread of plot.

harmonic starkness of this music is precisely Gluck's revolution, his method of banishing baroque scrollwork, of leading both melody and rhythm forth in naked power.

But *Alceste* was not indeed so revolutionary, so set against the other employers of Metastasio, as was the preface to the published edition (1769) of the opera. In this, a single sentence crystallized the aim and creed of an operatic school that has waxed and waned throughout the whole history of the art: "I have tried to restrict music to its true office of serving poetry by means of expression and by following the situations of the story without interrupting the action or smothering it in a useless superfluity of ornaments. . . ." Later in this brave document, Gluck (or Calzabigi for him) wrote: "I did not think it my duty to pass quickly over an aria's second section, the text of which is perhaps most impassioned and important, so as to repeat regularly four times the text of the first section and to finish the aria where its meaning may perhaps not end, this for the convenience of the singer, who wishes to prove that he can capriciously vary a passage in a number of ways. . . . I have felt that the overture should inform the spectators of the nature of the action to be represented . . . that the concerted instruments should be introduced in proportion to the interest and intensity of the text. . . . I believed that my greatest effort should be devoted to seeking a beautiful simplicity, and I have avoided making displays of difficulty at the expense of clarity . . . and there is no rule that I have not thought to set aside willingly for the sake of an intended effect."

Except one, these sentiments are beyond criticism: some of the greatest composers of opera and song could never have been forced to agree that the true office of music is to serve poetry. More than once a strong case has been made for exactly the opposite proposition: that in song and opera the true office of poetry is to serve music. But the Calzabigi-Gluck manifesto stated the tenets out of which they had produced *Alceste,* and after which, in 1770, they were to produce *Paris and Helen.* Although both are superior operas, neither pleased Vienna. With the relative failure of *Paris and Helen* (which contains *"O del mio dolce ardor,"* one of the most persuasively amorous of arias), Gluck left Vienna. Soon he was established in the Paris that, two decades earlier, had fought the *guerre des bouffons*.

Gluck found himself famous in Paris, not so much because of his music as because of the preface to *Alceste* and the scarcely less forceful one to *Paris and Helen*. An audience was waiting to applaud him when he would apply the Calzabigi-Gluck principles fully to a libretto in French. The far-seeing composer had already composed most of such an opera, *Iphigénie en Aulide*. In 1774 this took Paris completely. It is a great way removed from the ornate decorativeness of typical late Neapolitan opera or from a concert in costume. Grand, simple, dramatic—in short, the result of one way of mating text and music perfectly—*Iphigénie en Aulide* is an indivisible work of art. Gluck may have thought that his music was serving the indifferent poetry supplied by his French librettist, but in fact he had absorbed that text into his music, coalescing the two elements into something greater than the sum obtained by adding together the virtues of each.[4]

But the Parisians, while appreciating Gluck, loved "wars" and were realistically hospitable to more than one kind of opera. An Italian appeared, or was brought to Paris for the fun of a war, and was built up into a rival for the Austrian. Niccola Piccinni was a very talented composer of late Neapolitan opera. Hoping for something as scintillating as the *guerre des bouffons,* the Parisian amateurs were gravely disappointed when both Gluck and Piccinni declined to fight, each remaining content with the sort of opera he could compose best. Modern taste has forgotten Piccinni; it has remembered Gluck, though dimly and incompletely. But this is far from indicating that Gluck's "revolution" triumphed decisively or that the tuneful, demonstrative Neapolitan style, with its emphasis on *bel canto,* or the Lully-Rameau heroic opera, vanished forever. All sorts of opera, including several later varieties, have been composed since, in all purity and in every degree of compromise and combination. Gluck triumphed in another sense: he made magnificent musico-dramatic masterpieces that can be re-

---

[4] Gluck was to surpass the first *Iphigénie* with a second—*Iphigénie en Tauride* (1778), an opera worthy of the play by Euripides of which its libretto is a French adaptation.

stored to full life two centuries later. He reasserted the dramatic
ideals of the Florentine founders of opera, reasserted them in musical terms more complex than theirs, and passed them on to the
future. Without his intervention or that of someone holding his
beliefs, opera might have degenerated into a form neglecting
drama entirely. What Gluck's best operas achieved and preserved
was to be of major importance to composers as varied as Mozart,
Berlioz, Wagner, Verdi, Debussy, Puccini, and Richard Strauss.

As Dante was the first universal genius in Italian literature, Cer-
vantes the first in Spanish, and Shakespeare the first in English, so
Mozart was the first in the history of music. He did everything musical with mastery, understood all existing forms with ease, and
amalgamated contesting forces into satisfying artistic wholes. Before he was twenty-five he had composed *opera seria* and *opera
buffa* in Italian, as well as operetta [5] in German. In 1782 he wrote
The Abduction from the Seraglio, a comic opera in German. With
spoken dialogue between arias and concerted numbers, this type
of opera came to be known as *Singspiel. The Abduction* was nonetheless full of Italianate music. It required expert *bel canto* and
contained one of the most taxing arias (*"Martern aller Arten"*)
ever composed to show off the *colorature* of an agile soprano.
When Mozart was thirty (1786), he composed an *opera buffa, The
Marriage of Figaro,* that comes as close as any human product to
being entirely free of flaws. The next year it was *Don Giovanni,*
which he labeled a *dramma giocoso* (jocose or mirthful drama)
because it mixes tragedy and comedy, is neither all *buffa* nor all
seria. One of the greatest of operas, *Don Giovanni* mingles traits of
Neapolitan *opera seria*—including its florid, elaborately decorated
style—with traits clearly Gluckian. Three years after that, Mozart
almost matched *The Marriage of Figaro* with *Così fan tutte,* again
opera buffa. And in 1791 he composed *The Magic Flute* to a German libretto that stirs together Masonic symbolism, cheerful nonsense, and serious philosophy, putting into it some of the most ex-

[5] In the eighteenth century the Italian word *operetta* was used in its literal meaning of little opera; its later connotation, of light music intended wholly for entertainment, was then only hinted at.

alted music ever composed for the human voice with orchestra. He was a dying man at thirty-five, and in that same year he ended his operatic life with a reversion to unadulterated *opera seria, La Clemenza di Tito.*

Mozart possessed unique virtues as a maker of opera in addition to his stupendous, all but incredible, mastery of the techniques of composition, his surpassing fertility in melody, and his rarely failing sense of proportion. He has never been matched in the ability to depict a wide variety of characters in musico-dramatic terms. In *The Marriage of Figaro, Don Giovanni,* and *Così fan tutte* he was assisted by Lorenzo da Ponte, a more accomplished librettist even than Metastasio or Calzabigi. But though not even Mozart could have created so nearly perfect an opera as *The Marriage of Figaro* on a clumsy or poor libretto, it is certain that his finest operas multiply the best qualities of their texts—and that in *The Magic Flute* he triumphed over an often witless, sometimes pompous, and never solidly constructed libretto. In the creation of stage personalities who take their places among real human beings he is of the Shakespearean order, evoking men and women who, once familiar, can never be thought of as less than alive. With godlike swiftness and the assurance of genius, he gave to each protagonist in *The Marriage of Figaro, Don Giovanni,* and *The Magic Flute* music at once serenely or dramatically beautiful and entirely appropriate to his constant inward nature and shifting outward circumstance.

Mozart's music was not the servant of poetry. In this respect he stood midway between the expressed ideals of Gluck and those at the opposite extreme. His music was elaborated for its own sake, for those aesthetic-psychological effects of symbolic communication which only music (or music best) can achieve. So delicate was this balance that Mozart not only absorbed libretto into opera as Gluck had absorbed it, but also created drama—comic, tragic, or both together—out of musical characters in the round both on the stage and in the mind, characters who live precisely in the music he assigned to them for expressing the texts of their roles. Despite the universes of beauty in Mozart's symphonies, chamber music, and concertos, this special achievement—one never entirely

equaled by another composer—makes it seem to many that his
greatest work was the composition of opera.

By the time when Mozart composed his stage masterpieces, the
full eighteenth-century orchestra had evolved. In his sonatas, concertos, chamber music, and symphonies, the varieties of sonata
form had become mature, as they had matured simultaneously in
Haydn's symphonies and chamber music. With these two men the
rococo-classical forms reached peaks beyond which it was impossible for music to evolve without leaving the rococo behind altogether. Some new force, a tendency to another style, was required
if, after Haydn and Mozart, music was not to sink to repetitive
imitation. It matters not at which then existing technical element
or device of construction we look—whether it be orchestration, the
string-quartet style, modulation, the concerto style, opera, classical
harmony, whatever—it was used in Mozart's compositions and
those of Haydn's marvelous last years with perfection. Here was
the finest musical result of the gallant rococo world built out of
Austrian, Italian, German, and French elements, the world whose
end was symbolically announced by the fall of the Bastille in 1789,
when Mozart had but two years to live and Haydn was already a
man of fifty-seven.

Fourteen

CLASSICISM AND ROMANTICISM · BEETHOVEN
FORM AND CONTENT · STRING QUARTET
CONCERTO · PIANO SONATA · SYMPHONY
SCHUBERT · LIED · WEBER

———————

Faced with a discussion of Beethoven, a speaker or writer is especially wise to define his terminology, particularly those words referring to generalizations of style, manner, and content. What, that is to say, is "classical"? What is "romantic"?

One common use of the word "classical" with reference to music can be discarded immediately as useless to serious discussion. "Classical" music is not the opposite of "popular" music; for this necessary distinction between the supposedly weighty and enduring and the supposedly frivolous and temporary, no satisfactory terms have evolved.[1] Any attempt to make this distinction is often—as in the case of Johann Strauss's waltzes—bothersome and meaningless rather than helpful.

Another common musical use of "classical" has more value. This is as a historical label to cover the period from about 1750 to about 1800—that is, from the close of the baroque era, as represented by

[1] Many writers use such terms as "art music" or "serious music" when referring to whatever is not folk music or the music of light entertainment. But these terms will not serve: folk music is an art expression too, and the adjective "serious" weighs heavily on the pervading spirit of many a Haydn symphony, of *The Abduction from the Seraglio*, or of such a modern piece as Stravinsky's Suite No. 2 or Carlos Chávez' *Sinfonia India*, however serious their musical workmanship.

the death of Johann Sebastian Bach, through Mozart's life and
Haydn's creative life, and to a year selected because it is a round
number and coincided roughly with the appearance of new musical forces in the works of Beethoven and Schubert. In this sense
"classical" is a technical word: it remarks on the perfection of the
sonata form in varying raiment, on the ripe maturity of euphonious, predominantly diatonic, and consonant harmony—and on an
overtopping concern with proportion and balance among existing
musical elements. When "classical" is used to label the period containing the finest works of Gluck, Haydn, and Mozart—and the
early, more or less Haydnesque and Mozartean, works of Beethoven and Schubert—its opposite may be either of two other labels,
depending upon which way the speaker or writer is facing. If he
means to contrast the 1750-1800 period with what had preceded
it, the antonym of "classical" is "baroque"; [2] if with what succeeded it, the antonym is "romantic."

A third use of the word "classical" is common to all the arts. It
is difficult to define, and the indefinition of its boundaries has
made it a confusion for decades. Not only does "classical" always
necessarily suggest the meanings thus far mentioned; it also refers
to the art of ancient Greece and Rome. But ours is a psychological
age, and in it both "classical" and "romantic" have acquired psychological meanings vague in relation to their other, more closely
definable uses. In this sense, "classical" suggests art produced by
men whose preponderant interest is the creation of objective entities of certain size, shape, and content, impersonal (relatively
impersonal) works in which their own private personalities and
emotions are present only incidentally, as by-products; similarly,
the "romantic" artist is thought of as chiefly interested in "expressing" through his art his own character, personality, emotions, and
ideas—in using artistic creation as an extension of his self.

This psychological application of "classical" and "romantic" is
clear only at the extremes. Haydn can seem to few listeners to be

[2] The classical period, that is, was in one sense introduced by the evolution of rococo art, of which it became an extension and expansion. Despite the fact that
Gluck was a Bohemian, Haydn and Mozart Austrians, and Beethoven a German,
the most "classical" of their music is deeply marked by Italian and French manners.

telling them how he saw the world, loved, felt about God and the universe, or thought of his fellow men. But a Chopin scherzo or a suite of piano pieces by Schumann can scarcely help seeming to be—in addition, of course, to other things—an attempt by the composer to communicate his own emotions and ideas or beliefs. It has been said that "classical" music creates and evokes ideas and emotions in the listener, whereas "romantic" music communicates or conveys them from the composer. There are all possible shadings between such neat extremes, for which reason the terms themselves turn into battlegrounds removed from all reality. But there can be no doubt that this use of "classical" and "romantic" will go on plaguing all discussions of art, and of music in particular. It responds, that is, to a felt reality.

Artistic traditionalists cling to a belief that new forces and conditions could, if only they would, make use of old, perfected forms. Revolutionaries claim that forms are prisons of the past from which every present must escape. The history of any art is the graph of an oscillation between traditional "classical" and rebellious "romantic" periods, between insistence on formal probity, emotional reticence, and the increasing perfection of existing formal elements and periods shaped by the irruption of new or new-seeming ideas and forces and of those artistic personalities who tend to break up existing patterns, insert novel emotional tones, and dissolve the old mixtures. A "classical" era must be born out of a "romantic" one. It becomes more "classical" as it develops its patterns and practices, and then starts to break apart in the demanding presence of new forces that it cannot contain. The result of such a breaking is a new "romantic" period, always likely to look disorderly as it opens, but becoming more orderly as it extends itself in time and evolves toward another classicism. In this view, classicism is consolidation, romanticism is experiment.

Within this usage of "classical" and "romantic," Orlando di Lasso, Palestrina, Bach, Handel, Gluck, Haydn, and Mozart were all "classical." The era of Machaut, Dufay, and Okeghem, most of the musical seventeenth century, and the period from about 1800 almost to the end of the nineteenth century were all roman-

tic.[3] Obviously these periods were not sharply defined at either
limit: one extends into the other, and a composer is often alternately classical and romantic. What is important for us here is the
general statement, derived from observation of what has actually
occurred, that a classical period does not long outlast the apogee
of its particular perfections, that a romantic period tends from its
outset to become more and more classical.

The Viennese classical period could not prolong itself beyond
the culminating masterworks of Mozart and Haydn. Not only was
there a collapse of the world to which they responded; but also the
forms and patterns the composers had used were perfect only for
their purposes; they would not, *therefore,* serve the needs of a different day. The men appointed by genius and the nature of their
eras to fail at attempts to continue them, and destined in the process of failure to break up these eras and institute a new romanticism, were Ludwig van Beethoven (1770-1827) and Franz Schubert
(1797-1828).

Four of the musical genres in which Beethoven excelled were the
piano concerto, the piano sonata, the symphony, and the string
quartet. The earliest of his five mature piano concertos was composed in 1794;[4] the earliest three of his thirty-two piano sonatas
were published in 1797; the earliest of his nine symphonies was
composed by 1800 and published in 1801; and the first six of his
sixteen string quartets were also published in 1801. All of this music, then, was in existence within ten years of Mozart's death and
while Haydn was still completing *The Seasons.* What characteristics are common to Beethoven's Piano Concerto No. 2; his Piano
Sonata No. 2; his Symphony No. 1; and his earliest quartet?

They are all Mozartean-Haydnesque. They are all classical by
any of the definitions of that word discussed above. They are all
accomplished from a technical point of view. They are all fully

[3] An interesting case could be made for calling Carl Philipp Emanuel Bach the
center of a truncated romanticism containing little but his own music. For in the
view of those who depend upon the classical-romantic contrast, such a romantic
intrusion was essential between the baroque classicism of Handel and Bach and the
rococo classicism of Boccherini, Haydn, and Mozart.

[4] This is the "Second" Piano Concerto. The concerto now known as the "First"
was composed three years later, in 1797.

representative of a composer already about thirty years old; they are not juvenilia. Not one of them, in despite of numerous beauties, would have guaranteed Beethoven an important position in the history of music.

Beethoven's Piano Concerto No. 2 is shaped in the rapid-slow-rapid three-movement pattern favored by Mozart. It is altogether Mozartean, in fact, without approaching Mozart's rich mastery. In it almost every element is conventional and a little tame.

The Piano Sonata No. 2 uses the rapid-slow-minuet-rapid pattern favored by Haydn. It is altogether Haydnesque without approaching the stature or originality of the older man's best sonatas. Only in its final *prestissimo* movement is something un-classical suggested by pell-mell power and an insistence that threatens to pass the borders of the polite.

The first of Beethoven's nine symphonies suffers from a truly non-classical disproportion that has forced many apologists into tortuous explanation: it shows a composer not satisfied by the eighteenth century and not yet at home in the nineteenth. It is a comic work with traces of melancholy. Its orchestration, generally that of the string-dominated classical symphony orchestra, is over-weighted nonetheless in favor of wind instruments; Beethoven's voice is often drowned out by echoes of Haydn and hints of Mozart. This otherwise beautiful work is a little unsteady on its feet, being uncertain, there in the half-light of a new day, where the next step may be.

The String Quartet No. 3 (generally believed to have been composed first of the six quartets in Opus 18) is too close to both Haydn and Mozart for it to have occasioned great surprise had it been found among the published works of either.

Now let us look at the final examples of Beethoven's creative intentions in the same genres. The Piano Concerto No. 5 was completed in 1809; the Piano Sonata No. 32 was completed in 1822; the Ninth Symphony in 1824; and the last String Quartet, Opus 135, in 1826. In span of time elapsed between earliest and latest examples, Beethoven's piano concertos cover thirteen years, his piano sonatas twenty-five years, his symphonies twenty-four, and his quartets at least twenty-five. But in measuring the span of stylistic difference no mathematical gauge will satisfy. The last compositions do not sound so much like more mature works of the composer who had written the first as they sound like creations of another man, one somewhat influenced by the composer of the earliest works. Their very atmosphere, as contrasted with that of Beethoven's earliest compositions, represents a greater change than had ever occurred in one composer's creative lifetime. This shift is easy to hear; what is much more difficult is to isolate the most important of the technical means by which it had been brought about.

Hearing Beethoven's Piano Concerto No. 2 and his No. 5 (the "Emperor"), we may be struck first by their disparity in size—both the physical length and the size of development within that length. Then we notice that in No. 5 the second movement has no real ending, but closes on a whispered piano introduction of the chief melody of the final rondo—a bow in the direction of unifying the concerto by more than key relationships among the movements. More—late in that final rondo the violins comment briefly on that closing whisper of the preceding movement. Everything about No. 5 is grand, assertive, imperial enough to justify its otherwise meaningless nickname. No one can ever have thought of No. 2 as imperial, for in its every gesture it resembles an elegant, bright, by no means slavish courtier.

Now let us place the Sonata, Opus 111, beside the Sonata, Opus 2, No. 2. At once we see that the earlier piece is made up of equivalents of the four customary classical movements: fast-slow-minuet-fast.[5] Opus 111 has but two movements, fast-slow. As Beethoven labeled it a sonata, we have sensibly enlarged our definition of sonata to include it, but it is not a *classical* sonata. In one standard edition, the four movements of Opus 2, No. 2 occupy twenty-eight pages, the two movements of Opus 111 thirty-one. An examination of Opus 2, No. 2 promises no technical barriers to any pianist who can play the notes of an average Haydn or Mozart sonata. One

[5] The third movement of Opus 2, No. 2 is actually a scherzo rather than a minuet. But any hard-and-fast distinction between the two was not kept at the time. Scherzo (Italian for joke) came, in Beethoven's view, to indicate a more vigorous and wayward variety of a movement in ¾ time. The difference between a Mozart or Haydn sonata minuet and a Beethoven sonata scherzo is precisely the difference in personality, era, and technique we are discussing.

glance at the final pages of Opus 111, however, discloses such a passage as:

Here the technical problem is that of keeping three trills going at the same time, two in the right hand, one in the left. If the pianist is also a musician, he will understand that this new difficulty is a result, not of any desire by Beethoven to display virtuosity or dazzle by agility, but of a profound, unceasing search for ways to express new musical ideas, new compositional emotions. He will have found himself in a pianistic musical world far distant from the courtly grace of Opus 2, No. 2.

Placed beside the First Symphony, the Ninth looks like a monster. It is nearly twice as long. The First requires two flutes, two oboes, two clarinets, two bassoons, two horns, two trumpets, two kettledrums, and the usual groups of violins, violas, cellos, and doublebasses. To this the Ninth adds two additional horns, three trombones, four vocal soloists, and a mixed chorus. The First is shaped in the four classical movements: fast,[6] slow, minuet, fast; in the Ninth we find fast, faster, slow, fastest, the second movement being a minuet-scherzo in everything but label (it is headed *molto vivace: presto*). And in its opening chord the finale of the Ninth speaks a new musical world: it is an unvarnished discord:

[6] Borrowing a useful notion from Haydn, Beethoven introduces his first rapid movement with twelve measures of *adagio;* but this introduction does not alter the fact that it is an *allegro con brio.*

Quickly, too, this movement abandons the purely instrumental character of the classical symphony, introducing a recitative for the baritone voice, a quartet of vocal soloists accompanied by a chorus, a tenor solo with chorus, two choral sections, and a final vocal quartet with chorus. If the First Symphony might be thought of as a small bright star, the Ninth is a galactic system, large areas of which seem still to be in the active process of creation.

Beethoven's last string quartet, Opus 135, is not so far from his first as are some of the quartets that immediately preceded it. In Opus 130, for instance, composed in 1825 and 1826, he originally wrote a six-movement quartet of which the finale was a tremendous fugue. Not only were six movements too many for a Boccherini-Haydn-Mozart period quartet; also, several of these six were in musical patterns previously extraneous to the form, and the Great Fugue was in itself so vast that the composer's friends persuaded him to replace it by a less tiring *allegro* finale.[7]

In the quartet Opus 131, completed in 1826, Beethoven composed what in reality is a seven-movement work; because the movements are brief, are played without pause, and are closely interrelated in tone and character, the quartet seems to be in one continuous movement. Neither seven short movements nor one extended one would do for a *classical* string quartet. Over the third, slow movement of the quartet Opus 132, completed in 1825, Beethoven inscribed: *"Heiliger Dankgesang eines Genesenen an die Gottheit, in der Lydischen Tonart"* (Solemn Thanksgiving of a Convalescent to the Godhead, in the Lydian Mode). That is, the movement proffers autobiographical intentions, if not autobiographical contents. It is, further, not in a major or minor key, but has reverted to the ecclesiastical Lydian mode, here placed so as to be a scale looking much like F major. With a vengeance, this is, in any comparison with the period that preceded Beethoven, a search for new realms of expressiveness.

In the last quartet, Opus 135, Beethoven returned amicably to the four-movement classical form of the quartet-sonata. This is a relatively short work, and seems at first glance to be a return to

[7] The *Grosse Fuge* was published separately as Opus 133.

the truly rococo-classical manner of Beethoven's own earliest quartets. But above the final movement this curious legend appears in his own script:

Muss es sein   Es muss sein   Es muss sein

"Must it be? It must be! It must be!" Here is autobiography again, this time allied specifically to certain melodic fragments. What did the words signify? Probably, in view of Beethoven's biography, "Must I accept life as it is, illness, deafness, the stupidities of men, the infuriating minutiae of existence? Yes, I must. I must." And the atmosphere engendered by that non-musical question and its equally non-musical answer haunts the music. Here is one full-fledged aspect of romanticism: music used by the composer in an attempt to communicate personal thoughts directly to the listener. (Whether anyone not seeing the question and answer would suspect their existence by the sound of the music is another question.)

The point here is double, if not triple, and of first importance. Obviously, all music of all composers has always been influenced by their non-musical lives, as well as by the situations in which they found themselves while composing. When musical works were still largely composed to order, and their over-all character was thus defined for the composer in advance, his own state of mind nevertheless inevitably led him to choose certain sorts of melody, certain rhythmic devices, certain modes or keys, a certain length or brevity. When composers produced either what they thought would earn them money or what they were driven to by inner urge—Handel and Beethoven were among the first to compose primarily for these reasons—then the very forms selected were dictated, whether they knew it or not, at least in part by non-musical factors in their daily living. But there is a difference between that sort of non-muscial effect on music and the direct intention to make music communicate non-musical ideas or emotions.[8] Even

---

[8] It is true that about 1704 Johann Sebastian Bach composed a *Capriccio on the Departure of a Beloved Brother*. But in it nothing of the composer's non-musical feelings about that leave-taking can be proved present—though it does contain an imitation of the sound of post-horns.

Stravinsky, who once said that music cannot really communicate, cannot escape the first sort of non-musical effect on music. But the second sort is a determining characteristic of the *genus* romanticism. It could not help breaking up the harmonies, melodic styles, and formal patterns that had been the very containers and conveyors of classical music.

By its component nature, nonetheless, music cannot communicate specific emotions, logical thoughts and ideas, or pictorial and figurative statements with any degree of clarity. Attempts to make it do so must always be bolstered up with titles, captions, superscriptions, onomatopoeic imitations. And inevitably it follows that these attempts and their results cannot be the central reason for the existence of any good musical work. Early eighteenth-century composers delighted in elaborating huge pieces purporting to describe or evoke one or another famous battle. With a considerable portion of willing assistance from listeners, they came as near to success in this attempt as possible. But most of them were poor composers, and their battle pieces, one and all (including one by Beethoven himself, *The Battle of Vittoria*), are dead.

Yet if imitative, autobiographical, literary, or pictorial music is also good music in itself, there are no just grounds for taking a severe attitude toward titles, superscriptions, onomatopoeia, or other non-musical matter attached to music by its composer. The music is what counts, and there is no tenable law against calling a symphony *"Eroica"* or three symphonic sketches *La Mer*. In these cases what the listener must guard against is listening to the *"Eroica"* for its heroism or *La Mer* for its wetness.

Music that does not convey cogent musical ideas in musical terms will not convey anything else either well or long. But a strong musical fabric can be, often has been and is, sufficiently durable to carry by suggestion and imitation a freight of non-musical matter. Beethoven, bursting apart the purely musical reticence of the eighteenth-century classicism, introducing more and more "romantic," literary, and philosophical ideas into his inspiration, his titles and subtitles, rarely failed to weave his musical strands into fabrics of the greatest tensile strength.

Beethoven was a vividly energetic, mentally vigorous, and constantly dissatisfied, experimental man. He came, by force of necessity—a necessity growing from his own character and his many-sided relationship to the unsettled, stormy era in which he lived—to view the artist's existence as a contest with Fate, a lonely struggle with heartless Destiny, even a challenge to God. His musical talents were multiple; his grasp of the musical techniques he needed was all but absolute. But the chief single characteristic of his music is its unresting determination to be expressive in the way it bodies forth his fiery mental and spiritual attitudes. His experiments with melody, harmony, formal pattern, and the other elements of musical construction were direct ways of searching for this new, highly individual, romantic sort of expressiveness.

In sharpest contrast to Beethoven's vigorously dynamic, male personality stood the lyric, at times feminine, and always temperate musical character of Schubert, exponent of an altogether different aspect of romanticism. Schubert was almost never volcanic or doggedly assertive. His energy showed itself chiefly in the enormous number of his compositions rather than in any unusual forcefulness within single works. Schubert was not an intellectual, and whatever experimental steps his art took were the result, not of direct or conscious philosophical purpose, but of a different sort of search for expressiveness. His was primarily an art of sentiment, of a tenderness and intimacy of feeling to which his endlessly fertile musical imagination responded with hundreds of the most beautiful melodies ever penned. In Schubert's case, that is, the emphasis in the use of the word "romantic" must be placed largely on a kind of idealized love for—and responsiveness to—the intimate and quiet sides of man and nature.

Schubert touched most musical genres (though he never composed a concerto). He wrote operas, operettas, symphonies, overtures, chamber works in many forms, sonatas and other pieces for piano, songs, Masses, and many other sorts of music. In almost every genre he put some of the most heart-touching and beautiful of musical materials. In the song for solo voice with piano accompaniment, his mastery of expressiveness won him the loyalty of a world. In nearly six hundred songs Schubert presented lyric impulses, reactions to poetry, visions of a happiness he seldom knew. Such songs as *"Ave Maria," "Der Erlkönig," "Die Forelle," "Gretchen am Spinnrade," "Hark, Hark, the Lark," "Heidenröslein," "Serenade,"* and *"Who Is Sylvia?"* are simple-seeming, instantly convincing, and so winningly expressive that they have come to seem folk songs. Here is no restless, Beethovian mind seeking to force back the limits of its world or to assert man's central position in the universe.

Schubert did not "invent" the lied, but he did invent the Schubert lied, something unique and enduring. In this genre he has never been surpassed, though other composers—Schumann, Brahms, Hugo Wolf, Richard Strauss, Debussy, Fauré, Francis Poulenc—have written songs entirely outside his capabilities. But when, with the same equipment of melody and feeling, Schubert turned to more extended, more intellectual musical forms, such as string quartet or quintet or symphony, he brought to them, in most instances, no such shaping grasp or drive to the carving out of new, appropriate forms as the melodically less facile Beethoven knew. Whatever the exquisite beauty of many component parts, the least successful of Schubert's longer works, especially in varieties of sonata form, maunder and hesitate. For a symphony or piano sonata or string octet cannot be made entirely out of a single lyrical impulse, and its completely satisfactory elaboration requires an intellectual domination of musical architecture for which no impulse, however fresh, original, and momentarily beautiful, can be substituted. Nearly all of Schubert's extended compositions fail to supply that intense, specifically musical satisfaction which Beethoven almost always provides: the satisfaction of recognizing a form perfectly devised to house and present the musical materials it contains.[9]

In so unpretentious and lyrically enchanting a composition as the *"Forellen"* Quintet, so surpassingly expressive and movingly melodic a piece as the C Major String Quintet, so original and fascinating a piano sonata as the B♭ Major, or even so massive an

---

[9] In his tendency toward an attenuation of music's gift for making points swiftly, Schubert foreshadowed that nineteenth-century decrease of over-all tempo which at last led to the slow-moving monster compositions of Wagner, Bruckner, and Mahler.

achievement as the "Great" C Major Symphony, Schubert con-
quers by the lyricism of his melodies, the wonderful depth and
unexpectedness of his modulations, and his sensitivity to the timbres and individualities of instruments. But much of the time he
poured essentially songlike ideas and intimate melodies into patterns that he had misjudged or had failed to reshape to his needs.

Instead of breaking apart the classical forms and then remaking
them in his own romantic image—as Beethoven did—Schubert di-
lated them and filled them with song. He was not a hero; nature
and his background had not equipped him to lead any revolution.
Yet it would be senseless not to enjoy a Schubert symphony or
chamber piece—even so seemingly interminable a distention as his
F Major Octet—because it cannot give the satisfaction to be derived
only from the perfect fusion of material and form. Music supplies
other rich satisfactions besides the supreme sensation that material and form have become the same thing. But it is equally senseless to approach a Schubert work in sonata form in the expectation
of its providing the formal pleasure that Haydn and Mozart supply so bountifully in classical-rococo ways, Beethoven in an individual romantic way.

Beethoven the re-creator was certain to show the way to many
later composers; Schubert's historical effect is to be located especially in the remarkable efflorescence, after him, of the German
lied. The symphony, the quartet, and the piano sonata could have
evolved substantially as they did if he had not lived at all—then
we should have been deprived only of his works; they, whatever
their formal imperfections, are full, page after page, and piece
after piece, of music of an unparalleled, wholly cherishable, sort.

These men—Beethoven with his overarching urge to speak like
a hero and a god, Schubert with his intense lyricism—crossed from
the eighteenth century and its rococo perfections into the romantic unruliness of the nineteenth. Both began as classicists and
ended as romantics. But they did not enter all the portals to the
romantic movement, which in Germany was to have other emphases than those of the Viennese post-classical period in which both
Beethoven and Schubert matured. They did not reflect that aspect

of romanticism which related the word itself to "romanesque" and made it seem a revival of the artistic spirit of the eleventh and twelfth centuries. Such poets and literary philosopher-critics as Baron Friedrich von Hardenberg, known as Novalis (1772-1801) and Ludwig Tieck (1773-1853) reacted against what they felt to be the boring flatness of their own era; they preached and exemplified a return to the more flavorful manners of the romanesque Middle Ages, to the sense of mystery and wonder, to the knightly and the supernatural. Ernst Theodor Amadeus Hoffmann (1776-1822), composer and man of letters—and in this romanesque aspect, the most romantic of romantics—helped to recruit composers to the movement sponsored by Novalis, Tieck, and Tieck's friend Wilhelm Heinrich Wackenroder (1773-1798). Defining music itself as *par excellence* the art of subjective emotion, of longing and wonder, and saying that it is always romantic, Hoffmann called it *the* romantic art.

Concentrating on the subjective, the directly emotional, and the wildly picturesque, this sort of musical romanticism emphasized non-formal aspects of the art at the expense of formal considerations. In sacrificing the persuasions of formal balance and elegance in favor of ingenious attempts at direct communication between composer and listener, the lesser early romantics denied an important part of the special nature of music as an art. But they were unimportant extremists, and as the many impulses leading toward romanticism flowed together and were united by more masterly hands, the new sort of music began to evolve its own forms of discourse. Carl Maria von Weber (1786-1826) discovered the bases of his own romanticism in patriotism, a penchant for the grotesque and supernatural, and the setting of highflown opera librettos and other texts that have unfortunately but inevitably come to seem to later (and particularly non-Teutonic) generations too absurd to be tolerated.

The most enduringly remembered of Weber's larger compositions are three operas—*Der Freischütz* (1820), *Euryanthe* (1823), and *Oberon* (1826)—and the *Conzertstück* for piano and orchestra (1821). *Der Freischütz,* which found enormous popularity in Germany, deals with magic bullets, pacts with the Devil, and supernatural interventions in the lives of ordinary human beings. *Eury-anthe,* the plot of which is difficult to understand, deals with a wager between two courtiers of Louis VI, the subject being the fidelity of the betrothed of one of them. A monstrous serpent appears, a girl goes insane and is murdered by her bridegroom, and the soul of an unhappy woman named Emma is at last given peace when the tears of an innocent girl fall on the poisoned ring by means of which she had committed suicide. *Oberon's* cast of characters includes mermaids, the King and Queen of the Fairies, Puck, Harun-al-Raschid, and a pirate. Even the *Conzertstück,* according to Weber's own program for it, deals with a knight in the Holy Land, a sorrowing medieval lady, and the way his last-minute return to the castle saves her from a swoon of death. That most of this literary material now appears meretricious does not mean that Weber was led astray; it means that we have been carried a long distance from the heyday of German romanticism. Tastes have changed, but the qualities of Weber's best music have not.

Weber had a special gift for an unmistakable sort of richly curved melody, alternately nostalgic and declamatory, worked up on highly imaginative harmonic supports to climaxes of considerable intensity. Its texture is brilliantly colored and loosely knit, removed about as far as possible from the predominantly cool-tinted, tightly woven fabrics of the Viennese classical period. Weber was not Austrian, but very consciously German. His was perhaps the first deliberately chauvinistic music ever composed, his nationalism being a natural response of many young Germans to the waxing and waning of French Napoleonic imperialism. And in some manner that is psychologically unmistakable but impervious to analysis except in so far as its basis in folk practices can be pointed out, his private melodic-harmonic nature and nationalism coalesced to make his musical speech, for the Germans of his time, the very voice of Germany.

The mental universe in which Weber's music first sounded can only appear faded and quaint to most twentieth-century minds. It would be wasteful, however, to let that fact deafen us to the conquering fervor and horn-haunted mellowness of his music. His operas are probably beyond all possibility of stage revival: we

could not face their texts and stories with any measure of seriousness, and to face them without it is to deface their quality. But
they contain arias, duets, overtures, and other discrete sections that
bring Weber's unique quality across the fences of literary taste.
So magnificent an aria as Rezia's "Ocean, thou mighty monster" in
Oberon, so glimmering a breath of pure aspiration as Agathe's
prayer, *"Leise, leise, fromme Weise,"* in *Der Freischütz,* the expertly pieced-together overtures to those operas and *Euryanthe,*
the *Conzertstück,* and a handful of other excerpts and pieces bring
us his voice singing most convincingly—music being ever vaguer
about non-musical matter than literature is—of the spells, dedicated loves, midnight enchantments, and woeful virgins that we
would find unbelievable and perhaps ludicrous in the operas themselves.

It is true that Weber's music lacks larger formal perfection, that
seemingly inevitable progression of musical events in which every
expectation aroused, every promise made by what comes first is
fulfilled and kept by what comes next or at last—in which, to be
sure, musical ideas are placed last, first, or next largely to make
that arousing and satisfying of expectations inevitable. But not
to listen appreciatively to the best music of lesser masters is to deny
ourselves a whole world of secondary musical pleasure. Weber's
dashing or sighing emotional melodies, his rich, highly flavored
harmonies, his waywardly altering rhythms—these make E. T. A.
Hoffmann's dictum seem undeniable: this is *the* romantic art.[10]

In the musical practices evolved by Beethoven, Schubert, and
Weber can be found the beginning of the qualities by which the
music of the nineteenth century was to be defined and dominated.
It was to be emotionally expansive, often on the basis of underlying literary or philosophical ideas and ideals. It was to speak
much of love and struggle and death and redemption, to have

[10] Willi Apel in *The Harvard Dictionary of Music* sums up the virtues and defects
of high romanticism in a brilliant figure of speech. Having written that it tries to
shorten the distance between composer and listener by eliminating so-called "unnecessary formalism," he comments: "Not unlike a real short circuit, music has by
this method immensely gained in 'high tension,' but as might well be expected, at
the expense of sustaining power."

many utopian and supernatural visions. Restlessly seeking new forms—and in the process evolving some of permanent value—it was to aim less, or less successfully, than its predecessor at concision and balance. Its melody was to become more lush, its harmony richer and more highly seasoned. Seeking new musical means, it was to expand the size of the orchestra beyond anything Mozart and Haydn had required; it would experiment with many new instruments and new aspects of old ones.

Believing in personal communication, the direct transference of thought and emotion from composer to listener, the romantic musicians of the nineteenth century came to lean heavily on non-musical assistance, on programs, titles, superscriptions, thus tacitly giving away the game by admitting that music unaided and un-alloyed cannot directly *express* anything but itself, whatever else it may *symbolize*. As a response to increasing nationalism among the states of Europe, romantic music also developed national mu-sical dialects, still elements in the great international musical lan-guage of the preceding centuries, but each having its own increas-ingly noticeable peculiarities and distinctive habits. Specifically German, French, Italian, Spanish, Russian—and even Norwegian, Bohemian, and British—musical dialects would result. And each national "school," pursuing the necessary breakdown of the pre-ceding universal standards, would encourage the breakdown of its special dialect into an individual speech for each composer, mak-ing the style of each more and more personal, less and less like that of any other composer. It is possible to mistake some of Handel for some of Vivaldi, some of Telemann for Bach, some of Haydn (and early Beethoven) for Mozart—so much at each period in the eighteenth century was an over-all texture of music common cur-rency universally recognized and sought after. But it is not possi-ble to mistake Beethoven for Schubert or Weber, Schumann for Chopin, Berlioz for Wagner, Liszt for Mendelssohn, or any one for any other.

In music, nineteenth-century romanticism might be described as the great age of idiosyncrasy. It discovered the composer as a separate, unique individual and deemed individuality, rather than universality, a virtue. In a sense unknown to Haydn, a sense that

Mozart was at the very edge of reaching, each symphony, concerto, sonata, quartet, or trio by Beethoven is a world to itself. Each work by the composers of the classical period naturally contained its own special characteristics and differed markedly from every other composition in its genre. But it was clearly thought of—and it remains—the best example of that genre which the composer could create at that hour. It is a well-made, a lovingly articulated, even— if we will—an inspired, setting forth of the general over-all characteristics then considered native to the genre.[11] With the later-than-youthful Beethoven, this emphasis was drastically changed. That change is precisely what makes Beethoven's musical atmosphere so different from that of his predecessors and early contemporaries. What he was overtly symbolizing was his personal world, not the generally known world of music's universal material.

In an easily recognizable way, almost every late Beethoven composition in an instrumental genre is unique, as though in writing it he had evolved a new genre. Each was not so much the best music-making to which he could adapt the inherent capacities of a universally known pattern and form as it was the use of such an existing form as one of several means toward the presentation of a novel, a unique, world of musical matters related by various ties to a personal grouping of non-musical ideas. From earliest to latest, Haydn's symphonies, sonatas, and quartets, Mozart's concertos, sonatas, symphonies, and chamber pieces evolved and altered in inclusiveness and mastery, in expressivity and polish. But they remained instances of the same forms and patterns, used in all consciousness for the same, or for very similar, purposes, though used with firmer command as the composer matured. Between Beethoven's Second Symphony and his Third, between his Third Piano Concerto and his Fourth, at related points in the lists of his

[11] These remarks do not refer with equal cogency to music written to accompany, support, or collaborate with, words. Mozart's operas or Haydn's songs differ from one another widely because of the composers' sensitivities to the meaning, color, and weight of the text-words. It is in this respect that instrumental music, after the middle of Beethoven's life, tended to become more and more literary, more and more operatic. It was as though each instrumental composition were now the setting of a text kept secret. This becomes a certainty, of course, in the numerous cases in which the composer published or told fragments—or all—of the non-musical ideas and emotions he had held in mind while composing.

other compositions, much wider changes occurred. In this respect, the Second Symphony may be viewed as a straining at classical reticence, whereas the *"Eroica"* is wholly non-classical, a massive epic of the composer's interior universe. The *"Eroica"* is unlike anything else in music. Never before had it occurred to a composer of genius to use the symphonic pattern for so literary-philosophic, so poetically personal, a purpose.[12]

Classicism had operated by the principle of variety in uniformity. The composers of the nineteenth century transferred romantic ideas to music by breaking away from uniformity to shape their musical creations by the principle that each piece must discover or create its own nature and formal patterns, sometimes by altered use of genres from the past, but increasingly by performing the difficult double task of conceiving and presenting musical materials and at the same time evolving a pattern for them, a new pattern that could probably be used only once, being wholly native to the particular ideas at hand. All argument as to which method is more difficult, better, or more true to the nature of music as an art is pointless unless based on judgment of the success or failure of individual compositions, but the importance of recognizing the difference in basic attitude is great.

A modern listener finds it necessary to pay the closest attention to a classical composition if he is to be able to determine its individual characteristics, its particular expressivity, the ways in which it differs from other works by the same composer and by his near contemporaries. He must lavish the same care on romantic compositions if he is to discern in such of them as are labeled symphony, sonata, concerto, quartet, and quintet the uses they make of classical principles, their resemblances to other compositions similarly labeled. For the individuality and personal urgency of romantic music is often so intense and attention-capturing that its

12 This difference in fundamental conception of what a symphony is was the major reason why classical composers wrote symphonies in large numbers (Haydn more than one hundred, Mozart forty-one), while Beethoven composed but nine, Schumann and Brahms only four each. In the twentieth century the Russian composer Nikolai Miaskovsky, re-approaching the classical conception of a symphony as exemplary music-making rather than intense personal expression, astonished the post-romantic musical world by writing more than two dozen symphonies.

forms and patterns, the machinery of what may be called its uniquely musical attributes, are hidden from the unwary ear. It is far harder, but no less rewarding, to appreciate the architecture [13] of Beethoven's Fourth Piano Concerto, his string quartets of Opus 130, 131, 132, and 135, his Ninth Symphony, than it is to make the same essential conquest of even the most complex instrumental compositions of Haydn and Mozart.

Less assistance toward this understanding is to be obtained from knowledge of general principles or general awareness of formal usages. Although the final success of a composition of any complexity depends upon its use, adaptation, or creation of a formal structure substantially inseparable from its musical contents, in each romantic composition we no longer deal so much with a different example of a known quantity as with something entirely new and therefore comprehensible in formal terms only by greater effort. This, and no general failure of talent or technical ability in the composers of the full nineteenth century, is what allows us to view the Viennese classical period as orderly and serene (which it very often was not) and to see the romantic period as disorderly and tempestuous. Conversely, it has long underlain the crippling error of viewing the music of Haydn and Mozart as, by comparison, cool, superficial, and entirely unemotional.

[13] Musical architecture is not, of course, solely a matter of visible patterns upon the engraved page. It involves the appropriateness and interrelationships of the instrument or instruments used, the subtle effects of modulation and key relationships, and numerous other factors.

OPERA AND ROMANTICISM · BEETHOVEN · WEBER
ROSSINI · BELLINI · GRAND OPERA · MEYERBEER
EXOTICISM · CHOPIN · CHROMATICISM
DISSONANCE · FORM AND CONTENT · SCHUMANN
SONG CYCLE · PIANO SUITE · LISZT
SYMPHONIC POEM · WAGNER

Mozart had closed his operatic career with two astonishingly different works. *The Magic Flute* (1791) is a fairy-tale opera with philosophical and religious overtones; in it, music of mostly classical texture is married to a typically romantic libretto. Into its musical procedures there obtrude now and again—not unwelcomely or so as to destroy the opera's over-all integrity of style—hints of those romantic turns of melody, harmony, and instrumentation which had sounded so clearly in the last act of *Don Giovanni* (1787.) All to the contrary, *La Clemenza di Tito* (also 1791) is a setting of a remodeled *opera seria* text by Metastasio. Musically it often suggests a throwback to the stiffest classical works of an earlier day. Although *La Clemenza di Tito* contains beautiful and persuasive music, as an opera for the stage it was already an anachronism when Mozart composed it. So sympathetic a Mozartean as Edward J. Dent wrote: "For the stage of today it can only be considered as a museum piece." To listen to it in the hope of meeting those vividly living characters who people *The Marriage of Figaro* and *Don Giovanni* is to listen for the wrong thing.

The most indicative musical stage work between *The Magic Flute* and *Der Freischütz* (1820) was Beethoven's only opera, *Fidelio* (1805, later revised). Its theatrical values are indecisive, and it rises above other operas of the first two decades of the nineteenth century only because of its purely musical qualities. In the four overtures [1] that Beethoven composed for it, in separate scenes, every so often (but not all the time), *Fidelio* provides music of full Beethovian power. As a stageworthy opera, however, it has always failed to sustain itself. Music was drama to Beethoven, engaged in elaborating techniques for the communication of struggle and revolutionary conception. He had a wavering sense of theatrical activity in terms of those clashes of character by which it largely exists. It has been well said that there is more drama in the *Leonore* Overture No. 3 (not a part of *Fidelio* as Beethoven last revised it) than in the entire opera. When exceptional passages in *Fidelio* have been noted and admired (an outstanding one is Leonore's magnificent *scena*, "*Abscheulicher, wo eilst du hin?*"), *Fidelio* remains a patchwork of abstract music resembling Beethoven's instrumental works, of unliving but unremovable connective tissue, and of intermittently effective theatrical outcroppings.

Weber, who was theatrically gifted almost from birth, knew more about opera as stage music than Beethoven ever understood. In *Euryanthe* (1823) and *Oberon* (1826) he unwisely tried to compose integrated scores to librettos that were at times frivolous and always cumbersome. But his sense of what is theatrically right in musical terms, of what can be sung and what cannot, and of how to hold his audience's undivided attention was flawless. The faults we feel in his operas are not the faults of *Fidelio*. Weber's best stage works, further, were to beget a numerous line of recognizable descendants, while *Fidelio* has remained childless, whatever Richard Wagner and others have said to the contrary. Wagner was con-

---

[1] That is, in the so-called *Fidelio Overture* and in the three other overtures now known by the name of the opera's heroine as *Leonore* No. 1, No. 2, and No. 3. At least the last of these is a precursor of the symphonic poem or tone poem of later composers.

sciously, overwhelmingly, influenced by Beethoven, but by the
symphonist (and particularly he of the Ninth Symphony), not by
the composer of *Fidelio*.

First in the long line of German composers to show by close resemblance that he was Weber's artistic child was the now unjustly
neglected Heinrich Marschner (1795-1861). In such essentially
romantic, moodily macabre operas as *Der Vampyr* (1828), *Der
Templer und die Jüdin* (1829), and *Hans Heiling* (1833), Marschner built much of the bridge from Weber to Wagner. And as early
as 1841, in attempting a carefully unified setting of folklore
touched with the supernatural and the grisly in *The Flying Dutchman,* Wagner showed that he had been listening to both Weber
and Marschner. In throwing off extraneous influences, Wagner
was becoming more and more German, more and more Weberian—though with a difference. The early influences he had to cast
off, teachings and methods inimical both to his development and to
his success, had come from Italian opera, French opera, and from
the international works of a Frenchified German. These were foreign aspects of romanticism not specifically German or folkloric
enough to contribute successfully to Wagner's intensely Teutonic
concept of the art of music.

From the days early in the seventeenth century when Caccini
and Peri had initiated the long course of opera, Italians had composed and produced musical stage works in profusion. *Opera
buffa, opera seria,* and variants and combinations thereof had
flowed unceasingly from Italian pens. The last great maker of
opera buffa, filling it with romantic and sensuous overtones, was
Gioacchino Rossini (1792-1868). His *Barber of Seville* maintains
its place in the active repertoire because of its vigor and melodic
inventiveness, because of the effervescence of its musical wit and
humor. Its chief characters (whose later lives are recounted in the
libretto of Mozart's *The Marriage of Figaro*) are not living people
in the Mozartean sense, but they are enormously lively and funny
types, all that can legitimately be required of them in *opera buffa*.

The enduring qualities of *The Barber of Seville* are present in
almost the same quantity in others of Rossini's *opere buffe—La
Gazza Ladra, La Scala di Seta, La Cenerentola, Le Comte Ory* are

examples—but his position in the evolution of musical manners derives from his effect on recitative, on the inviolability of the text as composed, and on grand opera. He gradually gave up *recitativo secco* for recitative with orchestral accompaniment, thus tending toward its incorporation into the over-all texture of the music. And he forestalled star singers, formerly tempted (and able) to decorate a composer's vocal writing with flashy, difficult ornaments of their own devising—forestalled them by meticulously writing out all the ornaments and then insisting that they be sung exactly as written. Rossini's own vocal lines were difficult and showy enough even for singers in one of singing's golden eras, and so sopranos and tenors could find little reason to fight the losing battle against his insistence that music sung in one of his operas be his alone. The justice of Rossini's position in this matter can be estimated by trying to imagine a singer interpolating passages of extraneous music into *Die Meistersinger, Pelléas et Mélisande,* or *Der Rosenkavalier*.[2]

Somewhat younger than Rossini was Vincenzo Bellini (1801-1835), one of the most original of composers and a force out of all proportion to the brevity of his life. An artist of Keatsian temperament, Bellini evolved a sort of melody which was to echo down through the nineteenth century into our own, a long-lined, highly decorated *cantilena* of hushed, intense ecstasy, of all but perfumed melancholy. In his best operas—*La Sonnambula* (1831), *Norma* (1831), and *I Puritani* (1835)—he supplied the stages of Italy, and then of the world, with romantic serious operas as exquisitely fashioned (though not as lively) as Rossini's *opere buffe*. Their success made certain the prolonged cultivation of the art of exquisite singing and added to the vocabulary of musical romanticism that unmistakable melodic intensity which in our day is thought of as the invention of Chopin (who knew Bellini and admired his music).

[2] Sopranos, a persistent race, have triumphed over Rossini in one renowned instance. When the role of Rosina in *The Barber of Seville* was transposed from the contralto range for which Rossini composed it to that of high soprano, the music he had supplied for her to sing in the "Lesson Scene" was abandoned. Since then Rosinas have there sung everything from "Home, Sweet Home" to samples of showy brainlessness especially composed or arranged for them. It is perhaps unnecessary to point out that only when Rosina is sung by a contralto and the "Lesson Scene" consists solely of the music Rossini wrote for it have we any right to judge the opera.

That Bellini's operas are now seldom heard is to be explained mostly by the refusal of modern singers to undergo the years of training and practice needed to sing them effectively and well.

Perhaps the most remarkable of all the remarkable Bellinian melodies, equally astonishing for its length and for its poetic evocativeness, is that of the soprano aria *"Casta diva"* in the first act of the Druid opera *Norma*:

This was something new. As an expansion of the art's resources it proved to be as important in the final evolution of musical romanticism as Weber's coloristic orchestration and Chopin's chromatic harmony. Without these condiments, indeed, nineteenth-century music would have meant something other than the music we know, that music which—fortunately or unfortunately—still forms the large core of the standard repertoire.

An anomalous position both in musical history and in the living library of music is occupied by Luigi Cherubini (1760-1842), an Italian long resident in Paris. Cherubini's music was admired by Beethoven, Weber, Brahms, and other composers. Born when Mozart was four years old and dying fifteen years after Beethoven, Cherubini thus spanned the interim between the climax of the Viennese classical style and the full tide of romanticism. He was a magnificent artificer of lofty-toned Masses; he composed a Requiem that many critics have called the final representative of the great line of Italo-German religious music. Cherubini's operas (out of which we now hear only the Beethovian overture to *Anacreon*) were superbly made and so noble in ethical atmosphere that they fascinated Beethoven. *Fidelio* could scarcely have been composed without their example. Cherubini was a musician of vast learning, a powerful teacher and administrator, and a composer of all but the highest quality. But his music—semi-classical in a romantic age—now seems to lack the personal idiosyncrasy and warmth that might have kept for it the living place it otherwise demands.

Historically even more important than Cherubini was another interim Italian, Gaspar Luigi Spontini (1774-1851). Responding to the pseudo-classic, romantic pomp of Napoleon as emperor and conqueror, Spontini, having begun as a second-rate confectioner of *opera seria,* evolved into an inventor of grand opera. "Grand opera" is an abused term: the reality it covers is easier to sense than to define. For purposes of identification, it may be said to have the following characteristics: it has orchestral accompaniment throughout, and therefore minimizes the distinction between full song and recitative; it is preponderantly tragic in text; and it involves very large amounts of pageantry, panoply, and elaborate stage business. It characteristically employs chorus, ballet, procession, and set scenes of splendor and brilliance. Napoleon's glory brought it forth. Its first unmistakable exemplar was Spontini's *La Vestale,* produced at Paris under the patronage of the Empress Josephine in 1807. Romantic in its physical appurtenances, the score was almost Gluckian in its dignity, or so it seemed to those who heard it first. Its classicism now looks like romantic pseudo-classicism much resembling the pseudo-classicism of the Empire's painting, architecture, and interior decoration. And like those visible expressions of the First Empire, *La Vestale* has very considerable beauties. Basically sincere and moving, it is a little static and very self-consciously grand.

Spontini became grander with time. His *Fernand Cortez* (1809) required crowds of supernumeraries, a troop of horse, and complex stage machinery evoking the Conquest of Mexico. With *Olympie* (Paris, 1819) he finally set the manners of grand opera in a groove from which they could be turned only with difficulty. When *Olympie* was sung in Berlin for the first time on May 14, 1821, it seemed that Spontini's Italo-Napoleonic magnificence would conquer the Germanies too. To the struggling Weber the opera was anathema: *Der Freischütz,* essentially Teutonic and far from "grand," intensely romantic both innately and outwardly, was to be sung in the Prussian capital five weeks later. Weber realized that it altogether lacked the numbing magnificence of *Olympie.* But because it spoke to the inmost childhood memories and vivid nationalism of its first audiences, it triumphed. Spontini's German reign was cut short, and it seemed that the future of German opera was Weber's future. Paris could keep grand opera; Berlin and the other German cities and towns would take the Weberian *Singspiel* with its weird atmosphere, the folklike warm simplicities of its human relationships, its almost cozy musical colorings.

Yet Spontini had evolved a sort of opera that would dominate the opera houses not only of Paris, but also of other world metropolises, for much of the rest of the century and part of the twentieth. Grand indeed were *La Muette de Portici* (also called *Masaniello*), composed in 1828 by Daniel-François Auber (1782-1871), and *William Tell* (1829) by Rossini, both composed by men now remembered chiefly for their lighter, less ponderous works. And in 1831 Paris heard *Robert le diable,* a blazingly romantic opera of the very grandest proportions by Giacomo Meyerbeer (1791-1864). In Meyerbeer's synthesizing hands, grand opera was to achieve a Babylonian gorgeousness. In *The Huguenots* (1836), *Le Prophète* (1849), and the posthumous *L'Africaine* (1864), Meyerbeer purveyed operas of unfailing theatrical impact to the singer-enthralled publics of Paris, London, and New York. His purely musical talent was considerable, but his energies were chiefly expended in supplying instant stage effectiveness of the most reliable sort. At the business of showing off singers, of keeping costumers and stage designers lavishly occupied, and of supplying opportunities for dramatic, vividly pictorial stage groupings Meyerbeer has never been surpassed. He joined the sensuous melodic idioms of Rossini and Bellini to the Weberian orchestra; he took well-understood hints from everywhere. The popularity of his operas became so great and widespread that for decades other composers—Berlioz and Wagner included—found them blocking all roads to advancement, particularly at the greatest summit of all, the Paris Opéra.

Meyerbeer's influence was enduring and incalculable. It can be found without difficulty in Wagner's *Rienzi* (1838-40) and *Tannhäuser* (1843-5); [3] in Verdi's *Aïda* (1871); in Berlioz's *The Trojans* (1858-9); in Jacques-François Halévy's *La Juive* (1835); and in hundreds of other operas by Frenchmen, Italians, Germans, and Russians. Much of what has been called Wagnerian in operas by other composers (notably the late Verdi) turns out on examination to reflect Meyerbeer's taste and talent for expansiveness, grandeur, and theatricality.

In Weber's operas the orchestra's multiple voice had been romanticized by coloristic use of instruments. He had made special,

---

[3] Between *Rienzi* and *Tannhäuser,* however, Wagner composed *The Flying Dutchman,* a child of Weber—and more indicative of his own future style.

dramatic use of those sections of instruments' ranges (notably the woodwinds and brasses) which other composers had avoided in the belief that they were not the instruments' "normal" voices. He had made effective use of the mute, the device by which the tone-colors of violin and viola are rendered mysterious and muffled, if somewhat nasal. But he had been content, so to say, to individualize his orchestra without vastly increasing its size.

Meyerbeer, Berlioz, and Wagner expanded the orchestra to giant size, building it into an instrument capable of ear-shattering volumes and varieties of sound that would have surprised and perhaps repelled Bach, Haydn, and Mozart. Like grand opera, this vastness of means was an aspect of romanticism. Sometimes it illustrated the pathetic belief that size insures greatness. But music for eighty, ninety, or one hundred players is not necessarily mere furious sound. Here, as everywhere, the problem of evaluation is that of deciding, in each case as taken on its own terms and merits, whether or not the result justifies the means employed.[4] What must seem megalomaniac excess in the scores of a third-rate composer can be abundantly just in the outbursts of a Berlioz or a Wagner. Justified or unjustified, this enormousness of orchestral means became an important characteristic of the romantics' prolonged attempt to conquer new worlds.

Weber contributed considerably to the use of local color in nineteenth-century music. In various works he introduced actual folk or composed melodies, harmonies, and rhythms from Turkey, Poland, China, and Spain. Haydn, Mozart, and other earlier men had introduced Turkish, Hungarian, and other non-Western usages into their classical-textured music. But the prevailing idiom of music in that noonday of Vienna classicism was so absorbent that it diminished, rather than increased, the exoticism of foreign elements introduced into it. So to say, the classical composers of the

---

[4] When Weber, for example, divided his strings, simultaneously giving each of several subdivisions of the orchestral violins its own melody—and similarly multiplying the voice of the violas and cellos—he was not showing off. He needed the resulting harmonic richness for the expression of the musical ideas, for the creation of the musical texture he had imagined. Haydn, it is true, had composed great music without dividing his strings. But Haydn was not composing Weber's music.

eighteenth century had woven a few brilliant foreign threads into the homogeneous fabric of their music. With Weber, however, the exoticism of the Chinese melodies introduced into his incidental music for Schiller's *Turandot* or the Spanish ones in that for P. A. Wolff's *Preciosa* was a conscious attempt to produce noticeable foreignness, for which reason divergence from the manners of the classical idiom was insisted upon. Because of the harmonic implications of both real and imitation exotic melodies, often widely divergent from those of German, French, and Italian folk music and from those of classical music, they became ways of introducing new harmonic practices into the vocabulary of romanticism.

Of even greater importance than Weber in this respect was Chopin, who brought over into Western European music both Slavic practices from Poland (notably in his mazurkas and polonaises—both Polish dance forms) and those of his own highly original invention. It was said earlier that during the classic era harmonic evolution was marked by "rapidly enlarged importance of the tonic, dominant, and subdominant as harmonic centers; rapid modulation to remote keys, achieved both enharmonically and by passing rapidly through intervening keys." The influence of Weber's carefully cultivated exoticism, of Chopin's native Slavic coloring, and of the naturalization of the liberties that they and others had begun to legitimatize, was to initiate a gradual disintegration of all the harmonic suppositions and reticences of classicism. This psychological movement cannot be dated exactly, but it is useful to note that it began roughly in the 1820's and was complete by the 1920's.

In romantic nineteenth-century harmony the triad and its inversions [5] kept their central roles. More and more of their hints

___

[5] It will be recalled that four different triads may be based on any tone. Taking C as our fundamental, that is, we may build a major triad, CEG; a minor triad, C-E♭-G; a diminished triad, C-E♭-G♭; an augmented triad, C-E-G♯. Any one of these can be inverted once or twice. Taking our major triad as example, CEG may be inverted to EGC (first inversion), which in turn may be inverted to GCE (second inversion). The first inversion (EGC) is called a sixth chord because the interval between E and C is a sixth; the second inversion (GCE) is called a six-four chord, G to E being a sixth, G to C a fourth. The chords here discusssed are not separate events by themselves, but functions of harmonic development, necessarily or usually leading to other chords that in turn are functions.

and suggestions were explored and accepted, a result being that classical notions of consonance or concord were inevitably dropped. The romantic composers began to use as pleasant for their own sakes many combinations of tones that the classicists would have thought unpleasant unless used warily and with very special purpose.

Relatedly, though the nineteenth-century romantics still thought of diatonicism as the central fact in manipulation of keys and scales, they employed chromaticism with increased freedom. Chromatic alteration—*i.e.*, the use, at points in melodic development and harmonic movement where tones in the prevailing diatonic scale would formerly have appeared, of tones alien to that scale—became normal. Neither Chopin nor any other one composer, not even the nineteenth century collectively, "invented" chromaticism. It had appeared in the sixteenth century. Such a lonely experimenter as Carlo Gesualdo had used it for emotional effects. Both the principal melodies and the secondary melodies of fugues by Bach and others were often chromatic in the eighteenth and seventeenth centuries. Examples of chromaticism in patches, inserted by composers for specific effect, can be found in all varieties of music from *canzona* to concerto, from cantata to oratorio. But the Viennese classical composers had dispensed with chromaticism for the most part, or at least had not exploited its possibilities.[6]

Romantic composers later than Weber and Chopin began to hear almost constant chromatic alteration of tones as entirely normal. This naturally complicated the interrelationships of chords, making harmony more dense and rich. What these composers at first failed to recognize was that constant chromatic alteration could not, by its very nature and results, continue to be considered an "alteration" of diatonicism, but would at last establish chromaticism as parallel to diatonicism in validity and importance, having in itself become a melodic-harmonic scheme. That culmination of the chromatic revolt was finally to amount to a total (if

[6] A composer of any period who wrote a scale passage reading (upward) G-G♯-A-A♯-B-C or (downward) G-G♭-F-E-E♭-D-D♭-C was, obviously, writing chromatically. But in cadenzas or passages of *colorature* these scales were most often merely rapid effects, devoid of harmonic meaning or weight.

temporary) breaking down of harmonic relationships in the usual sense. It did not occur in that extreme form until the end of the nineteenth century or the beginning of the twentieth. Throughout most of the romantic post-Beethovian nineteenth century, the development continued to look like chromatic invasion of diatonic territory, resulting in richer and constantly more complex harmonic relationships.

Romantic composers increasingly asserted the freedom to employ "unprepared" and "unresolved" dissonances. A tone causing a dissonance is said to be "prepared" if it is the repetition of a tone just used—and consonant in that preceding use. Obviously, then, a tone causing a dissonance is "unprepared" if it does not appear in the preceding chord (or in that preceding chord is also used dissonantly). A tone causing a dissonance is "resolved" if it is followed immediately by a tone that would have been consonant if used in its place. A dissonant tone, then, is "unresolved" (at least, immediately unresolved) if it is not succeeded at once by a tone that would have been consonant in its place. Classical harmony placed great importance on both preparation and resolution. Haydn, Mozart, and their contemporaries would introduce unprepared dissonances or leave dissonances unresolved only rarely, and then for specially determined reasons. But Chopin and the later romantics not only disregarded the preparation and resolution of dissonant tones in chords; they extended that non-classical attitude to unprepared and unresolved dissonant chords. Of these perhaps the most structurally important is the so-called "*appoggiatura* chord."

Let us say that in a passage in A major a classically trained ear is expecting a chord consisting of C, E♭, G♭, and A♭, with harmonic support in the bass of a chord containing A♭ and E♭. Instead, the composer writes a chord consisting of B, D♭, G♭, and B♭—with A♭ and E♭ in the bass. In this position, the B and the D♭ are certainly *appoggiature* [7]—i.e., non-harmonic, dissonant, and sounded instead of harmonic consonant tones usually removed

---

[7] It is beyond the scope of this brief illustration to try to decide whether or not the B♭ is also an *appoggiatura*. In some views it would be so considered, but it can also be interpreted in other ways.

from them by the interval of a second. The B strikes the prepared
ear as taking the place of an expected and certainly consonant C;
the D♭ as similarly taking the place of an E♭. If neither the B nor
the D♭ was used consonantly in the immediately preceding chord,
both are unprepared, in addition to being dissonant and to being
appoggiature.

If, in the same progression of chords, the one succeeding our
B-D♭-G♭-B♭ does not read C-E♭-A♭—or, at least, if the G♭ in our
first chord does not disappear, the B move to C, the D♭ to E♭—then,
the dissonant *appoggiatura* chord remains unresolved, at least for
the time being. The lack of preparation and the failure of resolution would have been arresting and extraordinary in Mozart, but
it would cause little surprise in Chopin, and none in Richard
Strauss. This sort of unprepared and unresolved dissonance employing non-harmonic (often chromatic) procedure tended still
further to expand harmonic complexity and to debilitate the basic
assumptions of classical harmony.

Modulation, too, achieved extreme freedom. The necessity of
preparing the way for a change from one key to another, or of
moving from any established key to a distant key only by prescribed passage through intervening keys, was more and more disregarded. Schubert had begun to treat modulation with great freedom; later composers came to treat keys as units that might be
placed side by side almost as notes can be so placed. They began
to assume that the listening ear will take in without assistance of
intervening signposts the harmonic relationships involved, implied, and set up. Nor did late romantic composers have scruples
against employing major chords in predominantly minor passages
or vice versa. In fact, the formerly clear distinction between major
and minor began to become exceedingly, often excitingly, blurred.

If "thin" and "thick" can be used without implying a preference
for one condition or the other, classical harmony may be described
as thin, full romantic harmony as thick. And the leading result of
all this divergence from classical harmonic manners was the constant weakening of those types of musical structure which developed their logic and strength from the existence of a firm sense of
central tonality or key. In a much-used variety of exposition in

classic sonata first-movement form, for example, the pattern depended in part on its "first system" being in the tonic key of the
movement and its "second system" being in the dominant key if
the tonic were major, in the relative minor key if the tonic were
minor. Nearly everything in a typical classical composition or
movement existed in clearly felt relation to the basic key and to
the more and less important tones of its diatonic scale. But in an
advanced romantic composition that could no longer, in the same
sense, be true. Some of that sort of structural logic remained, but
not enough of it to give romantic composers the sensation of formal probity which they inevitably sought. Even while they still
thought of themselves as evolving their forms out of the harmonic
interrelationships of the classical period, romantic composers felt
uneasy, sensing (even when they did not intellectually understand)
that they were trying to remake old forms out of new materials
unsuitable to that activity. They increasingly sought out and invented new principles of organization. The evolution of the most
useful typical forms and patterns employed by the romantics must
be understood in true relation to the ever more fluid conditions of
romantic harmony, as well as in relation to the kinds of melody
that summoned up romantic harmony or appeared as its by-
products.

One of the commonplaces of unfriendly criticism often leveled
against romantic music by writers with classical prejudices has
been that such men as Chopin, Liszt, Schumann, Tchaikovsky, and
Brahms could not compose formally successful large works in sonata forms. This charge is made equally against piano sonatas,
symphonies, concertos, and chamber pieces. If romantic music is
approached and judged by classical standards, there is full truth
in this accusation. The reverse attitude—the judgment of classical
music by romantic standards—produces the same measure of truth.
The truths thus discovered are often nothing more than justifica-
tions of preconception. They damage our ability to listen to music
in the only honest and useful state of mind: that of approaching
each individual work as an individual case to be enjoyed and understood, so far as is possible, on its own terms, and to be judged

by its own successes and failures with its own solutions of its own self-created problems. The extension of preconceived classical and romantic standards to the post-romantic music of the twentieth century has blocked the enjoyment and stultified the understanding of much of the most important creation by our own musical contemporaries.

It is just possible that the careful elaboration of certain critical approaches could produce standards applicable to any individual work of music. But those approaches would have to be free of any lingering belief that the fully developed patterns and working methods of one musical period were in themselves superior to those of another. The varieties of sonata form, for example (and the prejudice in favor of that form is perhaps the strongest in existence, and therefore the most damaging to judgment), were evolved and employed by Haydn, Mozart, and Beethoven for the apt and convincing setting-forth of their musical materials. The musical structures they built by those means have proved enduring. But to assume that only they had the mental power to handle the sonata form is to convict oneself of arrested sympathy and to misunderstand the meaning of form. The sonata form provided a foundation of miraculous rightness for exactly the kinds of melody, harmony, and rhythm which the evolution of resources had placed within the classicists' reach. The exact degree of freedom in harmonic movement, the precise sorts of melody, and the shades of rhythmical relationships conceived and developed by the classical masters were what made the sonata forms, and proved them the miracles they were.

So great was the admiration of later composers for the sonata-based music of their predecessors that they naturally, all but unthinkingly, continued to work their own varieties of musical material into replicas of those forms. If the post-classicists can be convicted of intellectual absent-mindedness, that conviction must be based on their natural failure to realize quickly that their own melodies, harmonies, and rhythms would not supply the tensions, the measured interrelations, the levels of structural variety, that gave the classical sonata forms their special solidity. One result of this cultural lag was the romanticists' slowness in evolving those

new patterns and procedures which, alone, could bear to romantic
musical substance a structural relationship resembling that which
the sonata had borne to classical thought. Another result continues
to be the preposterous charge already mentioned: that composers
such as Chopin, Berlioz, Liszt, Schumann, Tchaikovsky, and
Brahms were deficient in mental power and simply could not learn
the sonata.

Let us consider a few romantic compositions: Chopin's B minor
and B flat minor piano sonatas and G minor cello sonata; Berlioz'
Symphonie fantastique and *Roméo et Juliette;* Schumann's symphonies, chamber music, and piano sonatas; Liszt's *Faust Symphony* and B minor piano sonata; Tchaikovsky's symphonies,
string quartets, and piano trio; and Brahms's symphonies, piano
sonatas, and chamber pieces. To approach this astonishing variety
of music, much of it endowed with original, vivid, and beautiful
musical ideas, in the hope of finding those ideas classically handled,
with Haydnesque or Mozartean clarity of formal interrelationships, is to invite self-defeat. Doing so, we are almost sure to miss
the real significance of the music. For the romantic intensity
crowded into short phrases by harmonic and rhythmic abundance,
the weakening of differences in key, the extreme liberty of modulation—all this rendered the sonata patterns of the eighteenth century useless as molds for re-use and at the same time cried out
unmistakably for the designing of new molds.

Like many arguments about aesthetic form, this one is in part
a war of terminology. If Chopin's B Minor Piano Sonata is a successfully contained piece of musical architecture, but not a true
classical sonata, then we must either enlarge our definition of "sonata" to include it or insist that Chopin should have called it by
another name. Neither mental process will tell us anything valuable about the music itself. This is not to deny the general point:
Chopin clearly placed obstacles in his own way and ours by trying
to force into sonata patterns musical ideas ill suited to them; then,
by using the still rigidly interpreted form-title "sonata," he invited
us to employ classical standards in judging what he had composed.

Romantic musical materials in general were suitable for extended treatment only in relation to literary texts, particularly

operatic; in the form of suites of linked short movements; and in new or adapted patterns evolved in response to their texture and weight.[8] To say this is not the same as saying that longer romantic compositions labeled sonata, concerto, symphony, quartet, or trio are inevitably weak in structure and unsuccessful as unities. It is to point out that to listen to them primarily in the hope of hearing them make *classical* sense is to act against them: they do not—and in most cases could not—make it. The typically romantic formal achievements lie elsewhere or are brief passages imbedded in these often moving and beautiful, but nearly always quite unclassical, forms.

Had Chopin composed nothing but two early piano concertos, three piano sonatas, a cello sonata, and a cello trio, he would not bulk large in the living repertoire or in musical history. But he was gifted with intense and unfailing formal insight, which he displayed in the elaboration of numerous short, perfectly proportioned pieces whose forms were at least as relevant to his musical personality as the sonata forms had been to Mozart's. In *étude,* ballade, impromptu, mazurka, nocturne, polonaise, *prélude,* waltz, and a few other categories, Chopin instinctively found the perfect homes for his musical children. The finest of these masterpieces-in-small lack only scope, a certain inclusiveness that can accompany only forms of greater extension, to belong with the greatest music ever written. Their very lack of scope proves Chopin's genius: for him to have distended the ideas of which he made them would have been for him to misjudge the nature of those ideas and to produce jerrybuilt structures. Small though they are, and compacted of the most intensely romantic inspirations, they have at their best the solidity of rock.

A few times, indeed, Chopin conceived groups of closely related ideas which demanded more expansion than any one of his exquisitely understood short categories permitted, but which he did not therefore unthinkingly and foolishly try to handle in sonata

---

8 It may be noted similarly that post-romantic music, opera having declined for both musical and non-musical reasons, found continuing valid use for the suite of short movements and the semi-literary, but text-free, ballet. An appreciable portion of the best twentieth-century music has been composed for dancing.

patterns. For them he evolved, through a process of intense intellectual concentration, new forms, romantic patterns of total rightness. These forms were, by the very necessity that had brought them into being, suited only to the materials out of which he had constructed them; they are not suitable to re-use by other composers, and Chopin did not re-use them himself. Examples are to be found in his four scherzos, his only barcarolle, and—most notably—in the F Minor Fantaisie. Either the Barcarolle or the Fantaisie proves, on analysis, to be so indissoluble a fusion of matter and manner that its mere existence should have prevented the ridiculous accusation that Chopin could not think consecutively or handle an extended composition. In thematic development, in subtlety and probity of key relationships, in rhythmic variety and justice, in harmonic tension and resolution—indeed, in every department of musical architecture—the Fantaisie is masterly.

Similarly Schumann. Nobody has ever been completely at ease with the formal setting of any of his four symphonies. His chamber pieces, rich though they be in melodic beauty, harmonic charm, and his unique epigrammatic concentration, are far from notable for formal proportion. But his songs and many of his short piano compositions are beyond the reach of negative criticism of their forms. In such chains of linked brevities as the piano suites called *Carnaval, Papillons, Fantasiestücke, Kreisleriana,* and *Études symphoniques,* in such song cycles as *Dichterliebe* and *Frauenliebe und Leben,* Schumann discovered for himself wholly apposite ways of making the presentation of his essentially undevelopable material formally satisfying through equivalents of long compositions. Even in Schubert's hands the lied and the song cycle had been romantic; in Schumann's they glow at the heart of romanticism. In view of them, of what importance can it be that Schumann could not obey the classical rules when playing the symphonic game or the sonata gambit? How should he have so played them when he lived altogether in an unclassical world?

Because of Chopin and Schumann, both the short piano piece and the lied, both the suite of piano pieces and the song cycle, as well as the extended piano piece in one unique movement, became available to other romantic composers, supplying characteristic methods of summoning forth and properly displaying their new musical ideas.

Franz Liszt, much more worldly and theatrical than either Schumann or Chopin, but entirely native to the same area of musical evolution as they, attempted again and again to build vast musical structures. Inevitably these proved inhospitable to his intensely romantic cast of thought; inevitably, that is, so long as he clung to the skeletonic outlines of classical pattern. Brilliant as many of the individual musical phrases are in the *Faust Symphony, Dante Symphony,* piano concertos, and B minor piano sonata, none of these shows inevitability of form in relation to content. But in the volumes of briefer piano pieces Liszt called *Années de pélerinage,* in separate piano compositions, and in songs, he drew closer to the special musical success. He went farther, taking hints from many other composers: in the process of evolving the "symphonic poem" he discovered how to present romanticism with one of its most useful procedures.

The symphonic poem descended from mixed ancestors. One of its forebears was the operatic overture. Others were the related overture to spoken plays and the concert overture. From the short *sinfonie* that early composers of opera had placed before their first acts, the operatic prelude had expanded, attracting ever greater importance and autonomy to itself. By the beginning of the nineteenth century it was dividing into two general types of diametrically opposed purposes. One type was a potpourri, the loose stringing together of a collection of the opera's chief or most alluring melodies. The other, retaining at first elements of first-movement sonata form, often had a more integrated purpose: that of prescribing the emotional atmosphere in which the opera would be played. Examples of the potpourri type are several of Rossini's overtures, including the extended one to *William Tell;* an outstanding example of the other type is Beethoven's three *Leonore* overtures. This second type suggested, or perhaps evolved into, the concert overture.

Somewhere between the opera overture and the concert overture in purpose are the musical pieces intended for performance before a spoken play. When the plays themselves drop from sight or are performed rarely, the overtures perforce become events in isolation. Thus Weber's *Turandot,* Beethoven's *Egmont* and *Coriolan,* Mendelssohn's *A Midsummer Night's Dream,* Schumann's *Manfred.* The true concert overture, however, was not really an overture to anything, but a composition written for performance by itself. Thus Beethoven's *The Consecration of the House;* Mendelssohn's *Hebrides;* Berlioz' *Le Corsaire;* Brahms's *Tragic Overture;* Tchaikovsky's *1812;* and innumerable others. Not one of these but was intended by its composer to carry philosophic, pictorial, literary, or other non-musical suggestions and conceptions.

When Liszt began to wrestle with the idea of the symphonic poem, he had before him, in addition to such of these overtures as were already in existence, the example of Berlioz' astonishing five-movement *Symphonie fantastique.* That blazing orchestral work was proclaimed by Berlioz to be the telling of an intense story. He said that movement by movement it recounted the adventures of a man delirious with opium and passion. The lesson of its apparent marriage to the actual machinery of story-telling was not lost upon Liszt. Also, he understood completely the great importance of Berlioz' so-called *"idée fixe,"* the short musical phrase that occurs in each of the five movements of the *Symphonie fantastique* to represent the hero's beloved. To represent a person or an idea or a situation by an easily recognizable musical tag was not a proposition original with Berlioz: Monteverdi, Mozart, and others had employed it, mostly in opera. But Liszt fastened upon Berlioz' special employment of his *idée fixe* as lending over-all unity to the separate movements of a long composition. Liszt so used this device in his symphonic poems that Wagner was able to evolve from it his complicated, subtle system of leading motives.

Understanding well the overture in its then most recent manifestations, and absorbing the lessons taught by Berlioz' program symphony, Liszt began to develop an extended one-movement orchestral form based on literary or philosophical materials and/or pictorial suggestion.[9] The earliest of his works to belong to the

[9] Liszt used the symphonic poem more for reflecting the pervasive character of the program than for rendering its narrative or pictorial details. He was not Richard Strauss.

class he later labeled symphonic poems was *Ce qu'on entend sur la montagne* (written for piano in 1840, orchestrated in 1849). The most lastingly known of them are *Orpheus* (1854-56), *Les Préludes* (1856), and *Mazeppa* (1858); most often played of them all is *Les Préludes,* said to be a musical translation of poetic lines by Alphonse de Lamartine, though it was not composed with them in mind and may originally have been conceived as illustrating an altogether different program—or simply as music devoid of extramusical ideas.

Gradually Liszt fabricated that highly original method of melodic-harmonic unfolding throughout a composition which has come to be called "transformation of themes," and by means of which he was able to give each of his symphonic poems a considerable amount of integrity. Making as much use as he wished or needed of strict key relationships, imitation, traditional modulation, and fragments taken from classical patterns, Liszt concentrated on the evocation of emotional intensity. Most of this he extracted from his flamboyant melodies by stating them and then altering them constantly, either one by one or in combinations. The fabric of such a consciously conceived symphonic poem as *Hamlet* or *Die Ideale* (both 1859) is continuous—and continuously more complex—though all of one piece, or nearly so. Here, in short, Liszt had developed a romantic form capable of extension and scope. It had arisen directly from the nature of his musical ideas and extra-musical philosophy, both of which were naturally related with closeness to those of his contemporaries. Liszt's symphonic poems have not, for the most part, stayed in the active repertoire, a fact that may be owing to what strikes many later listeners as his posturing and insincerity. It is almost certainly not the result of formal inferiority.

The symphonic poem quickly became a standard romantic form. Popular examples of it have been composed from Russia to Spain, from France to the United States. Nineteenth-century and twentieth-century concerts would have been incomparably less varied without—to name but a few symphonic poems—Debussy's *Prélude à L'Après-midi d'un faune;* Smetana's *My Country* (four linked symphonic poems, including *The Moldau*); Tchaikovsky's

Francesca da Rimini, Respighi's *The Fountains of Rome;* and Sibelius' *The Swan of Tuonela* and *Pohjola's Daughter.*

Almost the entire fame of Richard Strauss until he composed *Salome* in 1905 resulted from a series of tone poems (a label he preferred to "symphonic poem") which began with *Don Juan* in 1886, included *Death and Transfiguration* (1889), *Till Eulenspiegel's Merry Pranks* (1895), and *Also sprach Zarathustra* (1896), and concluded with *Ein Heldenleben* in 1898. With the last of these a climax of music as autobiography was reached: *Ein Heldenleben* portrays Strauss himself as the hero of the title, and quotes extensively from his earlier tone poems. Particularly as it does not offer Strauss's finest musical ideas, many modern listeners have difficulty in not finding it absurd.[10]

The music and composers generally classified as belonging to nineteenth-century romanticism present to the listening ear a far wider variety than the music and composers generally classified as eighteenth-century classical. From the later music of Beethoven and Schubert to the music of Wagner, Brahms, Tchaikovsky, Gustav Mahler, Anton Bruckner, and Jean Sibelius, the nineteenth century—extending, of course, a little back into the eighteenth and a little forward into the twentieth—included such shadings of character as the classical romanticism of Mendelssohn, the romantic classicism of Brahms, the theatrical romanticism of Verdi, and the nationalistic romanticism of the Russians and Bohemians. Almost everywhere, composers continued to produce pieces that they called symphonies, concertos, sonatas, and (intending the appellations as formal labels at least as much as they intended them as numerical descriptions) quartets, quintets, and trios. By the very nature of the common store of musical thought available to them in the atmospheres in which they lived, they were not writing classical music. Prevailingly, their melodies were freighted with more intensity and deliberate significance than classical melodies had been. Their harmonies were much more complex. Their

---

[10] Strauss's two largest orchestral works after *Ein Heldenleben—Sinfonia domestica* (1903) and *Eine Alpensinfonie* (1915)—curiously attempt to introduce essentially nonsymphonic procedures of the tone poem into the symphony.

rhythms were less decisive. Their prevailing tempo was slower. In the brief piano piece and the lied, the suite of piano pieces and the song cycle, the symphonic poem and the tone poem, they were successfully demanding of themselves the creation of new (or newly used) ways of relating their matter to self-justifying forms.

To enter upon highly debatable ground, it might be said that the notable failures of the most gifted composers of the romantic era to create extended compositions in which idea and form were indivisible were the result of a misreading of the nature of form. Those who feel that the symphonies of Schumann, Brahms, Anton Bruckner, and Gustav Mahler are magnificent failures—huge, un-unified structures in which the classical patterns add little or nothing of value—argue that these men, in these instances, were mistaken in their worship of the classical symphony; that they would have done better had they performed the labor of working out for the rich and attractive musical materials forms and patterns growing out of them rather than out of a merely formal tradition.[11] The writers and critics who have held this view define musical form as a constantly unique interaction between musical materials—melody, harmony, rhythm, and the rest—and the best patterns and other means of setting them forth.

Certainly the most gigantic, and in many ways the most interesting and influential, attempt on the part of any composer, at any time, to remake the art of music in his own image, to create very extended compositions, and to relate consciously all the elements of his own mind to the results of his composing was Richard Wagner's. Except for a few youthful works of little importance, he never composed in the classical patterns. He wrote one symphonic poem (*Siegfried Idyll*) and one piece that might be so classified (*A Faust Overture*). But most of his colossal store of energy and genius went into operas and the new sort of opera he preferred to call music drama. It is in Wagner's later stage works, and particu-

---

11 The opposite procedure has at times been followed with success. Sergei Prokofiev, for example, composed in 1916-17 his *Classical Symphony*, making use of the movement patterns of Haydn's and Mozart's symphonies, but deliberately creating the sort of material that would best fit into them. The result is an enduringly charming pastiche—not deeply expressive because it is an imitation rather than a native product of the composer's present.

larly in *Tristan und Isolde* and *Der Ring des Nibelungen,* that
the most challenging formal effort of nineteenth-century romanticism culminated.

Gathering together concepts exemplified by the late Beethoven,
the chromatic harmony of Chopin, the symphonic poems of Liszt,
the orchestral expansiveness of Berlioz, the folk romanticism of
Weber and Marschner, and the operatic magnificences of Meyerbeer, Wagner created musical syntheses of unprecedented size.
This would have been the merest megalomania if he had not been
a great natural musical genius. But until very recently it could be
said that no man composing music later than *Tristan und Isolde*
and the *Ring* has been free of Wagner's influence. Until only yesterday, that is, every post-Wagnerian composer was either a Wagnerian or an anti-Wagnerian; in either case Wagner stood colossus-
like in the near background, athwart history and aesthetics as the
overtowering summing-up of romanticism.

Sixteen

INSTRUMENTAL MEDIUM AND CHARACTERISTIC STYLE

OPERA · WAGNER · MUSIC AND NON-MUSICAL IDEAS

VERDI · LATER OPERA

Since the Renaissance, one of the constantly decisive forces in shaping new manners of composition has been the increasing distinction between vocal and instrumental music. Almost from its inception instrumental music differed from vocal music because instruments and the human voice possess differing capabilities. As the number of instruments grew, the variety of instrumental styles increased too: a given instrument has different capabilities from all other instruments. Within an orchestra, for example, a violin can handle well a musical line all but impossible for a trumpet, and vice versa. A symphony orchestra can obviously perform music impossible to a string quartet.

Such critical beliefs as that certain combinations of melody, harmony, and rhythm are properly "orchestral," "violinistic," "pianistic," or closely related to the capabilities of a string quartet or orchestra, became enormously more decisive with composers in the nineteenth century than they had been earlier. This is not to say that Haydn's materials and his manipulation of them did not differ when he was composing a piano sonata from those he used and manipulated when composing a symphony; it is rather to say that in Haydn's time this difference was commonly little wider than the separate mechanical natures of the media employed made inevitable. Comparing Mozart and Bach, let us say, we may sense that Mozart's textures, melodic shapes, rhythmic ways, and harmonic motion grew, far more ascertainably and directly than Bach's, from the special characteristics of the forces for which he was composing at the moment. The tendency to this sort of specialization increased swiftly during the eighteenth century. But when the comparison is extended from Mozart forward in time— to that of a piece for piano by him and, say, one by Chopin (born only fifty-four years later than Mozart), it becomes clear that early in the nineteenth century this tendency increased suddenly. The contours and manners of a Mozart composition for piano do not differ in materials and handling from those of a Mozart work for orchestra in the same degree as a Chopin piano piece differs from any piece of orchestral music whatever.

It is as though Bach had possessed (or had been able to imagine and embody) an endless supply of musical ideas complete in themselves as to melody, harmony, and rhythm, but unrelated to the technical abilities of a given instrument or ensemble. (This is exaggeration, but one that suggests a useful idea.) Setting these ideas down so as to make their performance possible, Bach assigned them to such instruments or groups of instruments and/or voices as he could command at the moment, as he had been ordered to supply music for, or as were equipped to project them—equipped, that is, because of the number of melodic lines required or because they had the power to sustain tones and make them clearly audible. By Mozart's time the process was different. Mozart responded to the problems of composing for a string quartet with musical ideas that would not have occurred to his imagination when writing for piano, for voices, or for orchestra. This was no longer a question, much of the time, of what instruments were at hand, what class of musical employers or patrons was involved, or which producing means could project a certain number of melodic voices or produce sustained or brief—and perhaps percussive—tones. It was far more than with Bach a question of conceiving simultaneously the musical materials and their means of projection. One aspect of musical creation reacted upon the other so constantly that they began to be inseparable steps of one process. When a

Mozart composition is transcribed for another medium, far more of its complete original nature is sacrificed than when a Bach piece is similarly transcribed: far more of the individual aspect of the music resides in the organic relation between its materials and its instrumentation.

With Chopin and other composers of the high romantic period, moreover, this process began to pass the line of relatively equal interaction. To some extent—and often to a very large extent—a Chopin composition for piano is an emanation of the piano itself, grows as it does partly because Chopin explored the piano's unique abilities and accepted musical materials suggested by them. A Beethoven piano sonata, particularly a late one, often sounds like orchestral music transcribed; no one of Chopin's piano works could have been conceived for any other medium. Nor could Berlioz' orchestral pieces have been composed for any other means than the orchestra, which is in itself an important component of their very size, shape, and physiognomy. This quality of characteristic relationship, in which the medium plays a definitive role in the shaping of music, is pre-eminently a nineteenth-century procedure that would reach its most intense application early in the twentieth century. Guesses from close quarters are dangerous, but it appears to be losing force as our century progresses.[1]

Bach composed *The Art of the Fugue* abstractly—*i.e.,* he did not indicate the instrument or instruments by which it was to be realized as sound. It has been arranged for two pianos, string quartet, and orchestra. Much of it can be performed successfully on the piano, and there is little reason why it could not be wordlessly sung by several accurate human voices. Mozart wrote a serenade for eight wind instruments (K. 388) and himself re-composed it

[1] Maurice Ravel, a master of instrumentation, composed *Ma Mère l'Oye* in 1908 in two forms, for two pianos and for orchestra. He composed the six-section *Le Tombeau de Couperin* for piano solo in 1917, and re-composed four of its sections for orchestra, repeating what he had done with his *Valses nobles et sentimentales* in 1911. He apparently felt that the other two sections of *Le Tombeau de Couperin*— the two which are not dances, and which seem to have grown most clearly from the piano's percussive qualities (*Prélude* and *Toccata*)—would be badly served by the orchestra. In Ravel's hands the orchestral versions are not "orchestrations" of the piano music, but entirely new compositions making use of the same (or very nearly the same) melodic, harmonic, and rhythmic materials.

for string quintet (K. 406); although he appears to have written
the wind version because he wanted to, the quintet version because he needed money, enthusiasts still dispute the relative quality of the two. But such orchestral transcriptions of romantic music
as those which have been made of Schumann's *Carnaval* and of a
group of Chopin pieces as *Les Sylphides* (both were made for ballet
use) simply denature the music: they remove from it one of the
important causes and reasons for its existence, its integral relationship to the piano. Similarly, a four-hand piano transcription of a
Haydn symphony loses much; a transcription of a Berlioz orchestral composition loses much more; any transcription of any mature piece by Debussy loses almost everything. By the time of
Debussy, the partnership between material and medium had become equal—if, indeed, it would not be more illuminating to say
that the medium had become a pervasive element of the material.
In extreme cases the piano or orchestra or other medium appears
to have played more part in shaping the music than the composer
himself.

The human voice can produce only one musical tone at a time.
But two voices can produce two tones, and one hundred voices
one hundred tones. These irreducible facts rule all vocal music.
The voice can, within the physical boundaries of breath-supply
and breath-control, sustain tones well for a relatively long time,
but it cannot produce well very *staccato* tones or sharply percussive
tones. These facts, too, shape all vocal music.

The violin sustains tones easily, can be made to produce *staccato* tones, but can produce not more than two tones at a time
and is limited in volume; whereas the piano excels at *staccato*
(it is often classed as a percussion instrument), can produce only
a relative *legato,* and (at the hands of one player) can produce
ten, at moments more, tones at one time. It has a much greater
potential volume than the violin. These facts explain much of
the difference between truly "violinistic" and truly "pianistic"
music. And the fact that a symphony orchestra—to which piano,
organ, and other not strictly orchestral instruments may be joined
—can produce all at once *staccato, legato,* loud tones, and soft

tones, and has a tremendous potential volume—all these physical facts dictate the kinds of music written for orchestra.

Critics often write of a composition that it is or is not well conceived for its medium. A composition for piano may produce in well-trained listeners an uncomfortable sensation that the composer was attempting to make the solo piano do what only an orchestra could really do—or do easily and without strain. Or a very percussive piece, largely of *staccato* tones, composed for a bowed stringed instrument may seem to them wrongly scored in that it would have projected its percussive nature better through the piano keyboard. When this aspect of criticism is just, the composer has failed as badly as he would have failed if his melodies were poor, his harmony awkward, or his rhythms monotonous. The important fact to notice is that these are nineteenth-century and twentieth-century critical conceptions, end results of the romantic concentration on coloristic, characteristic instrumentation.

Richard Wagner did not discover early in his career the amalgamated medium most germane to his ideas. The vastness of the musico-theatrico-moralistic beliefs that he was to evolve in his maturity would require not only the combination of orchestra and human voices, but of a monster orchestra and of voices specially used. He composed one symphony when he was nineteen; piano sonatas when he was sixteen and eighteen; other early piano pieces; seven settings of lines from Goethe's *Faust* when he was nineteen. These pieces were not only juvenilia; they were also false starts. But Wagner made a correct start, also at nineteen, when he began to compose an opera to a libretto written by himself: *Die Hochzeit,* never completed. Only in his own adaptation of opera was he to find his own way.

Wagner produced six operas from *Die Feen* (1833-34) through *Lohengrin* (1846-48) by following Weber and Meyerbeer, using a full orchestra, setting semi-historical and legendary texts written by himself. These six operas are typically early-romantic in both detail and over-all effect. Through them increasingly runs the underlying belief that opera could and should exemplify

and inculcate ethical and moral ideas. The texts of all six are
in dead earnest. They are serious works of art with messages
to convey. In short, they are romantic not least in being employed hopefully as a means of communicating non-musical
ideas directly to listeners. In all matters of musical grammar
and syntax Wagner's work became constantly more complex.
Through *Tannhäuser* and *Lohengrin* his form was still preponderantly that of eighteenth-century opera as adapted to
grand opera. It was made, that is, of an overture or prelude [2]
followed by a series of separable solos, duets, trios, and so forth,
connected (or separated) by orchestra-accompanied recitative,
arioso, and purely instrumental tissue. But Wagner made novel
use of the *Leitmotiv* ("leading motive") and showed signs of
something like Liszt's "transformation of themes." That is, he
was increasingly interested by methods of breaking down the
separate-number scheme of operatic architecture. He was moving toward new methods of over-all operatic unification.

Wagner had a peculiar talent for inventing short musical
phrases highly useful for identifying, expressing, or characteriz-
ing an idea, a character, or an object. He had begun to weave
these leitmotivs into a continuous musical fabric, subjecting
them to transformation, contrapuntal combination, and all variety of slight or major melodic, harmonic, and rhythmic alteration. By the time he came to compose *Tristan und Isolde*
(1857-59), the four operas of *Der Ring des Nibelungen* (*Das
Rheingold,* 1853-54; *Die Walküre,* 1854-56; *Siegfried,* 1856-71;
and *Götterdämmerung,* 1869-74), and *Parsifal* (1877-82), he had
succeeded in making operas in his own image.

In the later "music dramas," except where a special incident
in Wagner's own text called for a set number, formal arias and
other separable forms had been dispensed with. Except for
changes of scene, the texture was continuous and uninterrupted.
Full-blown melody in the classic manner or early romantic manner had given way to continuous semi-melody in which numer-

---

[2] In Wagnerian terminology an overture comes to a full stop before the stage
action begins, whereas a prelude leads without break into the opening of the act
following it.

ous leitmotivs appear and disappear in response to the hints of the text. Because Wagner desired continuous texture, he made his harmonic motions more and more chromatic and avoided those formal cadences which give the listener a sense of finality and break. He employed a very large orchestra and then demanded that singers be heard clearly against and above it—and therefore finally required not only a new sort of singing, but also the erection of his own theater for acoustic reasons including the proper location of orchestra and singers.[3]

Wagner believed himself a hero destined to revolutionize the art of music and, in doing that, to educate the German people for its leading role in world affairs. For combined genius, egotism, and force of will he has no equal in the history of art. What is more important than the fascinating story of his struggles is that he finally won a gigantic, a Wagnerian, triumph, enlisting across the world such hordes of intense admirers as are usually enlisted only by religious or political leaders. His belief in the desirability of a synthesis of all the arts—he at last intended his music dramas as nothing less—his beliefs about every aspect of music, his practice of the leitmotiv, his development of the continuously unfolding musical fabric, the effect of his mammoth orchestration and voluminous singers—all of his proclamations and achievements—seemed about to drown out the music of the past and obliterate that of his contemporaries.

The Wagnerian sovereignty over the musical world has only recently begun to fail. In order to understand Wagner, in order to comprehend the contemporary and later reactions to him, it is essential to examine some aspects of the techniques by which he created his most original masterworks: *Tristan und Isolde, Der Ring des Nibelungen,* and *Parsifal.*[4]

[3] Because of the sort of singing that Wagnerian roles require, the singers must be of ample physique and must nearly always belie in appearance the romantic youthfulness that many of them are supposed to express.

[4] *Die Meistersinger von Nürnberg* (1862-67), also an opera of Wagner's maturity, stands apart from the others. It is a comedy without magical or supernatural content. Its text, revolving about a singing contest, required some use of the set-number construction. Still, most—but not all—of the remarks made herein about the other music dramas apply equally well to it.

Tristan und Isolde is divided into three acts because its story requires three settings and three times: on shipboard, at a castle in Cornwall, and near a castle in Brittany. The Prelude to the first act merges into the opening of the shipboard stage picture without a break,[5] but each act necessarily comes to a concluding cadence giving a temporary sense of repose. Ernest Newman, analyzing *Tristan* in *The Wagner Operas,* quoted sixty themes, fragments of themes, and versions of themes, nearly every one of which has more than one symbolic meaning in relation to the text, or several shifting symbolic meanings. These motives appear, disappear, and reappear, winding sinuously in and out of the chromatic harmonic fabric woven of frequently chromatic melodies. The opening of the Prelude:

may be taken accurately to indicate that by the date of its composition Wagner had agreed to the full decay of the classic harmonic system and had made it inevitable that the harmonic development to follow his own works could be nothing short of conscious rejection of even so much of that system as survives in them. What key is this? There being no key signature, is it C major? No. A minor? Probably. Both C major and A minor? Possibly. Neither? That depends on the eyes, ears, and brain with which it is examined.

If, with Newman, we regard these measures as containing two motives—one from the opening A to the D♯ at the beginning of the second full measure, the other beginning with the G♯ at the opening of the second full measure and running to the final B—we can discover that one of the two is predominantly chromatic (A-F-E-D♯ being chromatic except for the first step), the other (G♯-A-A♯-B) altogether so. Wagner himself indicated the presence of two distinct motives here by assigning the first to the cellos, the second to oboes above a support of bassoons, English horns, and clarinets.

Slowly, with the deliberateness of much late-nineteenth-century romantic music, *Tristan und Isolde* grows by the addition of new melodic ideas and treatments that are not simply stated and abandoned, as in most older operas, but are referred to, hinted at, and used outright again and again throughout the acts. At moments of tension in the story, the melodic-harmonic intensity and complexity become very great, but rhythmic intensity is far less noticeable. The music induces a sensation of continuous, dreamlike unfolding which is formed from the sinuous chromaticism of melody, the slowly revolving richness of the chromatic harmony, and the pervasive (anti-Wagnerians would say the enervating) lack of well-defined rhythmic pulse.

A few sections of *Tristan und Isolde* can be detached from the entirety for concert performance or recording. The Prelude, in Wagner's concert arrangement; the Narrative and Curse sung by Isolde in the first act; the Love Duet in the second act; Isolde's Love-Death in the third act—these and a few other passages are often performed apart from the whole. But this questionable practice does not contradict the fact that *Tristan* is a continuous whole in three sections. If the listener's purpose be to absorb the meanings of the music (not to mention the text) or to judge Wagner by it, it is listened to adequately only as —or nearly as [6]—he composed it. The over-all form of this music drama is as relevant to its contents as the form of a Mozart concerto or Beethoven sonata is to its contents. By the time he reached his maturity Wagner had evolved a grasp and command of his complicated materials which were nearly absolute. Serious arguments with him must necessarily be conducted on the level of disagreement with his aims and purposes, never (or seldom) with his consciousness of what he was intending to do or with his success in doing exactly that.

[6] Few performances of any Wagner opera today are complete: they are nearly always staged with extensive cuts.

One peculiarity of the late Wagner music dramas is well exemplified by Isolde's Love-Death (*Liebestod*). A concert performance of this excerpt without a singer to perform Isolde's notes or an instrument to play them loses the narrative continuity, but almost nothing of the strictly musical structure or fabric. The notes assigned to the heroine are easily managed by a good singer; this is not awkward vocal writing. When properly sung they can be heard. But they add almost nothing *musically*. As Sir Donald Tovey pointed out (*Essays in Musical Analysis*, vi, 104), Isolde sings for sixty-eight measures, in twenty-five of which "she is able to deliver the main theme, constantly broken, sometimes quite awkwardly, by pauses and other necessities of declamation." During the other forty-three measures, the notes assigned to her are mostly non-melodic counterpoints, the omission of which in a concert performance by purely instrumental forces robs the music as music of nothing essential to it.

"Surely her [Isolde's] last notes should be memorable?" Tovey asks: she is the central figure of the entire music drama, and here she is dying of love. "They are the right notes in the right declamation; they easily penetrate the orchestra, and they will do justice to the most golden of voices. How many music-lovers can quote them? They have never been heard in the concert-room, except when a singer was engaged; but I should not be surprised if many of the music-lovers who go to every stage performance of *Tristan* found themselves unable to quote them." What Tovey describes here is a climactic example of a Wagnerian procedure: that of giving a majority of the musically important materials to the orchestra and of using the human voice largely for the prime purpose of pronouncing the text-words.[7]

---

[7] Any performance of the waltzes from Richard Strauss's *Der Rosenkavalier* represents only the accompaniments of various scenes. No effort whatever has been made, in arranging the waltzes for concert performance, to introduce instrumental equivalents of the notes given to the singers. Contrarily, concert and recorded performances of *"Sempre libera"* from the first act of Verdi's *La Traviata* usually assign to instruments of the orchestra (or to the piano if the aria is so accompanied) the notes supposed to be sung offstage by the tenor: the musical structure is incomplete without them. Thus opera in which the vocal line dominates differs in construction from opera (Wagner and Strauss) in which the orchestra is most important.

Tristan und Isolde is very long, but it shrinks beside the *Ring*, four complete operas constituting together perhaps the longest interrelated series of compositions in existence. The *Ring*, though not necessarily Wagner's greatest accomplishment, is the fullest demonstration of his unique manner of creating. In that huge concourse of musical means he summed up (and in some senses impaired the further usefulness of) romanticism's chief syntactical and grammatical contributions to music: the furthest development of chromaticism conceivable within the classical-romantic harmonic system; the effort to make music a language for expressing the non-musical, the didactic, the auto-biographical, and the philosophic; the doing away, in opera-construction, with both the aria and the lied and their deriva-tives; and the substitution for them of continuously unfolding melody pieced together out of themes and thematic fragments.[8] The clarity, crispness, and clearly outlined rhythms of classical music, as well as most of its transparency, are almost totally absent from the *Ring*. In their stead we find something like the flowing of a great river, a stream sometimes clear, but more often translucent; a stanchless flood flowing slowly except for occasional rapids and falls, a prehistoric current in which mon-sters lurk and the denizens of inhuman kingdoms carry on a strange sub-life.

Those who first fell under the intensely potent spell of the late Wagner were often as though literally bewitched; the in-creasing numbers of later listeners who can enjoy *Tristan,* the *Ring,* and *Parsifal* only in excerpts are most often found yearn-ing for the crisp sunlight or decorous candlelight of Viennese or French classicism, the sweet emotions of the Renaissance, or the anti-Wagnerian impressionism and relatively impersonal modern-ism of our later day.

The case of Wagner (and it is significant that Nietzsche, once an ardent admirer of Wagner's art, found it possible in 1888, five years after the composer's death, to write a book under that title) is unique. To be an informed and confirmed admirer of Monteverdi or Mozart or Beethoven it is not essential to know

---

[8] Analyzing the *Ring*, Ernest Newman found it necessary to quote one hundred and ninety-eight themes, fragments, and transformations.

what they as individuals thought or believed; on the contrary,
to be a confirmed Wagnerian it is inescapably necessary to ad-
mire even the messages imbedded in his texts. To an unprecedented extent, he really succeeded in making his music, his
texts, and his stage business indivisible. Nothing would have displeased Wagner more than to have learned that less than one
century after his death hundreds of thousands of music-lovers
would be familiar with all or fragments of his operas and music
dramas from *Rienzi* to *Parsifal,* but that among them only a
very few would know his artistic, philosophical, or religious beliefs. He would be positively shocked to know that a significant
number of today's admirers of some of his music has never witnessed a stage performance of a single opera by him.

At this hour the truth appears to be that Wagner survives as
a composer and as nothing else. Wagner the teacher, the arguer
about ethics, religion, theories of politics and race, the conceiver
of artistic syntheses—Wagner the dabbler in so many non-musical
fields of which he wished music to be no more than an equal
partner (if not a servant)—has ceased to matter except to historians, biographers, and a scattering of orthodox Wagnerians.
But some of his music, torn in fragments and patches from its
mammoth contexts, appears relatively immortal.

In a dramatic and persistent contrast to Wagner's evolution—
and significant both for producing music of enduring popularity
and for tending to mitigate Wagner's influence—was the comparatively calm development of Giuseppe Verdi. Born, like
Wagner, in 1813, the Italian by 1840 had produced two operas
(*Oberto, Conte di Bonifacio* and *Il Finto Stanislao*) not far removed from the *opera seria* and *opera buffa,* respectively, of the
era. If the name of Rossini or Donizetti were signed to both,
students would probably note that the operas were early, un-
developed works by those masters. They differ from, say, *La
Gazza Ladra* and *Lucia di Lammermoor* only in a certain ro-
bustness and muscularity—and by being inferior to them.

But Verdi lived more than sixty years after 1840, composing
twenty-four more operas and a Requiem Mass. Like Wagner, he

was always a full-blown romantic who felt somewhat the puis-
sance of the grand-opera manner of Meyerbeer. But his texts
were nearly always human in their action, devoid of myth and
legend, free of supernatural intervention. If Verdi held well-
formulated ethical, moral, religious, or political beliefs (beyond
a conviction that Italy should be free and united), they did not
appear in the texts he set, which were not of his own writing.
Except for the early *Il Finto Stanislao* and the late *Falstaff*—
completed when he was nearly seventy-nine—Verdi's are all tragic
operas. But none of them has any urgent non-dramatic or non-
musical message to convey. They do not attempt to communicate extra-operatic ideas directly to listeners except insofar as they
represent and support theatrical stories containing characters who
have such ideas.

The contrast in mental atmosphere between *Otello* and *Tristan
und Isolde,* between *Aïda* and *Der Ring des Nibelungen,* between *Don Carlo* and *Parsifal,* is in part national. But it is more
importantly individual, the difference between a man who aimed
at the noblest and most movingly human sort of musical entertainment and a man who believed that he was making a synthesis of the arts in the direction of a ritualistic philosophy or
a religion.

Musically, in all matters of grammar and syntax, Verdi was
nearly as complex in his earliest operas as he ever became. But
he tended, in a way distinctly his own, toward a continuous musical web freed in part from the separate-number plan of classical opera; through his long life his orchestration became at
once more effective and more complex. He made no extensive
use of the leitmotiv or the Lisztian transformation of themes,
but he occasionally employed methods related to them, uses noticeable and effective because of their rarity and because they
are climactically placed. In *Otello,* for example, the Moor, having just murdered Desdemona and stabbed himself, recalls the
rapturous melodic phrase allied, in their first-act love duet, with
the words *"un baccio."* The poignancy of this musical quotation is intense and quite un-Wagnerian.

Song and the dramatic interactions of human passion interested Verdi. He was a bountiful melodist, and many of his melodies have achieved almost the status of folk song. He learned how to characterize complex individuals musically in an almost Mozartean way: from his middle-period and late operas have stepped such rounded human beings as Rigoletto, Violetta, the elder Germont, Aïda, Amneris, Otello, Iago, and Falstaff. All of the characters mentioned, Aïda and Amneris excepted, had existed previously, though sometimes under other names, as personages in renowned plays, but the individuals created by Verdi from the materials handed him by his librettists are musical characters, not singing versions of personages created by Victor Hugo, Dumas *fils,* and Shakespeare.

Except for his increasing diminution of the distinction between aria and recitative, Verdi's plan of operatic architecture differed little from that of Meyerbeer or the Wagner of *Tannhäuser.* Yet *Rigoletto, La Traviata, Aïda, Otello,* and *Falstaff,* at least, are as stylistically unified as any operas ever composed. To the end of his long career Verdi maintained a seldom-flawed balance in the partnership of singers and orchestra. It is impossible to think of a transcription or performance of one of his arias or concerted numbers with the singer's notes omitted. Equally integral is his orchestration: piano accompaniment does small justice to his music.

Verdi expressed and incarnated few theories except purely musical ones and practical dramatic and theatrical beliefs. His harmony, increasingly subtle as he grew older, was seldom daring or experimental. His finest operas grew organically out of opera's past as interpreted by a dramatic composer of genius. They differ from Gluck and Mozart in myriad details and in atmosphere, but are recognizably blood descendants of all that preceded them. Even *Aïda, Otello,* and *Falstaff* nonetheless once looked old-fashioned beside *Tristan,* the *Ring,* and *Parsifal.* More recently their fierce sincerity, the masterliness of their vocal writing, the vital endurance of their characters, and their unbreakable mating of music and text have once again made them seem new. No more indicative revolution in musical taste has occurred in the twentieth century than that which has elevated Verdi to the universally recognized company of the very great. He was not Wagner's intellectual peer. He had not Wagner's all-conquering egoistic energy and drive. But there now seems to most students and critics no reason for the former tacit belief that Verdi's operas are, for these or any other reasons, inferior to Wagner's as works of musical art.

Wagner's influence on opera has not proved fertile or lasting. On purely instrumental music, his harmonic ripeness, his structural expansiveness, and his dedicated seriousness of intention have been fixed in several lines of descent. But the "music drama," that synthetic omnibus of the arts as he envisioned it, has not evolved beyond his own works, the last of which was completed and first performed in 1882.

The most obvious heir of Wagner was Richard Strauss, such of whose operas as *Salome* (1905) and *Elektra* (1909) made use of the Wagnerian continuous musical web, the assertiveness of Wagner's orchestra, and Wagner's usual separation of the voices from the meaning of the orchestra's music. But Strauss's are brief operas, for which reason they resemble a Lisztian symphonic poem or Straussian tone poem with added vocal lines. They are intensely serious, tragic works. In *Der Rosenkavalier* (1911), however, tragedy and earnestness gave way to a waltz-beguiled frivolity in which the discordant texture of the psychological tragedies made way for something sweeter and more old-fashioned. Engelbert Humperdinck's *Hänsel und Gretel* (1893) had also been Wagnerian in that its somewhat continuous music is evolved from melodic leitmotivs. A number of less successful, now largely forgotten, German, French, Belgian, and English composers tried vainly to follow in Wagner's large footsteps. But formally speaking Wagner proves to have been a massive door closing the operatic period of high romanticism rather than a gateway through which others could move forward.[9]

On the contrary, the influence of Verdi, a simple reaffirmation of long-standing Italian traditions, has been continuous and clear.

---

[9] *Pelléas et Mélisande,* Debussy's only opera, was in one sense a response to the Wagnerian music drama. See pages 275-276.

Giacomo Puccini, combining with some Verdian vigor the sort
of realism that Georges Bizet had handled successfully in *Carmen*
(1875)—but modifying both by his own less forthright, more feminine, personality—brought that phase of Italian opera to what
seems to have been its close. When Puccini's *Manon Lescaut*
(1893) and *La Bohème* (1896) followed close on Pietro Mascagni's
Cavalleria Rusticana (1890) and Ruggiero Leoncavallo's *Pagliacci*
(1892), it appeared to their contemporaries that a new school
of opera—called *verismo,* literally "truthism"—had been founded
on realism. But just as no German opera since *Der Rosenkavalier*
stays regularly in the repertoire of opera houses in the world
metropolises, so no Italian opera since Puccini's *Madama But-
terfly* (1904) has established itself with seeming permanence.[10]

Almost every important composer of the twentieth century has
composed at least one opera.[11] But because the production of
opera has become enormously costly, an opera must win the
support of the widest public to pass the test of the box office;
at the same time, the taste of the widest public and the style
of the foremost modern composers have diverged widely. The
result has been that most important modern operas have been
sung but a few times before being relegated either to silence or
to the less costly occasional concert performance. Also, the primacy of opera among musico-theatrical forms appears to have
ended in the close of the romantic nineteenth century and its
dying afterglow. The repertoire of opera houses has tended more
and more to the condition of a museum collection: opera houses
themselves are today mostly a means for displaying the art of the
past rather than a means for producing the art of the present.
In our century opera has lost to ballet its formerly unquestioned
position as the leading musico-theatrical form.

10 Operas such as Italo Montemezzi's *The Love of Three Kings* (1913); Ermanno
Wolf-Ferrari's *The Secret of Susanne* (1909) and *The Jewels of the Madonna* (1911);
and a few others have sometimes appeared to be on the verge of entering the mystic
circle of the "standard repertoire."

11 Alban Berg's *Wozzeck* (1914-21), regarded by many critics and enthusiasts as a
towering musical peak, is discussed in a later chapter. See pages 310-313.

LATE ROMANTICISM AND NEO-CLASSICISM

BRAHMS · VARIATION FORM · BRUCKNER

MAHLER · SIBELIUS

Later than the highly individualistic romanticism of the first half of the nineteenth century, but contemporary with or following the gigantic efforts to sum up romanticism and synthesize the arts, large-scale attempts to pour the new wine into the old classical bottles developed a classicizing movement. It formed largely around the massive orchestral compositions of two men: Johannes Brahms (1833-1897) and Anton Bruckner (1824-1896), important counterparts and extensions of whose formal acts were to become evident in the somewhat isolated later compositions of Gustav Mahler (1860-1911) and Jean Sibelius (1865-   ).

These four greatly dissimilar men shared a clear belief in the enduring disciplinary value of the sonata patterns, the symphony and the other large forms shaped by the classical eighteenth century. They did not question the wisdom of adapting these forms to musical matter and conceptions native to the nineteenth century and—with Mahler and Sibelius—to some extent, the twentieth. None of these four men ever composed an opera. Mostly they tried to use the originally dramatic sonata procedures for meditative, epic, philosophical, or other non-dramatic purposes.

In Brahms's earliest surviving music, the romantic contours of the melody and the ripe warmth of the related harmonies seem

direct reflections of Schumann, whom Brahms knew personally
and admired intensely. But the patterns over which the young
Brahms stretched this Schumannesque material were brought forward, little changed, from Beethoven's middle and late periods.
This unstable relation of matter and manner is particularly noticeable in the three piano sonatas and the piano scherzo composed
between 1851 and 1853 and the Concerto for Piano and Orchestra
in D Minor (1854). The musical personality and mind that this
music reveals are quintessentially romantic, whereas the employment of the extended formal patterns often reins in too soon the
material's intense, discursive nature or prolongs the development
of some of its sections beyond necessity. Brahms had not found the
perfect vehicle for transmitting his musical messages. It is notable
that during the last forty-four years of his life he composed no
more piano sonatas, though he composed much piano music and
several sonatas for other instruments with piano.

Brahms considered the symphony the loftiest of instrumental
forms. He approached the composition of his First Symphony
(1855-76) with timidity and extreme care, experimenting meanwhile with two orchestral serenades (1857-60). In the four symphonies, written between 1855 and 1885, classical patterns persist—
but whereas the models in the serenades had been largely Beethoven's chamber music, in the symphonies they were Beethoven's
symphonies. The melodies swell, conveying romantic, sometimes
fruity, emotion; the harmonies become more and more complex.
The formal conservatism, combined with the steady discipleship
to Beethoven, at time battles with the innate, self-sufficient nature
of the musical thought. In the eyes of others, this music won
Brahms the unwanted leadership of the anti-Wagnerian forces;
he came to be regarded as the white hope of classical romanticism
in the "war" against the formal as well as material romanticism of
Liszt and, particularly, Wagner.

But the mature Brahms did not compose only symphonies, the
gigantic Concerto for Piano and Orchestra in B♭ Major (1872-81),
and that huge parallel to Beethoven's *Missa Solemnis, A German
Requiem* (1857-68)—which, however otherwise admirable, do not
fairly represent successful effort to house his idiosyncratic musical

personality. He composed many lieder; in these, too, he was at first slavishly Schumannesque, but he grew to a song-writing method of his own by which he produced some of the most satisfying poetic settings of the post-Schumann era. Curiously, Brahms never made significant use of either the song cycle or the suite of short piano pieces, both of which forms Schumann had brilliantly made his own. But, perhaps influenced by Chopin's nomenclature (though not often by Chopin's melodic habits or persistently daring harmonic motions), Brahms composed many brief piano pieces —ballads, capriccios, intermezzos, rhapsodies, romances, waltzes, and *études*. In these, as in his finest lieder, the musical ideas and the forms by means of which they are projected are co-extensive. These later piano pieces are, in melodic and harmonic material, as unabashedly romantic as Schumann or Chopin, and by their individual formal successes they belong to the canon of romanticism's characteristic achievements. Of classicizing they are entirely free: they are, in fact, superb free forms produced simultaneously with and by the materials they contain.

For many decades, all discussion of Brahms was based on an assumption that he was a classic composer. This assumption began to lose its immediacy in the 1920's, when, for the first time since Brahms's youth, voices were to be heard saying that his claim to be considered an original master of music must be related chiefly to his lieder, his pieces for solo piano, and—in a formal sense—to his command of a new extension of the variation principle. These were voices speaking in the light of a critical axiom difficult to controvert. Any great artist is necessarily one of his own era's representatives in the unstopped stream of artistic change: he either perfects forms already existing or evolves new ones. No claim has ever been put forth that Brahms's use of sonata forms bettered that of Haydn, Mozart, and Beethoven. He was no more revolutionary than Bach or Handel, and the new criticism asserted that, coming as late in the romantic period as they had come in the baroque, he had to be romantic to be great. They were saying that he was not a classic master at all, but a romantic one, no rebel of the Liszt or Wagner or any other sort, but able and ready to forge his own forms nonetheless.

In a remarkable series of extended sectional compositions in variation form, Brahms hit upon, and then with great intellectual power perfected, a compositional method peculiarly fertile for him. In the sense of liberating and concentrating his own significance, it was here that Brahms's discipleship to Beethoven became most fruitful, formally speaking. Brahms found the preliminary hints for his variaton technique in such Beethoven compositions as the piano variations on a theme from the *"Eroica"* Symphony; those in the *"Appassionata"* Sonata, Opus 57 (*andante con moto*); those on a waltz by Diabelli; those on an original theme in C Minor; and—for orchestra—the *adagio* movement of the Ninth Symphony. His own sets of variations include those on a theme by Schumann (1854) and culminate in the Variations on a Theme by Haydn (both for orchestra and for two pianos, 1873); the Variations and Fugue on a Theme by Handel (1861); the *études* known as Variations on a Theme by Paganini (two volumes, 1862-3); and —for orchestra—the passacaglia finale of the Fourth Symphony (1884-5).

Variation is possible in many ways: on a more or less set progression of harmonies, on a melody, on a rhythm or group of rhythms. In the baroque and rococo periods, most continuous variation patterns and sectional variations maintained either a complete melody or a ground throughout. They were likely to maintain harmonic continuity between the varied theme and the variations. Up to Mozart, one notable aspect of all kinds of variation was the relatively small difference (harmonic, melodic, or rhythmic) between a theme and its variations. The differences, that is, were largely occasioned by slight shifts and decorations.

With Mozart, however, and more with Beethoven and Schubert, variation began to be interpreted in a more far-ranging sense. The interrelationship between the chosen melody or melodic fragment and the variations farthest removed from it was still usually easy to determine—but in the distant variations the melody, in particular, was often so altered that, if isolated, it became unrecognizable as a variant. Certain elements of the harmonic structure were preserved throughout, but the outline of the melody itself was at times almost altogether lost.

With Brahms, an element that might be called controlled way-wardness entered. This was a manner of evolving some variations from mere hints in the melody or from materials newly evolved in preceding variations. In his "Handel" and "Paganini" sets, whole groups of variations advance progressively, each variation being more closely derived from the variations before it than from the original theme. The most distant variations are related to the melody only by tenuous threads, but sound inevitable as placed in the new sequence of musical happenings. In all probability it was from the *alla fuga* that closes Beethoven's *"Eroica"* Variations and the fugue just before the last of the "Diabelli" set that Brahms adopted the plan of using, in the highly satisfactory finales of his "Haydn" and "Handel" variations respectively, a passacaglia and a fugue.

In the finest of his sets of variations Brahms welded impressive musical matter and impressively handled patterns into a true mu-sical form, one no less valuable because he never used it twice the same way. The Variations and Fugue on a Theme by Handel, for-mally speaking, is as great a triumph of romantic musical design as Chopin's Fantaisie or Schumann's *Carnaval*. Among the move-ments of Brahms's symphonies, concertos, and chamber pieces, few, if any, others display the composer so relaxed in certainty of power as does the stupendous passacaglia finale of the Fourth Sym-phony. Whatever else a passacaglia may be, it is not a dramatic form. Sir Donald Tovey brilliantly suggested (*Essays in Musical Analysis*, i, 116) that Brahms, having satisfied himself dramatically in the three first movements of the Fourth Symphony, desired his finale to be "free to express tragic emotion without being encum-bered by the logical and chronological necessities of the more dra-matic sonata forms."

This passacaglia is a theme, thirty variations, and something more. The theme, eight measures in length, first appears thus:

The extraordinary number of ways in which Brahms varies his treatment of this somber theme, altering it only by moving it from one register (pitch) to another, is a measure of the distance that one sort of variation had traveled between the seventeenth century and the nineteenth. The seventeenth-century *arie* had often consisted of a chief melody sung above an accompanying brief semi-melody sounded over and over (*basso ostinato*). Transferred from vocal-and-instrumental music to purely instrumental use, this pattern was often known as either passacaglia or *chaconne*. And the final movement of Brahms's Fourth Symphony is fundamentally nothing else: what differentiates it from a seventeenth- or eighteenth-century *chaconne* or passacaglia is the wealth of instrumental, harmonic, rhythmic, and contrapuntal methods that Brahms has applied to its unfolding. He has often so manipulated the unchanging theme as to all but obliterate it completely, making it for a time but one element in what amounts to entirely new music.

Although Brahms's passacaglia is one continuous musical fabric, it is actually plotted as follows: the theme itself, fourteen variations, sixteen more variations, and a coda. The second group of variations may be seen, in a typically Brahmsian sense, as variations on the first group of fourteen—though it must be noted again that the theme itself appears, substantially unaltered, in one instrumental range or another, as the base on which each section of the entire complicated structure is built. Of particular interest as an excellent example of the musical suggestibility that made Brahms a more original master of the variation than of the sonata forms, is his derivation of several satisfactory submelodies and counter-melodies from two small elements in the theme itself: the chromatic progression G, A, A♯, B in measures 3, 4, 5, 6 of the example, page 245 (and especially the A, A♯) and the descent of one octave from B to B (measures 6, 7 of the example).

In the twelfth variation, Brahms contrasts E major with the previously pervading E minor. When he begins the second group of variations with number 15, he indicates what might be called a re-beginning by returning to E minor. He employs numerous sorts of contrapuntal devices: variation 29, for example, is a canon. What is musically noteworthy about the entire passacaglia, however—as distinct from what is technically the cause of this quality—

is the sensation given the listener that he is being carried toward a climax: there is no *sense* of repetition. And when the rather agitated thirtieth (final) variation has entered upon a *ritardando,* the coda is able at last to give overwhelmingly convincing proof that the climax has been reached, that all complexities have been unraveled.

Up through the thirtieth variation Brahms has for the most part stayed rigorously in one key. The coda, again repeating (it at first seems) the original theme in the same key, gets through only its first four measures. Then Brahms uses the chromatic step and octave descent already mentioned, employing them as the convincing reason for a series of releasing modulations; employs an artful variety of imitation (the same theme two measures later and only a semitone higher); reiterates the theme in compacted quarter notes; and finds one last sad and solemn comment to make on it. The totality is a formal masterpiece as right for its communicative purpose as are, for other, more dramatic, less emotionally packed, purposes, the most superb uses of sonata forms.

Early in his creative life Brahms had mostly detractors, and the number of these was increased by mistakenly fanatic Lisztians and Wagnerians. Somewhat later, he became one of the most honored and popular of composers—justly for the loftiness of his musical aims, the creative grasp of his techniques, and the melodic and emotion-evoking richness of his finest works. But he was as mistakenly estimated in praise as he had been mistakenly depreciated in adverse, Wagnerian criticism. He became the very center of the mistaken attitude that (he being taken for a classical composer) the sonata was the one road to the highest achievement in purely instrumental music. In recent years, Brahms has once again been criticized adversely, but much of that criticism has actually been aimed at the mistaken picture of him. A fair statement of the most modern critical position regarding Brahms might be that he was unquestionably a great composer; that he was not a classicist, and in general used classical forms only to triumph over them rather than with them—to triumph by sectional beauties, noble melodies, and engaging harmonic variety, rather than by formal rectitude; that he took the variation principle to the most complex and

widely expressive stage of development that it has yet reached; and
that in lieder and piano pieces—the forms of the songs determined
by sensitive response to their texts, those of the piano pieces by
their basic musical matter—he was a great romanticist.

Since the late middle years of Brahms's life he has never lacked
very numerous admirers. Anton Bruckner, on the contrary, has
never (outside Vienna and some German cities) won more than a
handful of admirers. He was a religious man of somewhat naive
mentality, propelled by lofty ideals, but devoid of Brahms's genial
warmth, rather pretty sentiment, and earthy humor. Bruckner became an ardent Wagnerian (Wagner called him the only true symphonist after Beethoven), and unwary critics began to say that his
music was as Wagnerian as he. If his nine symphonies [1] be examined solely as music, they are discovered to be far more Beethovian than Brahms: Bruckner derived much of his musical philosophy and the patterns for carrying it from the Beethoven of the
Fifth Symphony. Gabriel Engel, a convinced Brucknerian, went so
far as to state that each of Bruckner's symphonies is based on this
formula: "I. The Drama of Inner Conflict (with the soul as hero).
II. Adagio. The Song of Faith (Prayerful Communion with God).
III. Scherzo. The Dance of Life (the Joys of Life in Nature). IV.
Finale. The soul's decisive struggle and the triumph over all oppo-
sition." With the slightest shifts, this might be taken as a crude
diagram of Beethoven's biggest symphonies.

Bruckner was fertile in melodies that he used for sonata-like
treatment, though they were most often romantic rather than classical in contour, and not in themselves of arresting beauty. Often
they were simply too extended to be happy subjects for any sort of
development. He strove understandingly and often with success
for rhythmic variety. His use of the orchestra was highly original,
deviating from the symphonic uses of earlier composers chiefly in
the employment of instruments in families. Again and again in

---

[1] Bruckner's First Symphony was composed in 1866; the Ninth (incomplete) in
1894. Of the nine, only the Fourth (1874) is anything but absolute music: the
Fourth, "Romantic," or "Wagner" Symphony has a vague program that Bruckner
warned his admirers not to interpret literally.

Bruckner's symphonies, an entire orchestral family (the brasses, the woodwinds, or the strings) is made to sound together; variety and a peculiar sort of forward movement are then achieved by silencing that family to bring in another. Bruckner's craftsmanship was everywhere scrupulous. He showed, in fact, most of the essential qualities of a great composer. But except in the eyes and ears of a fanatical few admirers he lacked all sense of punctuality; and he dangerously construed the sonata forms as epic. He used them for ceremonial and prolonged meditative and expositional effects rather than for the aspects of drama native to them both through ancestry and by innate structure. Many times he distended the component sections of sonata form until their dramatic contrast to the sections surrounding them was lost to the ear, however much they may be visible to the eye on paper.

The result of Bruckner's special combination of virtues and faults is that a Bruckner symphonic movement sometimes threatens to last forever as—sluggishly, with enormous pomp, and with persistent squareness—it moves by concentric motion toward no visible goal. Bruckner's String Quintet (1879), his only important chamber work, is one of his symphonies on an instrumentally smaller scale; it has the symphonies' flaws without their orchestral virtues. Only in his religious music, and especially in the concert Mass in F minor (1866) was Bruckner unable to impose upon himself the need to fill out at incredible length the sections of a pattern prescribed and strictly interpreted. There, reined in by a text, he could not challenge the logics of time and patience. His religious music forcibly suggests, as passages scattered throughout his symphonies suggest, that he mistook the very nature of formal truth, that he might have become the romantic master he was in many ways equipped to be if he had not held in blind adoration the letter rather than the informing spirit of Beethoven.

Gustav Mahler and Jean Sibelius are often regarded as modern composers.[2] They are more easily understood as prolonged after-

---

[2] Of Mahler's major compositions, only the first four symphonies and the song cycle entitled *Lieder eines fahrenden Gesellen* were composed during the nineteenth century; the later six symphonies (the Tenth incomplete) and the song cycles

glows of the sunset of romanticism and of a twilight attempt to re-establish adjusted classical forms.

Mahler was highly self-centered and intensely romantic. Every measure of his music is unmistakably colored by and expressive of his peculiar nature; he is as instantly recognizable and as unique as Chopin. Yet even one of his most vocal admirers (Gabriel Engel, quoted above in reference to Bruckner) states that Mahler's music "is in no respect, save in its unprecedentedly abundant employ-ment of solo-passages for all instruments, of a radical or revolu-tionary nature." Mahler, that is, attempted to confine his unique musical ideas in a cage of old usages and old formal patterns. As Mr. Engel points out, he did give an almost concerto-like impor-tance, within the texture and discourse of his symphonic orchestra, to one solo instrument after the other. He did introduce both solo human voices and choruses into several of his symphonies, perhaps reflecting Bruckner's special use of trumpet and horn statements as much as Beethoven's choral finale to the Ninth Sym-phony. But everything about the musical content itself was exuber-ant, idiosyncratic, nervous, and completely un-classical, not to say anti-classical. Not interpreting the symphony's patterns with Bruckner's literalness, and being willing to alter both the number and the order of the movements, Mahler nevertheless hewed to its broad outlines in nine completed symphonies, one incomplete symphony, and the huge song cycle, *Das Lied von der Erde,* really a symphony with voices.

The results of Mahler's twenty years of productivity are a body of music that has won a relatively small group of faithful admirers, a large body of indifferent listeners, and another small body of violent detractors. The admirers justly point out his music's origi-nality, its often charming "Viennese" melodies, its intermittently intense expressiveness, and the guiding effect of his "lineo-color-istic" orchestration on the composers who followed him. The crux of the argument over Mahler resides in their further claim that he created new forms in a "struggle to conform as closely to the

Kindertotenlieder and *Das Lied von der Erde* belong to the twentieth century. Except the tone poem *En Saga,* all of Sibelius' larger works were completed after 1900.

tenets of absolute music as a new content would permit" (Gabriel Engel). The indifferent listeners are most often merely unmoved by Mahler's length and diffuseness. And the detractors state that his symphonies simply fail to hold together, falling into shards out of sheer over-tension, from the over-development of highly personal musical materials either undevelopable by traditional symphonic procedures as Mahler altered them or appearing as self-sufficient units. For most listeners, there can be no doubt, Mahler must seem the final *reductio ad absurdum* of the nineteenth century's ever-increasing tendency toward sheer size, toward slow tempos, toward the pouring of increasingly inappropriate musical subject matter into distended, finally almost gaseously diffuse, versions of classical forms.

It is impossible to look upon Brahms's musical life as tragic: he composed much music that was and is greatly loved. But both Bruckner and Mahler may be seen as tragic in more than one light. Their music has always been more discussed than listened to, and the suggestion is inescapable that tragedy—apart from other, purely biographical, elements—lay in their attempt to achieve the impossible. They were anachronisms in that they failed to create for deeply romantic materials the related romantic forms. In the freedom of the symphonic poem or tone poem—or in forms that they might have evolved spontaneously from their own musical habits of speech—they might have evaded the unsuccess that clings always to their names. They are found guilty of a mortal artistic sin: they did not discover the integral forms by which their ideas could have satisfied the expectations aroused. From the noblest motives—and despite heroic wrestlings with formal problems—their own mental equipment and their position in artistic time led them to find in variants of existing patterns a supposedly eternal virtue that for them those patterns could not hold. This might not have mattered in a more superficial sense—they might have become as popular as Tchaikovsky—if they had been willing and able to succeed on any more superficial level and to curb their remarkably similar tendency to self-propelling discursiveness. But neither Bruckner nor Mahler was content to be anything less than a very great composer; neither was willing, as Tchaikovsky was, to be, in relative brevity, whatever he might be if he was entirely, unadventurously himself. The result now seems to have been that whereas Tchaikovsky was a highly successful composer of the second rank, both Bruckner and Mahler were failures.

Jean Sibelius appeared at first to have sprung, as a symphonist, straight from Tchaikovsky. His First Symphony was called "Tchaikovsky's Seventh," with reference to an earlier designation of Brahms's First as "Beethoven's Tenth." It is conventionally romantic in almost every detail. But Sibelius was no more a full-blown Tchaikovskyan romantic than he was a true descendant of Beethoven. He began to experiment with—and within—the symphonic patterns. Disregarding more and more the basic classical symphonic way of building drama from the contrast of strong and weak (or male and female) themes, he worked out a highly individual method of movement-construction. In many later Sibelius symphonies, a movement is built by gradual addition and grudging revelation. A fragment of melody is stated; a second fragment is added to it; only at the climax or conclusion does the complete theme appear. By this method Sibelius has wrought movements that possess great strength and solidity. By themselves they must be regarded as true examples of formal success. But this type of construction alters the inner relationships between a single movement and the other movements in a symphony. It tends to make the four-movement symphonic pattern unnecessary and undesirable, for it greatly weakens the contrasts on which that pattern subsisted. Sibelius himself recognized this: his Seventh Symphony (1924) is in one movement.

Sibelius' Seventh Symphony contains the rudiments of slightly altered classical symphonic form written in a type of musical shorthand and both condensed and run together. In one aspect it may be heard as a symphonic poem or tone poem without known program; in this view, its being called a symphony may appear mistaken piety. Yet Sibelius was still near enough to the dramatic bases of the sonata structures so that his claim that this is indeed a symphony must be regarded seriously. It suggests what no symphony by Brahms, Bruckner, or Mahler suggests at all: that it might be the dependable herald of a new, sonata-derived, formal classicism, if such a classicism were to become the musical atmosphere. Its musical ideas—whatever influence they show of the romantic effusiveness of the nineteenth century and of the harmonic restlessness of the twentieth, and whatever their attractiveness and power—are possible subjects for compact and condensed sonata-like treatment. The difference between Sibelius' Seventh Symphony and, say, his *En Saga,* composed thirty-two years earlier, is the difference caused by a long march toward classical concision.

Yet Sibelius' career is tinged by the tragedy more notably associated with the careers of Bruckner and Mahler: though he has at times—especially in England and the United States—won a far larger public response than they, he has not spoken convincingly to his most creative younger contemporaries, and the tendencies ruling twentieth-century composition have led music farther and farther away from him. His finest works are still often heard; but in the light of musical history he has long since become a noble, isolated anachronism. Much of the sometimes bitter appraisal of Sibelius derives from anger on the part of younger men that a composer of such obviously major endowments should have clung, even if half-heartedly, to the outward symbols of the past instead of passing over with them into a new day.

The foregoing paragraphs are not intended primarily as critical judgments of Brahms, Bruckner, Mahler, and Sibelius—all of whom could be discussed with wholly different emphasis from many other points of vantage. These pages intend, rather, to portray four men coming just before, at, or past, the end of the high romantic period of the nineteenth century, men who were not content or able to be adventurously romantic in formal behavior, as Chopin, Schumann, Berlioz, and Wagner had been, but who placed consistent lofty labor at the service of an attempt to revivify the symphony and other sonata-based forms. Each was a composer of ample talent. Brahms was a major master of music. Each demonstrated a belief that enduring value existed in sonata-like forms, almost without regard to the nature of the musical materials used to fill out those altered, but pre-existing, patterns.

It appears today that the future of music was not with them.
While Brahms was composing his Fourth Symphony, Mahler and
Bruckner their unfinished last symphonies, and Sibelius his Seventh Symphony, the whole itinerary and destination of the art of
music was abandoning romanticism and romantic adaptations of
classicism to set out on an uncharted new road. They were the
formidable last expressions of the nineteenth century. Alongside
their remarkable efforts to preserve or prolong the past, other men
with other ideals were—slowly at first, then swiftly—creating a present farther removed from them and their basic conceptions than
any musical period had ever been from the period immediately
before it.

Eighteen

LATE ROMANTICISM AND NATIONALISM · RUSSIA
TCHAIKOVSKY AND BALLET · THE NATIONALISTS

During every period since the Middle Ages there has usually been
a predominant, entrenched style in each of the arts—a manner or
group of manners already recognized and accepted as normal by
listeners, readers, and spectators. Parallel with such "normal"
styles and manners, and usually to some extent at war with them,
have been "modern" or "new" manners and styles not yet recognized as entirely acceptable by the widest existing public. In many
cases, though not always, these so-called revolutionary styles have
endured to become the predominant, entrenched styles of the succeeding period. Such "revolutions," frequently accused of being
anarchic and destructive both by the larger public and by the artists practicing the styles accepted by that public, have often been
the representative formal efforts of younger men. Whether musicians, writers, painters, architects, or sculptors, these newcomers
have been asserting their right to respond to their own world, as
distinct from that of their elders, in ways attractive and useful to
them. Sometimes this rebellion has been that of classicists against
romanticism; in the late Beethoven, in Schubert, Chopin, and the
early Berlioz, romanticism produced and was produced by men
struggling to force open the doors closed to them by a classicism
that had begun to lose the freshness and relevance by which it had
risen some decades earlier.

255

The nineteenth century was largely an expansive and emotion-cultivating period in the arts. Yet at the hours when the representative romanticists were working out their own formal and expressive problems, forces were gathering for the very necessary task of disintegrating their kind of highly personal creation, which was becoming less and less relevant to general currents of life and thought as the century sloped toward its close. As producing the musical art of our century, those forces were localized chiefly in three countries, in each of which they operated differently, by ways determined in the past and by what was being rebelled against. The countries in which post-romantic music—modern in the first-half-of-the-twentieth-century sense—burst from the enveloping embrace of romanticism were Russia, France, and Austria.

In Russia the hiatus between folk music and serious composed music had been all but complete for centuries, with vitality greatly present in the former and absent from the latter. For the folk music of the Romanov empire was, naturally, Slavic, more or less Oriental in rhythm, harmony, melody, and color, whereas composed music was slavishly Italianate, with late, occasional infusions of the Teutonic and the Gallic. In that slowly stirring giant of a country the first cause leading toward modernism turned out to be nationalism. It was most clearly expressed in the determination of a small group of only partly professional musicians to relate their art to the folk music and other truly indigenous expressions of Russian life.

The principal Russian composers involved, both before and after the self-conscious nationalist efforts, were Mikhail Glinka (1803-1857), Alexander Dargomizhsky (1813-1869), Alexander Borodin (1833-1887), Mili Balakirev (1837-1910), Modest Mussorgsky (1839-1881), Nikolai Rimsky-Korsakov (1844-1908), Igor Stravinsky (1882-   ), and Sergei Prokofiev (1891-1953). Also from Russia during the period covered by these men came two others: Piotr Ilyich Tchaikovsky (1840-1893), one of the most widely performed of composers during the six decades after his death, and Alexander Scriabin (1872-1915), an interesting musical eccentric. Both were outside the line of technical and stylistic inheritance which stretched from Glinka to Stravinsky and Prokofiev.

In France music had been nurtured since the earliest times on a close relation to folk music, and French musical nationalism was therefore impossible in anything like the Russian sense. The Paris rebellion that opened one road to modernism was revolt against a reactionary group of learned but imitative composers and academicians who controlled the schools and theaters under state supervision. This fight had been instituted by Berlioz, whose single-handed war had produced his own music and nothing else. In men who came later than Berlioz, the closest thing to signs of rebellion against the academicians had been the chromaticism and so-called "cyclical form" [1] of César Franck (1822-1890) and the feeble transplanted French Wagnerism of Ernest Reyer (1823-1909). In the sense of either leading to modernism or of actually evolving it, the composers of first importance in France after Berlioz were Claude Debussy (1862-1918), Erik Satie (1866-1925), and Maurice Ravel (1875-1937).

In Austria, following upon the widespread acceptance of Wagner, Brahms, and Richard Strauss,[2] rebellion took still another form, being directed against the idiom and size of romantic composition rather than against the emotional attitudes of romanticism. Largely intellectual in inception, it challenged at its foundation whatever remained of the classical harmonic system in romantic harmony, finally altogether denying the continuing validity of tonality. The important composers in this drastic revolution were Arnold Schoenberg (1874-1951), Anton von Webern (1883-1945), and Alban Berg (1885-1935).

Important aspects of twentieth-century music arose in other places than Russia, France, and Austria. But its salient characteristics could have existed almost exactly as they are without the in-

---

[1] "Cyclical form" refers to the building of a compositon out of several movements, in all (or at least several) of which the same melodies or other recognizable materials occur. The idea was not original with Franck, as has often been pointed out: Schubert had used it, for example, in his *Wanderer Fantaisie*. But Franck applied the idea in a way closely related to the Lisztian "transformation of themes," and made the repetition of materials from movement to movement as important an agency of over-all unity as key relationship. His pupils and followers, notably Vincent d'Indy (1851-1931), Camille Saint-Saëns (1835-1921), and Gabriel Fauré (1845-1924), were deeply marked by Franck's interpretation of cyclical thematic repetition.

[2] Strauss was accurately and suggestively described in 1920 as "the false dawn of modern music" (Paul Rosenfeld: *Musical Portraits*, 55).

tervention of any composer not in the above lists. One exception
to this statement may be called for by the music of the Hungarian
composer Béla Bartók (1881-1945). Bartók compressed into his
own creative span an evolution very like the course of Russian music from the folk nationalism of Mussorgsky to the highly individual, only vaguely nationalist, modernism of Stravinsky.

To understand the evolution of twentieth-century music, it is peculiarly necessary to take note of Tchaikovsky both in a positive
and in a negative sense. Positively, Tchaikovsky made possible the
international efflorescence of Russian ballet, without which whole
areas of twentieth-century music would never have come to be
what they have been.

Tchaikovsky composed three of the most popular symphonies,
one each of the most popular piano concertos and violin concertos,
and several other orchestral compositions that can be grouped as
symphonic poems which have been familiar for sixty years to anyone at all conscious of music. In those feverishly romantic, astonishingly convincing, self-revealing works he was, for the most part,
formally unadventurous.[3] Tchaikovsky was not a self-conscious
nationalist, being far more cosmopolitan in taste than most of his
Russian colleagues, but enough Russian and other Slavic turns of
musical thought found their way unself-consciously into his music
so that his enormous worldwide popularity has played a large part
in naturalizing them elsewhere.

Insofar as Tchaikovsky's large non-theatrical works won the
widest possible audience for serious music throughout the world,
they served as belated reinforcements of nineteenth-century romanticism. Standing almost as much as Wagner's music (and later
that of Brahms and Richard Strauss) athwart the path young men
wanted to find to the future, the music of Tchaikovsky was for a

---

[3] One of Tchaikovsky's signal deviations from usual procedure occurs in his
"Pathétique" Symphony. Its finale violates classic habits by being an *adagio lamen-
toso, i.e.,* a slow movement the opposite of triumphant or joyous in tone and effect.
Tchaikovsky was unquestionably led to this experiment by the feelings of a
troubled man in a troubling world. Because the experiment provided an entirely
satisfying capstone for the symphony, this finale is in its way as self-justifying as
the passacaglia finale of Brahms' Fourth Symphony.

time cordially and vocally hated, most particularly by the propagandists of modernism. Possibly no more instantly convincing and engaging music has ever been composed, and modern criticism now appears to be taking the attitude that a liking for Tchaikovsky indicates either a lack of musical sophistication or a sophistication so complete as to be impregnable.

Similarly, modern criticism often holds that Tchaikovsky's most galvanic contribution to musical evolution was made in his scores for ballet. This formalized dance, originally imported into Russia from Italy, had been popular in St. Petersburg and Moscow for at least a full century before Tchaikovsky turned to it. The music of pre-Tchaikovskyan Russian ballets either had been the thin, characterless, imitative stuff written for dancing by Frenchmen like Adolphe Adam (1803-1856), Germans like Peter Ludwig Hertel (1817-1899), or Italians like Cesare Pugni (1805-1870), or it had been Polish and Russian apings of their feeble compositions. The first great Russian ballet, musically speaking, was Tchaikovsky's *Swan Lake* (1876). To the elaboration of this music, carefully made to fit the ballet's scenario and choreographic necessities, he brought his abundant melodic gift, his richly romantic harmonic idiom, his apparently unending supply of rhythmic variety, and his genius for instrumentation. The result is a series of short musical pieces full of fairy-tale sorcery—and devoid of Tchaikovsky's sometimes wearying autobiographical neuroticism. It is, of course, futile to look for large formal patterns in what is, by its very provenance, a suite of small and often musically unrelated pieces; but there is no doubt that most of those pieces not only are flawless for their dancing purposes, but were shaped by an unfailing sense of small form.[4]

After *Swan Lake* Tchaikovsky composed two other ballets: *The Sleeping Beauty* (1889) and *The Nutcracker* (1891-92), both also to fairy-tale scenarios. After his death, the three ballets became (along with the compositions of later men) the basic repertoire of the Russian ballet companies that burst upon the cities of Western

[4] Great ballet scores had been composed long before Tchaikovsky and the era of Russian ballet. Lully, Rameau, Gluck, and many other composers had produced ballet music of magnificence.

Europe and America, bringing with them the folk-dramatic literature of Russia, its Oriental colors, and its tradition of ballet's high
seriousness. Tchaikovsky's ballet music and such of its offspring
as were continually more responsive to Russian nationalism provided the receptive atmosphere needed for the creation of that
later series of ballets by Stravinsky. In the scores of three ballets:
The Firebird (1910), *Petrouchka* (1911), and *Le Sacre du Printemps* (1913),[5] Stravinsky was to carry one sort of modernism out
of the picture-book realm of Rimsky-Korsakov's operas to perhaps
the highest point it has attained.

The romantic harmonic idiom of Tchaikovsky's ballet scores
was little different from that of his other music. Those who com-
plain that Tchaikovsky's symphonies sound like ballet music are
in reality only saying that they sound like Tchaikovsky. The historical importance of his three ballets is technical only in a balletic
sense: musically it consists of the fact that he composed them at
all—that a serious composer should have lavished all the compositional care he could on what, in Russia, had for some time been
considered proper work only for hacks.

With one hand, then, Tchaikovsky helped to increase the weight
and blocking power of that curious and often incomprehensible
body of music known today to impresarios as the "standard repertoire"—as Brahms and Richard Strauss similarly helped unwit-
tingly to impose its stationary standards on the great musical
public. With the other hand, however, Tchaikovsky liberated
ballet as a serious vehicle for modern music, signaling to many
younger Russians and foreigners a side-door by which they might
be able to slip their revolutionary idioms into the musical sanc-
tum. Among those who eventually took most telling advantage of
his example were not only Stravinsky, but Ravel, Hindemith,
Falla, Prokofiev, and Copland. The list could be lengthened considerably by adding to it composers of works not originally written

---

[5] Another composer of carefully and elaborately made ballet scores was Léo
Delibes (1836-1891). For the Paris stage, Delibes wrote *Coppélia* (1870) and *Sylvia*
(1876), both of which Tchaikovsky intensely admired, and which have kept their
delicate musical vitality.

to accompany dancing, but which have won acceptance, even wide-spread popularity, as adapted to balletic use.

Mikhail Glinka was a semi-professional, semi-dilettante composer trained in Western European methods both at home and in Italy and Germany. Much of his music is conventional nineteenth-century romantic tone-painting or Italianate opera different from other music composed during his lifetime only because of his occasional employment of synthetic and actual folk melodies, folk rhythms, and—to a smaller extent—harmonies derived from or colored by folk usage, largely Russian and Spanish. The wide popularity of such of his scores as the nationalistic tone picture *Kamarinskaya,* the *Jota Aragonesa,* and of at least sections from his two operas, *A Life for the Tsar* (1836) and *Ruslan and Lyudmila* (1842) served, as Chopin's polonaises and mazurkas served more importantly, to introduce to Western ears the previously unregarded textures and colors of Slavic-Oriental and Spanish-Gypsy-African music. The "Orientalism" of Viennese eighteenth-century "Turkish" music pales beside the splashed colors of *Kamarinskaya.*

Most of the salient characteristics of the Russian music of the second half of the nineteenth century and the first half of the twentieth are promised by Glinka's compositions. His use of orchestral instruments with great sensitivity to their individual and mixed colors, producing an over-all ensemble of notable brilliance and transparency; [6] his knowing use of choruses, particularly as an operatic method of expressing the tempers and natures of crowds; his tendency to build long compositions out of brief musical fragments; his Orientalism, with its consequent (but perhaps mostly unconscious) harmonic daring—all of these set the norms for much in the art of his successors.

In *A Life for the Tsar,* one passage of notably Russian-Oriental texture is the wedding chorus. This is in 5/4 time, a rhythm fre-

---

6 Glinka was a pioneer in enlarging the orchestra to include both the harp and the piano as naturalized members. He was also one of the first composers to write important characteristic parts for the English horn.

quent in Russian folk music, but largely foreign to Western Europe—so foreign that many Westerners cannot to this day feel it as anything but an artificial combining of two beats and three beats or of three and two. After Glinka it occurs often in Russian composed music, one of the most renowned examples of it being the second movement of Tchaikovsky's *"Pathétique"* Symphony. Another Glinka passage notable for its progeny is an example of melodic-harmonic daring derived from folk music. It is the leitmotiv that accompanies the baleful wizard Chernomor whenever he appears in *Ruslan and Lyudmila:* [7]

   This passage is cited frequently by historians as the earliest appearance in composed music of the whole-tone scale, later to become an important tool, particularly in the hands of French composers, for the destruction of the unique position of the classical harmonic system. On instruments of fixed pitch only two whole-tone scales can be played: C, D, E, F♯, G♯, A♯, B♯ (C) and C♯, D♯, F, G, A, B, C♯, either of which may of course begin and end on any tone it contains—and either of which can be annotated in flats. Nowhere in these scales are to be found two of the intervals central to the classical system of major and minor tonalities: the perfect fifth and perfect fourth. Nor does any whole-tone scale supply the half-tone (minor second) step up to the tonic—as in C, D, E, F, G, A, *B, C,* or in A, B, C, D, E, F, *G♯, A*—which is of fundamental importance, particularly to closing cadences, in both the major and minor modes. It is theoretically possible to build whole-tone melodies into a system of whole-tone harmony, but such a system must always lack the sensation of a "home" or tonic founda-

   [7] The theme is quoted here as it appears in the finale of Act I. It is in the first notes of each of the bass tremolos: G, F, E♭, D♭, B, A, G, F, E♭—an uninterrupted succession of whole-tone intervals.

tion to which all other tones have affinities and kinetic relationships. The importance of the whole-tone scale from a creative point of view has proved transitory, but it was useful in lessening the hold of the classical harmonic system on composers' mental ears, and it supplied Debussy and a few other composers with additional means for exploiting exotic and impressionistic effects.

A Life for the Tsar and *Ruslan and Lyudmila* are as fragmentary and unintegrated (both as to libretto and as to music) as any operas ever composed—and this episodic lack of development, this failure of (or simple lack of interest in) integration were also to be characteristic of much Russian music later than Glinka. This kind of fragmentariness, as has often been pointed out by students of Russian culture, is also to be found in much Russian literature, including its greatest creators except Turgenev. This is perhaps to say that all Russian music, and perhaps all Russian art, of the nineteenth century is romantic art, in which the what is of greater importance than the how.

The libretto of *Ruslan and Lyudmila* was based on a fairy tale by Pushkin, who became as important to the evolution of Russian opera as Ariosto and Tasso had been to that of seventeenth- and eighteenth-century Western opera. Alexander Dargomizhsky likewise based his first important work, the opera *Rusalka* (1856), on a Pushkin play. But Dargomizhsky was unhappy over the intervention, between the poet and his audience, of a librettist, whether himself or someone else. His second, incomplete, opera, *The Stone Guest,* therefore attempted the excessively difficult, perhaps impossible, task of setting to music Pushkin's version of the Don Juan legend exactly as the poet had written it.

In *Rusalka,* Dargomizhsky took long strides toward the naturalization in composed music of harmonic implications and rhythms native to true Russian and Eastern folk song and folk dance. But he was a creative musician of intermittent and uncertain power, and in attempts to identify his music psychologically and pictorially with Pushkin's characters and scenes he sometimes sacrificed all musical interest to a prosy, unmusical declamation not unlike the least communicative recitative in older operas. He believed that music could be made "to express precisely what the words express," a delusion particularly damaging to his music in those parts of a libretto which a more dramatically wise composer would simply have refused to set, knowing them unsuitable for musical treatment.

In *The Stone Guest* an entire opera is built out of what Dargomizhsky called "melodic recitative," an endless almost-melody whose rise and fall respond mechanically to the meanings and accents of Pushkin's words. Except in those passages in which Dargomizhsky the composer rises to his very best, the opera is theatrically ineffective because the text is more alive than the music.[8] This dogged application of a crippling theory of operatic construction, however, led Dargomizhsky to harmonic combinations never before seriously written down.

Because *The Stone Guest* is so frequently couched in harmonic combinations foreign to the true constitution of major and minor tonalities, Dargomizhsky noted it without a key signature, again foreshadowing later composers. The opera contains several melodic passages in whole tones, and at times seems to be at the verge of attempting a harmonic system depending from them. Thus, though the opera's juiceless, stiff texture and the intermittence with which Dargomizhsky's imagination supplied him with arresting and expressive materials leave *The Stone Guest* thankless on the stage, its influence was lasting because of the hints it supplied to composers far more gifted than Dargomizhsky.

Dargomizhsky's harmonic unconventionality had almost as deep an influence as the politico-literary tenets of nationalism upon Borodin, Balakirev, and Mussorgsky, the three central figures of the "mighty handful," known to non-Russians as "the Five." [9]

---

[8] Dargomizhsky also subjugated his orchestra to the singers' unending recitative, thus unquestionably suggesting to Debussy something of the vocal-instrumental balance of *Pelléas et Mélisande,* a suggestion that Debussy transformed in his own musically far richer way.

[9] The other two members of the group were César Cui (1835-1918), more memorable for his sponsorship and championing of nationalism than for his generally mediocre practice of composition, and Rimsky-Korsakov, an erudite musician on whom Dargomizhsky's theories about operatic "truth"—as apart from his coloristic use of Russian, Caucasian, and other Eastern folk idioms—had almost no effect.

With the ably argued assistance of the critic Vladimir Stasov (1824-1906), Balakirev was the very heart of Russian musical nationalism, being both the intense supporter of a "war" against Westernism and an accomplished practitioner, in pure form, of folk-based musical creation. In his symphonic poems *Tamar* (1881) and *Russia* (a revision, 1882, of an earlier work) and in his piano fantasy *Islamey* (1869), Balakirev composed music that both sums up intense Russianism and Orientalism (much of which he had absorbed in the Caucasus) and displays the unique and integral method of setting them forth. Borrowing— or creating by imitation—musical ideas essentially self-sufficient and therefore impervious to classical development, he made strength out of what might have been debility. Realizing the sectional nature his extended pieces must inevitably have, he employed many kinds of variation.

Although nothing *develops* in *Tamar, Russia,* or *Islamey,* their component melodies, harmonies, rhythms, and decorations are strong and attractive, and interest is raised to climaxes and then diminished with remarkable sense of the material's staying power. If "form" be used to indicate the fusion of material, pattern, and other methods, these pieces undoubtedly possess satisfactory form. Their structural devices have been used to present and display completely the musical ideas they contain.

Islamey in particular is the legitimate ancestor of many Russo-Oriental compositions, both real and simulated. It consists almost wholly of two melodies, both varied by decoration. A Western composer earlier than Balakirev might probably have considered the first melody unfit for any sort of musical extension—by variation or any other method—the second too weak to play an important role anywhere. Yet out of these unpromising basic materials Balakirev developed a brilliant piano composition of satisfying proportions. Despite its fragmentariness to the eye, in it he managed, by apt variation and understanding use of the piano's peculiar possibilities, to produce a fairly long composition. In the deepest sense, perhaps, *Islamey* lacks real variety, as it certainly is without any sense of struggle or drama.

It nevertheless holds the listener's attention without wearying it.[10]

If all but the greatest compositions of "the Five" are looked at for their similarities, it may be seen that both their virtues and their flaws are those of *Islamey*. Except for the master-pieces of Borodin and Mussorgsky, these brightly colored, melod-ically pungent, rhythmically vigorous, and harmonically seduc-tive Slavic-Oriental compositions substitute surface variation for the real development foreign to the possibilities of their very subject matter. They are fragmentary; and their sections are generally short-winded, gaining length only by repetition.

Only Borodin among the nationalists and Tchaikovsky among their Russian contemporaries succeeded occasionally in creating extended organic compositions in which musical ideas really de-velop, in which some of the drama that gave birth to the sonata and the symphony is worked out without patchiness, or at least without patchiness that too obviously shows. Borodin composed three symphonies (the third incomplete) and two string quartets that are structural marvels in view of the excessive difficulties with which the composer faced himself by using melodies of Slavic-Oriental cast which can be manipulated by sonata tech-niques only through great and concentrated effort, both because of their very definiteness and because of the harmonic meshes they generate. Borodin's symphonies and quartets are suavely euphonious. And yet, for all their superb facture they are some-what boring. In the first movement of the Second (B Minor) Symphony, for example, the opening melody, repeated again and again, at last becomes highly unwelcome, however justified its reappearances may look on paper.

No such reservations are possible about Borodin's tone pic-ture *In the Steppes of Central Asia* (1880) or his incomplete

10 It may be said that *Islamey* is "virtuoso" music that will not hold the attention through numerous hearings. If this is true—and general experience suggests that it is—the flaw is in the folklike themes themselves, recalcitrant to treatment other than decoration, a form of applied variety that has strict limitations in music as else-where. Certainly *Islamey* seems monotonous and shallow if contrasted with a fine movement from a classical sonata, with Schumann's *Carnaval*, or with Mussorgsky's *Pictures at an Exposition.*

opera *Prince Igor*. In these the fragmentariness persists. But in
the symphonic poem the form is produced by the material, nowhere required to do more than it is able; and in the opera
—actually a series of pseudo-historical tableaux, a very conventional old-fashioned set-number opera completely without musical development in any Wagnerian sense—the charmingly relevant Oriental coloring, the handsome use of choral effects, and
the sensitivity with which most of the music is related to the
fragmentary libretto combine to make the musical fragmentariness unobjectionable. Borodin has often been criticized for banalities in this opera, many of which have proved, on careful examination, to be additions by Rimsky-Korsakov or Glazunov,
who completed it. The very undistinguished overture, for example, is far from pure Borodin.

It is both fair and useful to criticize the Russian nationalist
composers adversely for their obvious failures to find or evolve
the proper formal means for sustaining their musical materials
—fair and useful, that is, when their attempts to adapt forms
extrinsic to their basic materials make failure both certain and
obvious. But such criticism is unfair and useless when it leads
to belaboring *Islamey* for not being a sonata movement, *Boris
Godunov* for its lack of Wagnerian symphonic development,
Pictures at an Exposition for not being a classical suite, or *The
Golden Cockerel* for not being profoundly serious. A general
rule of critical behavior covers all these cases. If a work of art
succeeds in being exactly what its creator intended it to be,
criticism of it for not being something else is gratuitous nonsense, though criticism of the creator's intentions may not be.

True folk music is of fundamental service in refreshing by
suggestion the idiom of composed music, but it is almost im-
possibly difficult to manipulate in strict forms—as difficult, in
fact (and for much the same reasons) as the German and other
high romanticists had found their individual, intense musical
ideas. Its basic self-completeness, shortness of musical line, and
sharp, quickly revealed color make it peculiarly useful in songs,
in regional and historical effects in opera, and in the building
of extra-musically inspired symphonic poems or piano pieces of

self-determining brief patterns. The later Russian composers who have written symphonies, concertos, string quartets, and sonatas to popular approval or critical acclaim or both have drawn away more or less completely from the use of actual folk tunes and rhythms and from overt imitation of them. Serge Rachmaninoff (1872-1943) and Prokofiev were intensely Russian, as is Shostakovich—but none of these men can be classified as a nationalist in a sense that Balakirev was. Even in the Soviet Union, the nineteenth-century type of folkloric nationalism appears to be left to second-raters like Aram Khachaturian.

In opera, contrarily, Glinka's suggestive employment of folk materials mated to stories from national legend, history, and literature signaled the dawn of a truly brilliant, prolonged outburst of highly colored masterpieces. If the Five had produced nothing more than Borodin's *Prince Igor,* Mussorgsky's *Boris Godunov* and *Khovantshchina,* and Rimsky-Korsakov's *The Golden Cockerel,* it would have justified completely its major tenets. The creation of scenic atmospheres; the reflection, underlining, and creation of character; the lifelike evocation of historical periods; and the musical pictorialization of the fantastic supernatural— none of these has been more happily carried out elsewhere.

The sadness of unfulfillment that pervades much of the musical story of the Russian nationalist composers is borne out by facts. Dargomizhsky's *The Stone Guest,* left unfinished, was "completed" by Cui and orchestrated by Rimsky-Korsakov. Borodin's *Prince Igor,* in turn, was completed by Rimsky-Korsakov and the mediocre Alexander Glazunov (1865-1936); his Third Symphony was "set in order and scored" by Glazunov. *Boris Godunov,* though existing complete as Mussorgsky arranged it for performance in 1871-72, is known only in a revision by Rimsky-Korsakov which prettifies it, and in "versions" tampered with by other composers. Mussorgsky completed a vocal score of four acts of *Khovantshchina,* but did not orchestrate them, and left the fifth act in rough sketch; the opera was "arranged" by Rimsky-Korsakov. *The Fair at Sorochinsk,* another opera left incomplete by Mussorgsky, has been "completed," "arranged," and "orchestrated" at least three times.

Elements in the lives of both Mussorgsky and Borodin can be blamed in part for their failure to complete so many works. But it may also be just to lay some blame for the incompleteness of their works on technical incompetence, if that phrase is nicely interpreted. Borodin and Mussorgsky were musical geniuses of a high order; the music of both deserves the enthusiasm any critic may wish to show toward it. But neither of them was either highly trained or successfully self-trained in the overcoming of small difficulties that a thousand of their inferiors could have solved without either thought or talent.

No such technical and formal uncertainties beset the earlier nationalists when composing songs. The cosmopolitan Tchaikovsky wrote beautiful and moving songs touched by Slavic gaiety and Slavic melancholy. But Mussorgsky's songs—such as the six called *Sunless* and the four *Songs and Dances of Death*—are often great dramas in small, evidencing the talent for musical character revelation which makes *Boris Godunov* a masterwork of musico-literary art whether or not it suffers from over-all formal flaws. Mussorgsky's emotional power and genius for pictorial evocation of the most convincing verisimilitude are also evident in his suite of piano pieces, *Pictures at an Exposition*.

Rimsky-Korsakov is a peculiar figure among the nationalists. He was prodigiously learned, an accomplished professional composer. His techniques, most notably as an orchestrator, were certain and unbounded. He believed that music was a brightly colored deception, and he devoted his chief energies to a series of pictorial folktale and fairy-tale operas that can be compared to splashily painted illustrations in the way they lack all depth. His ability to imitate the exteriors of other men's styles was astounding. He paid obvious tribute to Glinka in the operas *May Night* (1878) and *Snyegurochka* (*The Snow Maiden*, 1880-81); to Dargomizhsky in *Mozart and Salieri* (1897); to Borodin in *Sadko* (1894-6) and *Kitezh* (1903-4); and to Mussorgsky in *Pskovityanka* (*The Maid of Pskov*, written and rewritten between 1868 and 1893).

Rimsky-Korsakov's operas attempt no musical character creation as Mussorgsky and Borodin understood it. In his best fairy-tale opera, *The Golden Cockerel* (1906-7), this fact is unimportant,

at least on the first few hearings. The opera is crammed with
superficially very attractive melodies, gay rhythms, and harmonic
effects that pall only with familiarity. His symphonic poem *Scheherazade* and the scarcely less renowned *Capriccio Espagnol* and
Russian Easter Overture are mines of instrumental effects from
which other composers have been extracting ore ever since. On
the surface, much of Rimsky-Korsakov's music is as instantly winning as Tchaikovsky's. But Tchaikovsky was putting his entire being into what he composed, whereas Rimsky-Korsakov often
appears to have been creating a collection of dazzling effects. Suffering from the same inabilities of formal development as the other
nationalists, he did not—as at least Borodin and Mussorgsky did—
compensate for that lack by intense expressiveness. He was one of
the last men in Russia who should have tampered with the musical
works of his betters.

In addition to completing fifteen operas in thirty-nine years,
Rimsky-Korsakov also composed three symphonies, numerous fantasias, symphonic poems, overtures, a piano concerto, and chamber
music. Although he believed that he was composing in various
styles, he had only one style, one dictated by his taste—and all but
unparalleled talent—for a Glinka-like transparent instrumentation in primary colors. In his operas Rimsky-Korsakov simply
added the voice to that individual palette. His great supplies of
technical knowledge and his pervasive conviction that music is a
decorative deceit combined to lend almost everything he composed
a childlike thinness. He evoked a storybook Russia distant from
the bitter realities summoned forth by *Prince Igor, Boris Godunov,* and *Khovantshchina.* Harmonically he was a pedant and a
conservative. But he was also a nationalist, and therefore admitted
into his rule-governed harmonic world harmonies related to the
folk and folklike melodies he borrowed and invented. Historically
speaking, the result was that he, too, played some part in the final
overthrow of the classical-romantic interrelations among form,
scruple, manner, and euphony.

The styles, methods, and mannerisms of Mussorgsky and Rimsky-Korsakov, indeed, so polar to one another, did indeed jointly
affect the evolution of both Stravinsky and Prokofiev, though in

different ways than those later men were affected by Tchaikovsky. Mussorgsky disdained the accepted norms of musical procedure, partly because he never fully understood them, but more importantly because he was not going toward the musical destinations to which they led. His music is frequently modal—in passages that grew spontaneously from the modal uses in Russian and Oriental folk music. In opera, unknowingly, he was a descendant of Peri and Caccini, of the manifestoes of Gluck, and of some of Dargomizhsky's and Wagner's theories: he wanted operatic music not to be an end in itself, but to be one more means of projecting the text and of realizing the characters.

Mussorgsky did not care at all whether one chord "correctly" succeeded another in the convention derived from Western practice during the eighteenth century and later. If the sounds of two chords in succession appeared to him to assist in projecting the significance of the libretto or in drawing the lineaments of an individual or a crowd, he used them. He disregarded the theoretical proprieties of modulation, moving from one tonality to another without preparation as, and exactly when, he was impelled to by the meaning he was trying to convey or invoke. He was much more interested in what he considered to be dramatic truth than in smoothness or euphony. His orchestration was rough, powerful, and not always capable of producing exactly the results at which he directed it. He was not a polite or well-bred composer, but the vividness and physical force of his best music *as he wrote it* [11] are unique. That vividness and that force were the native qualities of his creative imagination, but they survive for us because of the means he evolved for representing and conveying them. To regard Mussorgsky as a fumbling illiterate is to misconceive the meaning of musical originality. That he was not more secure technically is sad only because it prevented him from achieving and completing more than he was able to compose in his forty-two years of life.

[11] Maurice Ravel's orchestration of *Pictures at an Exposition* is not a prettification of the original in the sense that Rimsky-Korsakov's version of *Boris Godunov* is. Ravel's instrumentation is an attempt to re-create Mussorgsky's suite in another medium, and it leaves the highly original harmonies intact. Even so sympathetic and comprehending a transcription should never, of course, be mistaken for real Mussorgsky.

Mussorgsky's contribution to musical evolution—quite a different reality from his value as a composer—was in operatic realism,
in the song as a faithful intensification of its text, in harmonic
freedom, and in still further disintegration of what remained of
the classic harmonic system.

Notable is the fact that no member of the Five composed a ballet, though Borodin, Mussorgsky, Balakirev, and Rimsky-Korsakov
all composed large amounts of of danceable music. The Dances of
the Persian Slaves from *Khovantshchina,* the Polovtsian Dances
from *Prince Igor,* the Hopak from *The Fair at Sorochinsk,* and a
dozen excerpts from Rimsky-Korsakov's operas—including the
familiar Dance of the Buffoons from *Snyegurochka*—entirely demonstrate not only their ability to write music for dancing, but also
the special applicability of their styles to the expressive, panto-
mimic, and evocative powers of ballet. But whatever of their music (notably *Scheherazade*) has played any part in the story of ballet has been adapted to that purpose later rather than being conceived for it.

Now, long after the fact, we can see that an important chapter
of the history of ballet and an equally important one in the evolution of twentieth-century music lay in the combining of Tchaikovsky's serious handling of ballet music and the harmonic freedom
and rhythmic variety of the Five. What was needed to bring about
that combination was an impresario of daring and fresh vision.
Opportunely, he appeared. He was Sergei Diaghilev (1872-1929),
whose brilliant theatrical sense, knowledge of advanced pictorial
art, and hospitality to the latest manifestations in music were to
affect deeply the history of twentieth-century music. Diaghilev
found the composer able to combine Tchaikovsky's attitudes toward ballet with the musical idiom of the Five—and particularly
of Rimsky-Korsakov and Mussorgsky—and to go on from that con-
fluence to become the single most influential composer after Wagner and Debussy. That composer was Igor Stravinsky.

Nineteen

THE END OF ROMANTICISM AND AFTER · DEBUSSY
THE BREAKDOWN OF CLASSIC-ROMANTIC HARMONY
EXOTIC SCALES · ANTI-ROMANTICISM · SATIE
TWENTIETH-CENTURY CLASSICISM · RAVEL

Despite the works of Berlioz, Debussy, and Ravel—to name only three French composers out of many—an idea stubbornly persists that France has been a comparatively unmusical nation since the days of Rameau. Whatever part of this misjudgment is not merely a holdover from the musically pro-German second half of the nineteenth century has derived from the smooth conventionality of most French nineteenth-century music before and after Berlioz. Additionally, the nineteenth century having for far too long been foremost in the minds of music-lovers, the fact that many of the musical luminaries of Paris during that century were foreigners— Chopin, Liszt, Rossini, Meyerbeer, and Offenbach are examples— has added to the apparent plausibility of the belief in France's musical decadence. The talented, agile, and musically learned Camille Saint-Saëns, the soberly classic-romantic Gabriel Fauré, and the stately, somewhat pedantic Vincent d'Indy, producing pleasant, delightful, even enduringly beautiful music part of the time, failed to make the native French musical scene very lively. The first intensely and disturbingly original composer in France after Berlioz (Franck was a Belgian) was Claude Debussy.

Others in addition to Chopin, Liszt, Berlioz, and Franck had imported techniques of musical romanticism to conservatory-dominated Paris; others, too, had evolved new elements of romanticism on the spot. But the first large and significant French attempt to relate music to literature and the other arts, so characteristic a desire of German romanticism, occurred when the central technical means of nineteenth-century musical romanticism had begun to wear thin elsewhere. And so it happened that the oblique mentality and peculiar imagination of Debussy evolved music related to symbolism in literature and impressionism in painting. Except in technique, Debussy was a romantic; for most of his creative life he was a technical post-romantic composing the last bright notes of romanticism. Only very early and very late in his life did he compose notable music that made no use of verbal text or poetic-plastic title: his String Quartet (1893) and the three chamber sonatas of the final three years of his life. Between these poles in time lay many compositions of exquisite facture, unquestionable technical rightness, and revolutionary originality—compositions entirely able to engage the mind without reference to their flowery and suggestive titles. Nonetheless, this music is related with remarkable appositeness to the names by which Debussy identified it.

Debussy's art, beginning in feeble echoes of Saint-Saëns and of the ardent lyricism of Gounod and Massenet, drove constantly toward concision, self-sufficiency of form, and an emotional reticence directly contrasting to the expansiveness and assertiveness of high, and particularly German-Austrian, romanticism. He found comparatively small use for classical forms (the sonata included), attacking instead the central romantic task of unifying form and material freshly in each given instance.[1] Falling under the spell of Wagner after visiting Bayreuth in 1888, Debussy became acquainted with his own different future the very next year, when he came to know Mussorgsky's *Boris Godunov* and to hear southeast Asian music at the Paris Exposition Universelle.

Within a few years Debussy had composed the *Prélude à*

---

[1] This was, of course, the central romantic task even when the form used was theoretically pre-existent: romantic material made the task inescapable under any condition.

L'Après-midi d'un faune, the String Quartet, and the three unexampled *Nocturnes (Nuages; Fêtes; Sirènes)* for orchestra. As early as 1880 he had begun setting Paul Verlaine to music, and shortly he was using texts by Paul Bourget, Théodore de Bainville, Alfred de Musset, Stéphane Mallarmé, and Pierre Louÿs. His music for the solo piano, beginning with innocuous salon pieces, by 1904 included the three *Estampes (Pagodes; Soirée dans Grenade; Jardins sous la pluie),* in which his mature style is unmistakable. Between 1892 and 1905 he completed, besides much else, his largest masterworks, the opera *Pelléas et Mélisande* and the "three symphonic sketches" (really a tripartite symphonic poem), *La Mer.* He was to add to the list of his compositions in almost every genre, but it was with these large central works that he influenced the entire course of Western music.

Debussy was interested by shadowy and fine-spun emotions, by the "iridescence of decay," by powerful, but subdued, eroticism—the very aspects of life available to the symbolists. He was also moved by the shifting, momentarily fixed, evanescing play of light and tint which the impressionists were painting. Whatever was compelling, likely to depart, and (at least on the surface) charming, all that seemed aristocratic and rare, impelled him to composition. Reflecting the sources of his literary and plastic inspiration in the structure and coloration of his music, he evolved and perfected a stylish technique that has remained unique (for the easy belief that Ravel imitated it is false). He dissolved rhythm and remade it in smooth complexity. He debilitated harmonic logic without making use of astringent dissonance. He mixed instrumental colors much as Monet and Seurat mixed pigments and as Mallarmé and Rimbaud mixed words. Debussy was seldom awkward and never excessive. He used the whole-tone scale, but followed its implications only as far as they could be fitted into solid structures retaining a sense of tonal "home"—and then dropped them, or mixed whole-tone passages with his own version of diatonic and chromatic harmony.

In Maeterlinck's symbolic drama *Pelléas et Mélisande* the lovely heroine, first encountered lost in a forest, does not know whence she came, why she lives, or why she must die. The members of the exalted family of Golaud (whom she marries) and Pelléas (whom she loves) inhabit a gloomy castle above caves at the edge of the sea. As closely as such an impossibility can be approximated, Debussy's score for this misty text simply retells it in music. Nothing in the score is definite or clear, but everything in it is relevant. There are no arias, no set pieces of any sort. There are no crowds,[2] no triumphal scenes, no dances—none of the things that made grand opera grand. All flows, mounts, continues, subsides. Debussy believed that he was composing an anti-Wagnerian opera. But in disposing of the sectional construction of *opera seria* and most grand opera; in reducing what is sung to a kind of continuous heightened recitative; and in performing on a continuous web of interrelated drama and music, *Pelléas* is perhaps the most Wagnerian opera composed after *Parsifal*. Yet Debussy was correct: *Pelléas* is anti-Wagnerian. Its entire ethos and atmosphere are subdued, non-imperial, un-Teutonic, Gallic. It triumphs by restraint and half-statement. When Wagner would have repeated and enlarged, Debussy blurred and hinted; where Wagner would have gathered a towering climax, Debussy shifted a color from one end of the gamut to the other.

Even at his most massive and voluminous, as in *La Mer*, Debussy denies the nineteenth century and its tendency toward highly personal direct communication, its prolonged attempts to storm Parnassus with shattering masses of sound. When his brasses cry out, they cry briefly just before sinking back into the heaving, murmurous orchestra. In this seascape there are no people (just as, in reality, there is no water), not even Debussy himself. No attempt whatever is made at communicating non-musical, ethical, moral, religious, or other ideas from composer through performer to listener. *La Mer* is music for its musical sake, title and subtitles notwithstanding.

Even more impersonal—so reticent, indeed, that romantically minded listeners often mistakenly find them meaningless—are the Sonata for cello and piano (1915), the Sonata for flute, viola, and harp (1915), and the final Sonata for piano and violin (1916-17).

---

[2] Significantly, the only true supernumeraries in the opera—three blind beggars—are seen only once, and that once are asleep.

These are as French as Couperin *le grand,* and of a refinement almost dandyish. The subtly sensual composer of *L'Après-midi,* the *Préludes* and six *Images* for piano, and many of the songs has here shed the last remnant of his own romanticism. These sonatas are pure abstract constructions of patterned sound. They show as little trace of either non-musical intention or extra-musical support as a Haydn symphony. In the second decade of this century they indicated, though perhaps not for the first time, the change of musical weather which was later to be called neo-classicism. As Edward Lockspeiser said (Preface to the third edition of his *Debussy,* 1952), they are the "creations of a hedonist who had become a stoic." Journeying from his own image of romanticism to a new classicism, Debussy paralleled the artistic career of Berlioz. But Berlioz had lived too early to stem the swelling tides to which he himself had given great impulse, whereas Debussy matured at a moment strategic for the emergence of a new classicism.

Debussy's influence on rhythm, which he helped to re-subtilize and make nervously responsive, and on harmony, which he conducted ever farther from classical-romantic norms, was enormous. Even more original was his way of composing for the piano. He found the means to make the percussive giant murmur and glide, left it speaking mistily and with clangor. He exploited chords and successions of tones in which struck tones emphasized the overtones of others previously sounded. He made the piano evoke and whisper, suggest and dance. On that instrument, as on the orchestra and the human voice, he imposed his enigmas, his personality and aesthetic meaning, investing it with impressionist-symbolist magic. In this the immediate future was not with him: the last decade of his life and the more than three decades since his death have heard the piano sounding as percussively as possible at the bidding of later composers.

Debussy almost never made the foredoomed attempt to transfer visible, audible, tactile reality into musical terms. He used his isolated art to evoke a universe of vision, sometimes nearly of hallucination, a universe that existed nowhere before he imagined it. By unexpected, instantly self-justifying modulations, by swift, quiet, sudden irruptions of tones, he composed a world.

How did Debussy mold an art so striking in its originality, once it had emerged complete? By rhythmic, harmonic, and melodic idiosyncrasies that he seems to have developed because he knew that music could not sound as he needed it to sound if he went on with the dynamic, dramatic classical romanticism of Beethoven or the chromatically rich, rhythmically sluggish romanticism of the nineteenth century, especially the Austrian nineteenth century.

Debussy treated both consonant and dissonant chords as though they were single tones. Constantly present in his music are the dissonances that result when seconds, fourths, sixths, and sevenths are added to triads, and these are most often left unresolved. But they are not so characteristic a part of the Debussyan technique as is the way he placed them. For Debussy ignored, whenever he chose, the germinal tenet of harmony as it had been comprehended for two centuries: that chords have normal functions, are mostly the result of what has preceded them and mostly move on by logical resolution to other normal chords. He placed both consonant and dissonant chords in series with no regard to their harmonic functions, quite baldly because he liked the way the series sounded.

Parallel motion—successions of chords differing from one another only in pitch, and therefore containing the same intervals in the same relative positions—was considered improper by classical harmonists. In the case of parallel fifths it was flatly forbidden. But Debussy used parallel motion freely, not only for thirds, fourths, and ninths (which, under urgent circumstances, classical purists might have approved in moderation), but also for fifths and octaves. As early as 1888, setting poems by Verlaine, he began *"C'est l'extase"* with "side-slipping" or "gliding" parallel ninth chords.

In one of the most popular of Debussy's piano pieces, *"La cathédrale engloutie,"* he suggested the undersea tolling of cathedral bells by an unclassical (in one sense, totally un-harmonic) series of parallel octaves. Handling chords so, as though they were complex single tones, Debussy mixed his characteristic colors. More of them reside in the whole-tone scale. In such a *prélude* as *"Voiles,"* an extreme example, the misty, unsettled nature of the music derives almost wholly from the whole-tone progressions, totally unclassical. Nor was Debussy afraid of that *"diabolus in musica,"* the tritone (augmented fourth), which earlier composers had labored to avoid. His music is starred with tritones: such combinations as F-B, A-D♯, and G♭-C. Where classical harmony had sanctioned this interval only as one component of a more complex chord, Debussy delighted in its unfamiliar effect for and by itself, feeling no compulsion to resolve it, denying by implication that logic which required resolution. Similarly, he often disregarded the "leading-tone" principle: the upward approach to the tonic of a scale by a half-tone step. In strict usage of the whole-tone scale, of course, no half-tone was present anywhere, but even when Debussy was not moving entirely by whole-tone steps he saw nothing wrong, when closing a phrase, section, or composition, in having his melodic lines approach their tonics by other than half-tone intervals.

Another color-giving chemical applied to Debussy's strongly individual palette was the employment of modal passages not native to any diatonic major or minor scale (and not derived from the whole-tone "system")—and therefore still further disrupting and rendering impossible the logical implications of both classical and romantic harmony. He came to place chordal and tonal tints much as Monet and Seurat placed primary colors side by side, using unprepared and inexplicable irruptions for contrast and integral decoration. His harmony, if so it may be called, was that of a sensualist more interested in—and more certain of—effect than in physico-acoustical logic. His methods are dangerous in that they depend on an extremely sensitive composing ear, on "logics" of a highly idiosyncratic sort. No one but Debussy has ever employed them with complete success, for the seemingly similar art of Maurice Ravel differs from Debussy's results both spiritually and technically.

In developing the pattern of a composition, Debussy very often avoided long phrases and dramatic conflict, finding more germane to his conceptions a type of mosaic formed out of fragments of divergent sizes and shapes. Again his inner ear was triumphant, but he did not develop means that would serve other composers well. In his melodies too, he eschewed clear, sharp profiles delimiting onward movement, creating instead a new sort of melody that moved up and down in zigzags, with apparent willfulness and its own finally convincing and unmistakable logic. Melody in most of the compositions of Debussy's maturity is in fact no longer a separable element any more than is rhythm, harmony, or counterpoint. Melody has been assumed into fabric until it is no longer, in the classical or romantic sense, melody at all. Better it might be said that everything has been merged in melody, melody subtilized, refined, broadened, and softened. Seldom has a composer amalgamated the musical elements in this degree, mixed them until they can scarcely be isolated.

Debussy's musical cosmos was doomed except as it endures in the music by which he created and evoked it, for it depended entirely upon him. It was intensely romantic in every meaning but that of technique, a belated summation in musical atmosphere of the romantic world of Baudelaire, Verlaine, Rimbaud, and Maeterlinck. And by 1900 romanticism was expiring, even in Paris. Neither Satie nor Ravel was, in that sense, romantic at all except on rare occasion.

A highly accomplished jester, Erik Satie helped both to orient the very late Debussy toward a sparseness related to new views of classicism and to laugh out of countenance among younger French composers the more sensuous and idealistic aspects of musico-pictorial-literary romanticism. He kept his harmonies and textures unclothed to the point of nakedness. He deliberately exploited vulgarities of music-hall brashness. He used composition titles and musical directions that were most often nonsensical or utterly cryptic. Not a composer of great strength, he nonetheless came justly to be regarded as a *petit maître* because he helped to clear the air and reduce somewhat the too-indoor temperature in which Debussy had chosen to live. If, as Gerald Abraham has said, Debussy's music is concerned "with sensation instead of emotion (and hence often with the sensation of pure sound for its own sake)," Satie's is devoid of emotion altogether and is concerned with the wittiest arrangements of pure sound.

Satie was a full anti-romantic, being opposed by the scope of his musical techniques to the subjective expansiveness of late German-Austrian romanticism and by temperament to the technically advanced but characteristically impressionist-symbolist romanticism of Debussy's middle (and longest) period. By such of his titles (having nothing whatever to do with the music they head) as *Embryons desséchés, Heures séculaires et instantanées,* and *Trois Pièces en forme de poire*—and whatever the nature and value of the music—Satie laughed publicly and successfully at Debussy's poetic nomenclature. More important for the future, he laughed at all combinings of music with literature and painting. In his ballets *Socrate* and *Relâche* and in the wistfully antique *Gnossiennes* and *Gymnopédies,* with the merest wash of ambiguous and silvery emotion, he adumbrated the aristocratic and dandified classicism, the sheer delight in craftsmanship, that were to characterize much of the music of Ravel and younger Frenchmen. This was dandyism mixed with music-hall echoes and snatches of folk song. It was much else, but even in its lack of attempted personal communication it was not a return to the eighteenth century. What was clearest about it was that it had bade a willing farewell to the nineteenth and to all of Debussy except his unfaltering taste and some of his newly wrought technical devices.

Ravel began much like Debussy, in the sentimental train of Gounod and Massenet. But they had known nothing of his sardonic heartlessness, his sheer delight in highly varied sonority as an aim of composition divorced as much as is humanly possible from the composer's non-musical beliefs and emotions. Although the music of the mature Ravel has been called *pointilliste* because of its use of tiny areas of color, its structural outlines suggest the draftsman more than the colorist. He was a master of the modern orchestra, a composer of songs of persuasive charm and peculiar expressiveness, a composer for the piano able to proceed from the point at which Debussy had desisted, a man capable of following the implications of purely musical logic to a cold orgiastic frenzy. Scarcely one of Ravel's admirers has failed to sense that even his best-made music lacks

something with which it might have been great, but they are
surely correct in protesting that to condemn him to mediocrity
is to speak foolishly—and probably to confuse non-musical with
musical weight. He had not the adult Debussy's implacable sense
of proportion, but the composer of *L'Heure espagnole, L'Enfant
et les sortilèges, Miroirs, Le Tombeau de Couperin,* and *Gaspard
de la nuit,* of the best songs, and of the chamber pieces was not
an imitator or an empty vessel. He repays the most careful listening.

Like Debussy, Ravel made telling use of parallel chords in
series, notably sevenths, with which Debussy had concerned his
texture but little. He mostly avoided the whole-tone scale and
its chords, too misty and formless for the sharper outlines he
desired. In the *Sonatine* for piano, the Piano Trio, the String
Quartet, two piano concertos, and some other music, he adapted
classical forms to his own very different purposes, not scrupling
to season them with borrowings from American jazz. He wrote,
in such a piece as *"Scarbo"* from *Gaspard de la nuit,* virtuoso
piano music that recognized procedures in Fauré and Debussy
as ways of proceeding with Liszt's intentions. He composed much
music about the world of children, but not for them—in *Ma
Mère l'Oye* of a sophisticated adult's vision of fairyland, in
L'Enfant et les sortilèges (to a libretto by Colette) playfully,
but sometimes brutally, sardonic.

In his music Ravel became what Debussy—thirteen years his
senior, and as a composer much more warmly sensuous—had
not been: a twentieth-century man, abraded by twentieth-century
frictions, the framer of entirely post-romantic sensations and structures. Greatly admiring the *clavecinistes,* notably Couperin and
Rameau, he brought something of their refinement into his own
fully modern terminology, writing (as in *Le Tombeau de Couperin*) music of which past manners and meanings may be said to
be the subject rather than the significance. And in *Daphnis et
Chloë,* a ballet composed for Diaghilev, while not matching the
tonal violence of *Le Sacre du Printemps,* he proved that his techniques could be applied with complete success to the typical pur-

pose of the actor, that of making emotions and meanings foreign to his own nature the very stuff of a convincing performance.

With both Debussy and Ravel something peculiarly modern had occurred in the relations between melody and harmony. Harmony, freeing itself of rules and becoming an element of musical texture which required more and more of the listener's attention if he was to understand the composers' intentions, had begun to lose its individual importance. Having evolved originally as the logic of the relationships among simultaneous and successive sounds, having, that is to say, come out of counterpoint as a servant of melody, it had gradually asserted its own autonomy. But romantic chromaticism was, in this connection, self-defeating, for as composers began to treat chords and their interconnections with complete freedom, chromaticism lost its original significance: it could no longer be looked upon or heard as a "coloring" of predominantly diatonic music when diatonicism itself no longer prevailed.

This appears to be a paradox: that harmonic liberty again reduced harmony to the status of servant to melody. But it is no paradox. For when composers had come to treat the most complex chords as though they were single tones—and had gone on to write what might be called chord-melodies, melodies of which the constituent integers were groups of simultaneous tones, harmony could be nothing more than a method of widening or "thickening" melody. When chords (both those academically considered "consonant" and those frowned upon as "dissonant") were being moved *en bloc* from pitch to pitch, they were being treated melodically. Debussy and Ravel were not the initiators of this peculiarly twentieth-century manner of creating texture, but they first brought it to fruition. In the mature compositions of both men melody had taken harmony (and what remained of counterpoint) back into itself. At the very moment when an understandably bewildered wide public began to feel that melody was wasting away, it was reasserting its primacy among musical means. This is easier to hear in Debussy and Ravel, who had not discarded the repetition of melodic sections and the use of melodic series, than it is in the music of the polytonalists, atonalists, and twelve-tone composers— who in their search for great brevity have generally avoided the

smallest repetition. But it is still true that there can be no music
without melody; it is the special characteristic of contemporary
music that melody rules all, even the characteristic employment
of instrumental and vocal colors, the intense complications of
rhythm, and the other devices that also denote it.

Following (when it did not accompany) the music of Debussy,
Ravel, and Satie went the nose-thumbing, often deliberately vulgar
music of the *"Six,"* most notably that of Francis Poulenc and Darius Milhaud. Under the pyrotechnic cover of Jean Cocteau's wit,
Paris heard, during the 1920's and later, the small explosions of
a sort of music which delighted in transmuting banalities into destructive humor, sentimalities into oblique exegesis. The Parisian
modernists adapted from the more emotional and intellectually
violent modernisms of Central Europe, Germany, and Russia only
those spiritual attitudes and technical ways which could best serve
them in their own anti-romantic quests. Polyrhythm, polytonality,
exploitation of jagged rhythms, even atonality in measured portion tickled rather than seared the ears of their French and out-
land audiences. Seldom attempting to erect the largest structures
or convey their own personal or sexual feelings, their music
sounded trivial to ears bewitched by Wagner—and even by Debussy—but it is useless to proclaim that the composers were out of
joint or that music must be overtly romantic to be music at all.
Milhaud, Auric, Poulenc—these are men not at all frightened by
the seeming truth of the charge that they are not great poets or
likely to become culture-heroes in any Beethovian sense. They
were—and are—interested in music as music, and are entirely and
sensibly willing to leave poetry to poets and heroism to heroes.
It would scarcely be absurd to say that the "meaning" of French
music from the 1880's to this hour (aside from the welcome reassertion of entertainment as a good) is the divesting of non-musical
accretions from music, the reiteration of the incontrovertible
statement that what music can do best is what music alone can do
at all.

Twenty

THE END OF CLASSIC-ROMANTIC HARMONY

STRAVINSKY · POLYTONALITY · NEO-CLASSICISM

Igor Stravinsky, the most influential inheritor from the musical legacies of late nineteenth-century Russian music, began as a close disciple and imitator of Rimsky-Korsakov. Even the earliest of his played music is extremely clever and well made, but nothing about it suggests a revolutionary experimenter or a great composer. Only when Stravinsky began to compose for Diaghilev's seasons of ballet in Western Europe did he start along roads of his own discovery. The first Diaghilev-Stravinsky ballet was *The Firebird* (1910); in atmosphere and technique most of it strikingly resembles pages from Rimsky-Korsakov's operas. In it, however, lies the "Dance of Katshchei." Katshchei is a demon out of Russian mythology. His dance is accompanied by jagged rhythms, explosive bursts of dissonant sound, a brutality that was new in music. This music is closer to the witches' sabbath at the close of Mussorgsky's *A Night on Bald Mountain,* nearer to the harmonic novelties of Dargomizhsky and Mussorgsky altogether than it is to the idiom of Rimsky-Korsakov's fairy tales.

The Firebird was succeeded by *Petrouchka,* a landmark in the music of the first half of the twentieth century. As in *The Firebird,* the libretto deals with purely Russian matter, but with an important difference: the three central characters of *Petrouchka* are not mortals and supernatural beings, but marionettes that come to temporary life to act out an abrupt tale of faithlessness and tragic jealousy. Stravinsky's musical clothing for this melodrama (1910-11) is remarkable for the degree to which it reflects the semi-human nature of these animated toys, in its ways of reducing the world to their spiritual, mental, and emotional dimensions without diminishing its own suggestiveness and power to engage the listener. The score is naturally fragmentary if listened to or looked at apart from the choreography, but even then it is clear that it has peculiar psychological verity and that its rhythm and its metrical constitution are both something new. *Petrouchka* is a last farewell to the harmonic, melodic, and rhythmic manners of the nineteenth century, even the Russian nineteenth century. Into it, further, Stravinsky has introduced rhythmic and harmonic manners without which the later music of the twentieth century would have been something other than what it is.

In *Petrouchka* Stravinsky gave to shifting meter and rhythm—to definite, noticeable, but constantly altering beat—an importance that it had never before been allotted in the composition of either Russian or Western music. He elevated rhythm as a compositional element to a position as central in the achieving of a composer's conscious purposes, as significant to his listeners and disciples, as the places long held by melody, harmony, and counterpoint. To some extent, of course, characters in ballet had always been revealed to rhythms intended to be characteristic of them; but in *Petrouchka* the three central characters are not so much accompanied as created by the rhythmic profiles of the music associated with them. In themselves the rhythms of *Petrouchka* presuppose and prefigure choreography.

The Firebird had been Russian nationalist music marked by only enough new elements to suggest that its year was 1910, not 1890. With a difference, *Petrouchka* is a further refinement of that nationalism. Stravinsky was reducing to skeletonic essentials the folk-derived melodic contours and consequent harmonies and rhythms that had distinguished the scores of Balakirev, Borodin, Mussorgsky, and Rimsky-Korsakov from all other composed music of the period. So reducing them, Stravinsky propelled himself along a one-way road toward a new musical idiom in which force-ful, constantly shifting rhythmic beats would be a major tool of musical construction.

One of the passages in *Petrouchka* which evoked most comment from its early critics was this:

About this passage the historically significant fact is that it is composed in two simultaneous tonalities or keys: C major and F♯ major. The four introductory notes in the right-hand part are CEGC (CEG, the tonic triad of C major, with the root [C] doubled at the top); the four simultaneous notes in the left-hand part are A♯-C♯-F♯-A♯ (F♯-A♯-C♯, the tonic triad of F♯ major, inverted to A♯-C♯-F♯, again with the root tone of the chord [A♯] doubled at the top). In the eleventh measure of the example, note that while the left-hand notes remain unaltered, the notes played by the right hand, still in C major, make up the triad built up from its dominant, G (GBD, once more with the root doubled at the top). By some views of analysis, these notes may be looked at as *appoggiature,* especially when, in the measures immediately succeeding, Stravinsky spreads all the notes out like this:

Nevertheless, as introduced and worked from, this is an example of bitonality, of music couched in two keys at the same time. This post-harmonic device was to become of great utility to Stravinsky himself, as well as to many other twentieth-century composers, notably Milhaud. When, at times, more than two keys came to be used together, the practice became known as polytonality, which, by extension, is now used to cover bitonal usage as well. Whatever its enduring value *per se* [1]—*i.e.,* as distinct from its occa-

1 Although polytonality appears not to have been the most important ruling texture of any compositions of first quality, it is always too early to know what use a great composer may make of any musical method or device.

sional use for special effects—polytonality became one possible component of all specifically dissonant modern harmonic texture.

The ear is capable of hearing several tones at once, the mind of paying attention to them—else we should be unable to apprehend chords. The listening mind can follow two or more melodies at once, or polyphony would be a meaningless jumble. So the first supporters of polytonality asked: why not two, three, four—more—tonalities at once? And the answer was epithets: "Anarchy! Impossibility! Ugliness!" But *Petrouchka* and music far more extensively polytonal became popular stage and concert fare nonetheless. The ears of more hospitable and better-trained generations have found Stravinsky's score at first exciting and then acceptable. To sophisticated ears, indeed, *Petrouchka* now contains no measure that for any harmonic reason sounds incorrect, ugly, or anything but justified in its place. It has come to seem little more "advanced" than *Boris Godunov*.

In 1913, two years after *Petrouchka*, the Diaghilev-Stravinsky collaboration culminated in a ballet whose score stirred up such tempests of commentary as remain unparalleled in musical anecdotage, a score that to those who first accepted it as a surpassing masterpiece still tends to be the central fact of Stravinsky's career —and therefore of an entire hemisphere of twentieth-century music. This was *Le Sacre du Printemps* (*The Rite of Spring*). Unlike the music of *Petrouchka,* which was still sufficiently respectful of romantic-classical concepts of tonality so that its printed score shows several temporary key signatures, that of *Le Sacre du Printemps* dispenses with signature altogether. For in it tonality has become an element that may be taken advantage of here and disregarded or suspended there. The ballet employs a huge orchestra (see page 166), and goes forward from the jagged rhythms of the "Dance of Katshchei" to a rhythmic insistence that has never been equaled for nervous, kinetic force. The final seven measures of the full orchestral score of *Le Sacre du Printemps* are given on pages 290-291.

Here thirty staves are required. The constant changes in time signature (5/16, 3/16, 5/16, 3/16, 4/16, 3/16) are typical of many

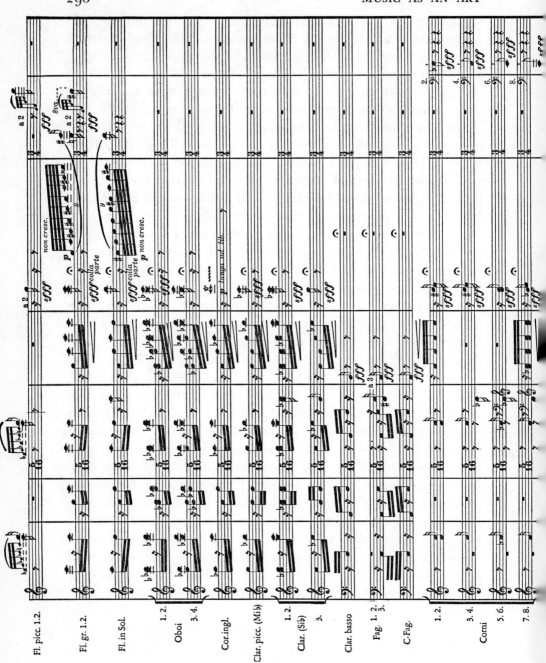

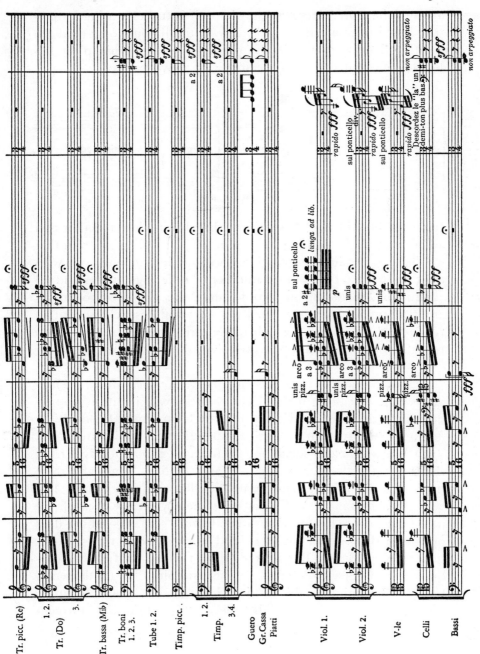

areas of the score.² Here, as elsewhere, it is full of searing, unprepared, and unresolved discords. Try, with all your force (and the assisting fingers of two friends), putting down on a piano the following chord (first beat of measure 5 of above example):

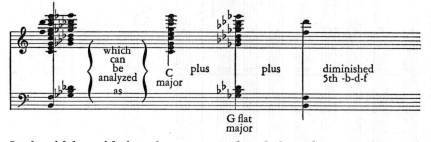

It should be said that these notes, played thus close together and all in one timbre on the piano, sound an effect different from that which they produce as played by various instruments and with the tones spread out. But no number of differing timbres and no amount of "spreading-out" could make this chord consonant in any traditional sense. It is only one of hundreds as dissonant in *Le Sacre du Printemps,* which temporarily marked the complete rejection of the musical textures evolved during the two preceding centuries.

Although many of those who first heard *Le Sacre du Printemps* attacked it by calling it the death of melody, it is music—and by definition therefore inevitably in part compacted of melody. A dozen or twenty entirely distinct melodies can be isolated from this score; part of its shocking effectiveness, in fact, derives from the contrast between the simple, mostly diatonic tunes and their intricate harmonic, instrumental, and rhythmic investiture. The startling simultaneities of tones are somehow greatly appropriate to the pagan pre-history that is the ballet's scenario—which does not mean that similar music existed in pre-historic times, which it certainly did not. But it is rhythm, rhythm set free from sequence and repetition of the same groupings of fundamental beats, which animates this music, which gives it savage, hypnotic power. At its most powerful, indeed, this music acts, through

² Mussorgsky had similarly alternated 5/4—that favorite Russian rhythm—and 6/4 time in the "Promenade" that occurs several times in *Pictures at an Exposition.*

rhythm, directly on the auditors' nervous centers while many of its other elements—melody, harmonic texture, tone-color, variation in tempo and volume—affect those reacting centers to which all composed music later than Gregorian Chant has directed itself.

Whether *Le Sacre du Printemps* really lifted the lid of a musical Pandora's box or not, as its enemies have asserted, it appeared to have done so to all musical conservatives who lived through the two decades following its first performance in 1913. Experiment, become habitual and self-conscious, led to vitality, but it also led —especially during the 1920's—to considerable vacuous nonsense from the studios of the untalented. For a time it seemed that all rules, beneficial or constricting, and all points of reference had been lost or thrown away. As though aghast at the anarchy of which he was being accused, Stravinsky himself pulled back, starting almost at once to be less and less "modern" in the terms of *Le Sacre du Printemps* and moving toward the special revaluation of musical methods and aims which has come to be called neo-classicism, a poor term and misleading label.

Meanwhile, however, *The Firebird, Petrouchka,* and *Le Sacre du Printemps* continued to be very much heard, the first two as both concert suites and as ballets, the last only in concert. More and more ears grew adjusted to the purposeful revolution they made; today thousands of music-lovers can listen with pleasure to Bach's *B Minor Mass,* Beethoven's Ninth Symphony, Wagner's *Tristan und Isolde,* and *Le Sacre du Printemps* without sensing that a deep rift yawns between Stravinsky and any other greatly talented composer of unlimited technical prowess. No listener in all his senses listens to the *B Minor Mass* when his state of mind and attention calls for a Mozart piano concerto, Bizet's *Carmen,* or Virgil Thomson's *Four Saints in Three Acts;* there is no sane reason for trying to obtain from *Le Sacre du Printemps* a sense of Christian resignation (it is a pagan program-piece) or quiet entertainment (it is in part very loud), or, indeed, anything but what it pre-eminently supplies and evokes: deep excitement, the suggestion close at hand of primeval mystery and blood-violence. In forty years, however, it has established itself in the canon of musical creations, and to refuse at this date to listen to it with an open mind and very unprejudiced ears is to fall victim to a peculiar trick of history.

The widely held belief that great composers suffer personally from being misunderstood because they live and create ahead of their times is not completely validated by a study of music's history. But it represents a measure of truth: any important new artistic creation, particularly in modern times, is different in several of many possible aspects from everything that has been created before. Especially was this true during the second half of the nineteenth century, when—in music as in painting and other arts—the breakdown of academic legislation became very rapid. Listeners scarcely had opportunities to begin catching up with one new aspect of musical texture before two or three much newer ones had begun assaulting their ears and minds. The gap between the harmonic techniques used by the most advanced composers, for example, and those familiar to (and therefore accepted by) the great body of listeners to music began to widen. By 1913, the year of Stravinsky's *Le Sacre du Printemps,* it had become dangerously wide: to many implicated individuals there seemed to exist a real danger that it was already too wide to be bridged—or to be bridged in time.

The situation that then resulted, comical when its tragic possibilities were not too patent, was perilous to the continuing vitality of the ancient art of music. Composing scores that stirred immediate, enthusiastic responses in the minds of a highly trained small group of their admirers, men like Stravinsky learned that their most advanced music struck the great public (only recently converted to Richard Strauss's tone poems) as meaningless, ugly, and infuriating. This could have signaled the stultification of the change that is the very ongoing vitality of any organism. What actually happened? *Le Sacre du Printemps* (1913) and *Les Noces* (*The Wedding,* 1914-17) proved to be a forward territory beyond which Stravinsky's own personal sort of rhythmically dominated, dissonant, harmonically free music was not to advance. Stravinsky himself faced toward other regions; his disciples and imitators began to search out diverging paths. And gradually the chasm between the Straussians of 1913 and the small advance guard began to be filled in by the detritus of time itself. Very slowly, and with some painful puffing, the giant steps that Stravinsky had taken from 1910 to 1913—from *The Firebird* to *Petrouchka* to *Le Sacre du Printemps*—were accomplished by the Western world's audiences for serious music.

But the comical-tragical results of Stravinsky's career as the foremost composer of his era had not ended when the music of his three big ballets had been imbedded firmly in the "standard repertoire." For by that time he himself had left them far behind. He had begun to react against their traces of romantic emotion, their increasing expansiveness, and their exploitation of extra-musical material. *Les Noces,* which achieved its definitive form as late as 1923, when Diaghilev staged it, was one of the first large movements away from *Le Sacre du Printemps*. Although it was described as "Russian choreographic scenes in four tableaux, with song and music," it was mechanistic in its stylistic abstractness, another evidence of twentieth-century music's determination to be unliterary, non-philosophic, unpictorial—inhuman, if necessary.

Increasingly involved in the elaboration of pure music built out of the essential elements of melody, chordal relations or lack of relations, and rhythmic pattern, Stravinsky went through a period of using the styles of earlier composers as subject matter. In the "ballet with songs" *Pulcinella* (1919) what the music was "about" was really the compositions of Pergolesi, from which much of it was derived. In *Oedipus Rex* (1926-27), an opera-oratorio anatomized the musical personality of Handel. *Le Baiser de la Fée* (1928) dealt with aspects of the sound-world of Tchaikovsky. Although adverse critics suggested that Stravinsky borrowed the styles—and even the melodies—of other composers because he had no style and little melody of his own, the truth was that he was merely asserting sharply that the most important value of the art of composition lies in what is done with basic materials rather than in the provenance and exact nature of the materials themselves. This stoic impersonality alienated larger audiences almost as certainly as had the kinetic and discordant violence of *Le Sacre du Printemps*. To listeners still under the influence of nineteenth-century romantic communication, this "neo-classical" abstraction seemed devoid of the very warmths and pleasures that characterize music.

Yet Stravinsky continued to please the *avant-garde,* that often derided but nevertheless extremely powerful group of highly attentive and trained intellectuals which often seems either to be closely allied to the evolving spirit of the age or to be producing that spirit. He remained "the style" in world capitals, not with the mass audience of symphony orchestras and opera houses, but with the critics and performers who are covertly looked up to even by many "average" music-lovers who pretend to deride them. His music, which he continued to send forth with something like abundance, would not down. It was—and is—*par excellence,* music that must be listened to with intense attention again and again. Doing little to be gracious or winning, it nevertheless wins and has grace. Increasingly, man after man, music-lovers who at first found Stravinsky's later music unappetizing if not altogether desiccated and dead have begun, much later, to "hear" it. Then it becomes clear to them that its business is the business of, say, *The Well-Tempered Clavier:* that of building musical structures out of inner tensions and relationships. Of Stravinsky's mastery over the means and manners of his art there has never been a question; his eventual vindication was another question of time.

Stravinsky and his celebrants have often confused those who paid more careful attention to pronouncements than to music. His often-expressed intense admiration for Weber and Tchaikovsky has appeared paradoxical from the lips of so assured a nonromantic. And then, in his autobiography, he wrote: "For I consider music, by its essential nature, powerless to express anything at all, whether a feeling, an attitude of mind, a psychological mood, a natural phenomenon, *etc.* . . . . Expression has never been the immanent property of music. That is by no means the purpose of its existence. If, as is nearly always the case, music appears to express something, that is only an illusion and not a reality. It is simply an additional attribute that, by tacit and inveterate agreement, we have lent it, thrust upon it, as a label, a convention —in brief, an aspect that we have come, unconsciously or through force of habit, to confuse with its essential being." Affronted, commentators seized on one section of this statement—that music is "powerless to express anything at all"—and said that they were shocked, that this showed Stravinsky to be an anti-Music. What they neglected to notice was that what he said was true: that the non-musical "anythings" we believe music to be "expressing" are not in the music, but in ourselves, however much we have agreed to let the sounds symbolize them. Here, as everywhere, Stravinsky was merely asserting in simple terms the autonomy of music as an art, its right to be musical.

And so, despite the obvious disappointment of those who waited for Stravinsky to go on from the romantic *Schrecklichkeit* of *Le Sacre du Printemps,* and despite the wrongheadedness of those who have hoped to find a return to the textures of romanticism in each of his new compositions, Stravinsky has gone on being a master. It is not suggested that every single item in the list of his works (which now includes symphonies, concertos, ballets, an opera to an English libretto, and numerous small works) is a great masterpiece. But if the passing decades have taught us anything about him and his creations, it is that with a little effort we can catch up with him and find that catching-up worth all effort. His craftsmanship is his most sincere tribute to the art he has practiced so long; whoever cannot enjoy craftsmanship in any art cannot really appreciate that art at all, for if he enjoys it nonetheless. it is certain that he does so for non-artistic reasons.

Even at its apparent wildest, none of Stravinsky's music has entirely abandoned some sense of "home" tones and "home" chords to which other of the composition's tones and chords bear a distinguishable relation. The most important tones in any passage from a Stravinsky composition, that is, are heard with a sensation that they are placed by him in relation to an at least temporarily established fundamental tone. In fact, the remoteness and complication of his most remote and complicated measures are remote *from* something present or understandably implied—but in either case soon established in the listening mind—and are complicated in relation to a fundamental simplicity likewise present or implied. While inviting the music-lovers of his time to share his enormous gifts for design, structure, and internal relevance, Stravinsky has journeyed as far as seems possible within the borders of tonality. It was in the third leading branch of twentieth-century music—the Austrian—that tonality itself was deliberately left behind. If judged by the procedures permissible under the harmonic government of Mozart's time, the state of rule in much of Stravinsky's music looks like anarchy. But in reality Stravinsky's harmonic rule is a very liberal democracy preserving significant elements of the procedures evolved during one thousand years of musical creation and codified to some extent during the eighteenth and nineteenth centuries. From the same base the harmonic government of Arnold Schoenberg at its strictest would have to be judged an autocracy from which tonality has been exiled by ukase, an arbitrary replacement of the past's constantly evolving ways by a series of complex formulas imposed by fiat.

Driven to verbal explanation and the compounding of abstract formulas by some necessity to justify the promptings of forces within their artistic selves, composers from time to time have experimented with abstruse harmonic "systems" without divinable connections to the audible physical habits of sound. Scriabin, for example, was natively fascinated by chords built up out of fourths (the conventional chords, it being remembered, are basically superimpositions of thirds). One of these, a central fact in his orchestral "poem of fire," *Prometheus* (1909-10), he permitted his religiously tinctured mind to call the "mystic chord"; it was simply a series of fourths: C-F♯-B♭-E-A-D (or A-D♯-G-C♯-[F]-B-E) and slight variants thereof. As Scriabin—a composer whose value has been unduly depreciated by lack of sympathy with all the non-musical freight he asked his compositions to carry—employed these synthetic chords and built a harmonic pseudo-system on them, they unquestionably lent his musical textures a peculiar, momentarily original sound. But the flaw in his pseudo-system was double: only those who learned it outside the music could really "understand" the music in which it was set forth, and they proved to be few in number; the resulting harmonic textures defied con-

structive evolution, and the result of that defiance was music of
necessity centripetal, rhapsodic, and static.

Experimentation itself, as has already been suggested, is a romantic activity, classicism being defined as creation out of materials accepted as being in a satisfactory state of evolution, and
originality being demonstrated in ways of manipulating it. To
this pattern Scriabin fitted: everything about his personality and
the non-musical machinery attached to his compositions places
him full in the nineteenth-century romantic atmosphere, however
harmonically advanced his idiom may appear to be. Equally romantic was a much more stern and rigorous defiance of ordinary
concepts of key and tonality which came from Vienna, specifically
out of the ideas of Josef Matthias Hauer and the compositions and
statements of Arnold Schoenberg and his most ardent disciples.
Today, nearly fifty years after its first appearance, both this overt
defiance of tonality and the system—a remarkable mental achievement—that it demanded are subjects of acrimonious debate. On
the side of Schoenberg speaks a group of ardent, convinced ad-
herents; against him speaks the indifference of most audiences,
some facts about the mathematical constitution of musical sound,
and the circumstance that even after forty years, his work still is
performed only very occasionally.

Adapted, mixed with older elements, and thereby somewhat
contradicted, the Schoenbergian techniques have produced one
towering masterpiece, Alban Berg's opera *Wozzeck,* and several
other compositions that have won a modicum of acceptance. In
undiluted form they have produced nothing that has been able
to cross the bristling boundary between cult and audience.

Schoenberg was born in Vienna in 1874. At the age of twenty-
five, he composed *Verklärte Nacht,* a string sextet. Passionately,
yearningly romantic, this conventional piece—in both its original
instrumentation and as expanded for string orchestra—won and
has maintained world-wide popularity. Unless the most advanced
harmonic speech of Brahms and Wagner be considered modern,
Verklärte Nacht is not modern. The only other composition by
Schoenberg which has ever won a fraction of music's larger audience is the *Gurre-Lieder,* a vast cantata or oratorio for soloists,

chorus, and orchestra. It is as romantic as *Verklärte Nacht* and has no more to do with modernism. By turns it is Brahmsian, Wagnerian, Mahlerian, Debussyan, Brucknerian, and Straussian; it was completed in 1911. In its full romantic expansiveness it is a product of the romantic strain kept blooming in Vienna from Schubert to Brahms and beyond: it is only mildly experimental, being entirely friendly to tonality and to chromatic and other aspects of late-romantic harmony.

Before Schoenberg completed the *Gurre-Lieder,* however, he had composed three short piano pieces whose implications were to rock the more intellectual sectors of the musical world—and to keep them rocking to this day. The *Drei Klavier-Stücke,* opus 11, composed in 1908-9, occupy but eleven pages; they were followed, among other things, by the *Sechs kleine Klavierstücke,* opus 19 (1911), which occupy seven (only the first is more than one page in length, and three of the six contain only nine measures each). Their explosive content, out of all proportion to their size, resulted from their flat, complete denial of the principle of tonality. Thus briefly and assuredly did Schoenberg contradict the basic assumption by which the music of Western civilization had been held together for the centuries since the earliest counterpoint.

Critics and other writers at once called this music "atonal." Schoenberg objected to the application of the term to the fabric of this music. He said, in effect, that this "a-tonal" music has "tonality," but added that the music thus miscalled was composed by "means of twelve tones [1] among which there is no relationship except the relationship of one of them to another." The very reason of tonality being that, in a given instance, the temporary functions of certain tones lend them a significance of which other tones are devoid, the last part of Schoenberg's phrase must seem to non-Schoenbergians the definition of a musical texture to which the term "atonal" perfectly applies.

In the piano pieces of Schoenberg's Opus 11 and Opus 19 there is no home tone, no point of rest or finality, no dominant or leading tone. Chords, mostly dissonant, are arbitrarily built, having

[1] He refers to all the steps between any tone and its octave, as A-A♯-B-C-C♯-D-D♯-E-F-F♯-G-G♯, the component parts of a chromatic scale of one octave.

been dictated solely by the interior reasoning of the composer's psychic-aural-intellectual being. The organizing principles of these compositions defy both deduction and imitation—a fact that Schoenberg himself came to admit when he acknowledged somewhat later the need for imposing principles on "atonality" from without and by rule. This music, then, is without "meaning" in the usual sense of musical significance—except as there is some modicum of "meaning" in any non-accidental arrangement of musical tones.

For the ordinary listener there is no "way" to listen to the *Klavierstücke* except that of letting the unobstructed sound of their arranged tones act on him; nothing he brings to such listening, no memory or preceding concept of musical pleasure or comprehension, can prove anything but a barrier preventing this music from reaching him at all. In most cases, the experiment of such pristine listening proves comparable to that of facing an entirely abstract painting or sculpture that suggests nothing or of reading one of Gertrude Stein's most abstract arrangements of words: the listener may be baffled, irritated, pleased, or amused. What he cannot obtain from these piano pieces is any of the responses he has been accustomed to experience when hearing earlier seriously intended Western music, from Gregorian Chant to the most extreme experiments of other, non-atonal modernists.

Schoenberg did not move directly from the deliquescent, over-ripe romanticism of *Verklärte Nacht* and the *Gurre-Lieder* to the several *Klavierstücke*. Some of his earlier pieces had been richly flavored by a taste for romantic harmony lush with chromaticism and complex counterpoint. And in the D Minor String Quartet, opus 7 (1905) and elsewhere he had composed architecturally baroque music in which the extreme complexities of chromatic and other counterpoint had carried him to the farthest edge of tonality. In this music a definable tonality is always to be discovered by looking, but cannot always be heard by listening.

A Viennese, pervasively romantic by nature, Schoenberg was driven by an interior demon. A man of formidable intelligence, he was, once convinced, utterly logical—and fearless of the results of logic. Not every composer could have faced the consequences of Schoenberg's steps. In the F♯ Minor String Quartet, opus 10 (1907-8); the cycle of fifteen songs with piano accompaniment on texts from Stefan George's *Das Buch der Hängenden Gärten,* opus 15 (1907); and the *Klavierstücke* already mentioned, he did several things that in sum resulted in what was clearly atonality though he said that it was not. He combined all previously existing harmonic practices—including whole-tone scales and chords, and chords not unlike Scriabin's towers of fourths—and added new devices of his own. He moved indecipherable chords sidewise by *en bloc* progressions. And the result was a final and complete absence of tonality.

Now, development in the classical or the romantic sense is by definition an activity within tonality. So Schoenberg wisely let development follow tonality into oblivion. This tended to curtail the native expansiveness he had demonstrated in the *Gurre-Lieder.* Another force tending in that direction was the sharply defined limitation of the amount of continuous non-tonal texture which even well-disposed listeners can listen to with concentrated attention. And so Schoenberg's first consciously atonal pieces were gnomic, cryptic, silent before the ear and mind could absorb any impression except that of much present discord and the total absence of any familiar landmark. The number of performances which these epoch-shattering pieces have won in the decades since their composition is smaller than that which has been awarded to any other pieces of like renown. They have no wiles with which to seduce those who come to them without preconceptions, with only a full musical background and willing attention. Again excepting converts, no matter what the nationality of the listener, these pieces always seem to him to be in another language than his own.

In 1912, however, Schoenberg composed, to German adaptations of moodily romantic French poems by Albert Guiraud, his Opus 21, *Pierrot Lunaire,* described as "three cycles of seven poems" and as a "melodrama for recitation and chamber orchestra." In this expressionist [2] masterwork, the female vocal soloist

---

[2] Expressionism—borrowed, like impressionism, from the vocabulary of painting—was a term often applied to Schoenberg and his disciples. It covered their attempts

is required to speak the heated, overwrought words on definite
pitches, which are indicated throughout the score. Schoenberg
had used a "reciter" among the soloists in the *Gurre-Lieder,* and
this employment of song-speech, known as *Sprechstimme,* is terri-
fyingly effective for the neurasthenic, sometimes almost demented,
meanings of the text of *Pierrot Lunaire.* Equally effective are the
intense, seemingly dislocated and arbitrary lines of the melodies
Schoenberg here sets forth by means of a chamber orchestra used
in delicate fragmentation. The result is a literary-aural experience
of shattering power. With the best will in the listener's heart and
mind, and despite the passage of forty years, it is difficult to think
of this power as a strictly musical function; but to escape its impact is even more difficult.

   Pierrot Lunaire at once suggested to wary listeners two ideas
about Schoenberg which time has done nothing to contradict:
he would always find the best employment of atonality in relation
to a verbal text; his whole conception of music was pre-eminently
suited to the support of exacerbated nervous conditions and de-
ranged mental states.

   Despite the relatively few performances of Schoenberg's music,
he went on being a very active composer. Following *Pierrot Lunaire* came *Vier Lieder* with orchestra, opus 22 (1913-15); *Fünf
Stücken* for piano, opus 23; a Serenade, opus 24 (first performed
in 1923); and a Suite for piano, opus 25 (1924). In this uncom-
promisingly atonal [3] music it gradually became apparent that
Schoenberg was in the process of forging for his atonality a system
logical and workable enough to satisfy a mathematician.

   Schoenberg commanded fabulous contrapuntal learning, a ti-
tanic grasp of harmonic and contrapuntal practices from every musical era, which made him the century's greatest preceptor and
theoretician. Using old contrapuntal methods, he inverted his
often widely skipping melodies; he reversed them and combined
the original form with the reversion; he built them into canons

to express in music the contents of their real, or subconscious, selves. In a technical
sense expressionist music is almost exactly co-extensive with atonal and twelve-tone
music. Its psychoanalytic pretensions are, of course, added—and non-musical—
qualities.
   [3] Schoenberg in his later years occasionally wrote tonally.

and crab canons. From about 1915 onward both his music and his remarks made it clear that he was at work on a system for imposing order on atonality. Any such system could only be abrupt, complex, and difficult.

Hints for important sections of this system were taken from the music and writings of a remarkable man whom most of the musical world has forgotten, Josef Matthias Hauer. A prolific composer, Hauer also published a series of pamphlets and monographs in which he advocated grouping the twelve component tones of a one-octave chromatic scale into patterns he called *Tropen*. Hauer's theories partook somewhat of mathematical legerdemain, of the sheer fun in discovering the number of different ways in which the twelve tones could be arranged. Schoenberg's ideas were different. What was important to Schoenberg in Hauer's conceptions was the idea of making a particular "row" of twelve tones— a melody of twelve tones in which none is repeated—the basis of a composition in somewhat the way that a tonality had been the basis of tonal compositions.

Coming fully armed at last from Schoenberg's formidable brain, this second of his history-altering steps was soon known as the "twelve-tone system." This frankly arbitrary imposition of laws from without, however hard to understand by hearing its music, is easy to explain in words:

1. Each twelve-tone composition is built out of a tone-row containing all twelve tones of a chromatic octave-scale. Arranged at will, these twelve tones (none of which is repeated within a row) are presented over and over in the same unchanging sequence or one of three variants thereof;

2. Besides the original order of the twelve tones in the row designated, they may at any juncture be presented upside down (inversion), backwards (retrograde progression), or both upside down and backwards (retrograde inversion);

3. Both in its original form and in any of the three legislated variants thereof, the tone-row (called *Grundgestalt*) may at any time be transposed whole so that its first tone is any tone at all— but then the row's internal pitch relationships must be renewed intact in that new pitch;

4. Any of the twelve tones of the designated row may at any time appear in any octave; they may be presented vertically (in chords) as well as horizontally (in melody);

5. Both melodies and chords may be derived from the tone-row, but all twelve tones of the row, in whichever of its forms, must be employed before the series is re-begun.[4]

If any arrangement of the twelve tones within an octave is to avoid sounding like a simple chromatic scale, it is necessary that few of the tones appear in contiguous sequence; the typical Schoenberg tone-row therefore contains many wide skips. Here is the "basic tone-row" or "basic set" from his Wind Quintet, opus 26 (first performed 1924):

As used inverted at a descent of one octave, this row reads:

And here is a comparatively simple passage from the Wind Quintet which demonstrates one actual treatment of this row to create musical texture:

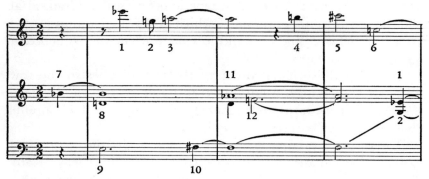

4 In later manifestations of the twelve-tone system, Schoenberg somewhat relaxed this rule. He himself sometimes used sections of a row without completing it each time.

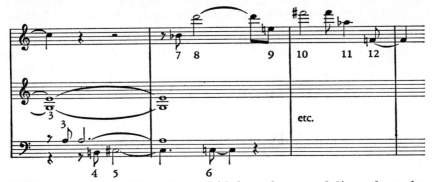

"This example," Schoenberg said in a lecture delivered at the University of California at Los Angeles in 1941, "shows how an accompaniment can be built. As octave doubling should be avoided, the accompanying of tones 1-6 with tones 7-12, and vice versa, is one way to fulfill this requirement." This explains not only the method but the ineradicably dissonant and mechanistic "counterpoint" always characteristic of twelve-tone music in pristine purity.

These examples from the Wind Quintet show the twelve-tone system in relative simplicity and absence of complication. The invitations to fabulous complexity with it are highly numerous, and Schoenberg and his disciples accepted most of them. In some of their scores the examining eye is all but prevented from following the tone-rows. And it is difficult, often to the point of impossibility, for the listener to hear what is really happening in such cross-textured music, though this would, of course, be entirely unimportant if the music were available to him without such knowledge. Of most of the rows or basic sets it can only be remarked that, though they certainly are non-accidental successions of tones and may very well be melodies, it is possible to hear them again and again without being able to hear them as performing a truly melodious function. In fact, it is possible to hold a naturally hospitable attitude toward any music presented (or even to cultivate a conscious preference for *le dernier cri*) without being able to obtain from much of Schoenberg's music any specifically musical values—to obtain from it, at last, any sortable impressions whatever.

Certainly this does not mean that any intelligent listener should simply write Schoenberg down as a charlatan or a tragic catastrophe. First, he must face the lively possibility that the familiar time-lag is here in operation: that he will one day be able to catch up with Schoenberg as he can catch up with the late Stravinsky and as the whole musical world caught up with Wagner and Debussy. Second, he must recognize in Schoenberg's twelve-tone system this century's most single-minded attempt to give musical form solidity. In effect that purpose of constructing whole compositions from one germinal idea (the tone-row) goes back beyond the sonata forms to the baroque principle of unity through singleness—or, if looked at another way, makes variation on a single thematic integer the central principle of musical pattern. And, last, it may easily turn out (though I am much inclined to doubt it) that the quality in Schoenberg's music which so sets on edge the teeth of many originally well-disposed listeners is not its techniques but its dogged and decayed romanticism.

Mosco Carner, rightly calling Schoenberg "a typical exponent of late German romanticism," spoke bluntly of his "monomaniac urge for unrestricted self-expression." Schoenberg's compositions in tonal manner—both the early ones and those he interspersed among the atonalities of his later periods—confirm this judgment. For both personal and historical reasons Schoenberg was an unhappy and often a neurotically disaffected man. Being a clear product of romanticism, but living in a technically modern age, he became an expressionist. And his music, tonal or atonal, expressed *him,* both as all creation somehow expresses the creator and self-consciously, by fierce determination. When he used his atonal, expressionist, twelve-tone techniques in support of a literary text, they were perhaps best used. But he chose texts that conveyed in literary terms the exacerbations, neuroses, angers, frustrations, and violences of his own uprooted nature—and in this way the very integrity of his self-expressive purpose denied us the benefits we might have won if he had been capable of objectivity either in selecting texts for opera, cantata, and song or in the creative use of his talent and magnificent knowledge.

Because atonality and the twelve-tone technique were demanded by the logic of one historic line of development, they have value. It is, in a sense, our duty to give their foremost exponent the benefit of every doubt, to take as many steps as we can toward meeting him halfway. Still, not ruling out the hopeful possibility that we shall one day come to accept his products as integral parts of the canon of meaningful music, we need not discard altogether the possibility that we shall not. There is certainly some reason for supposing that even in the hands of a more balanced and sanguine human being (supposing that such a composer would find Schoenberg's techniques relevant to his personality and purpose) unmitigated atonality and the twelve-tone technique would still prove a musical side-road leading to a dead end. It may easily turn out that all this gigantic mental effort has produced, in the light of subsequent musical evolution, a few technical devices to be absorbed into the general texture of the art, there to have no more enduringly important a place *per se* than the whole-tone scale or Scriabin's chords of superimposed fourths.

Of the two foremost Schoenbergians, Anton von Webern was an atonalist and twelve-tone composer of uncompromising conviction. His extraordinarily brief compositions might be the music of another planet or another form of life, so little resemblance do they bear to anything we considered music before they were composed or have come to accept as music since. He even added new rules, new limiting clauses to the legislation of the twelve-tone system: in his ensemble pieces, for example, he allowed no single instrument to sound any two tones from a row in succession, thus presenting the components of a row in a predetermined variety of timbres. About the most that these cryptograms suggest is unmotivated intensity and a curiously selfless dedication.

The other leading Schoenbergian was Alban Berg.[5] A composer of genius, he was not so orthodox. His finest works suggest, more forcefully than any argument, that atonality and the twelve-tone system will eventually find their proper places when employed

---

[5] In *Style and Idea,* a book published in 1950, Schoenberg wrote: "The harshness of my requirements is also the reason why, of the hundreds of my pupils, only a few have become composers: Webern, Berg, [Hanns] Eisler, [Karl] Rankl, [Winfried] Zillig, [Roberto] Gerhart, [Niko] Skalkottas, [Norbert von] Hannenheim, [Gerald] Strang, [Adolph] Weiss. At least I have heard only of these."

for special purposes among the numerous other musical techniques evolved in the past ten centuries.

Berg too was a belated romantic, and like Schoenberg sought
roads to self-expression. But his self was less insistent on iron
introversion; his sympathies were broader; humor never deserted
him for long—and he was finally more interested in music than
in any theory or system. Schoenberg was doubtless the most important influence on his practice, but he was even more clearly the
child of Brahms, Bruckner, and Mahler—and of Debussy. He died
in 1935 when only fifty, and he had by no means been prolific.
The subsequent curve of his reputation and the insistence with
which his opera *Wozzeck* was kept alive by discussion until it returned to the living stage suggest what nothing that has occurred
with Schoenberg's music suggests at all: that Berg's work will take
its place in the active repertoire as the fascinating final postscript
to Viennese nineteenth-century romanticism.

Berg approached atonality spontaneously and by stages. But he
had already composed his *Vier Stücke* for clarinet and piano, opus
5 (1913), dedicated to Schoenberg, and the more important *Drei
Stücke* for orchestra, opus 6 (1914) before he began *Wozzeck*. The
orchestral pieces, entitled Prelude, Round, and March, strain the
then-existing means almost to the snapping point. Elaborate directions to each player indicate an intense occupation with dynamic
values; the counterpoint is extraordinarily luxuriant; no melodic
voice is doubled anywhere; there is, in any conventional sense,
no development; the insistence upon the individual timbre of each
instrument is final; and great care is taken to make each chord
not only a combination of tones, but also a combination of instrumental timbres, for each note of each chord is assigned to an instrument of its own. This music—and notably the final section—
is as complex and as difficult to hear as anything in Schoenberg;
but a *sensation* that understanding will follow, that this multiplicity of learned means is at the service of a meaning that we shall
finally be able to extricate from it, can precede even any rewarding
study of the score. Everything about the facture and presentation
of this highly romantic stuff indicates, even to an unfriendly ear,
that the intelligence at work behind it is primarily at the disposi-

tion of a truly musical urge rather than a primarily intellectual one or a complex of self-revelation.

In May 1914 Berg was deeply moved by a staging of *Wozzeck,* an incomplete, disorderly, but powerful drama of poverty and hallucination by Georg Büchner (1813-1837). This loosely related series of twenty-five scenes, some of them of extreme brevity, was peculiarly germane to Berg's twentieth-century moods and perceptions. He worked at making a usable libretto from it, completing this part of his task in 1917, having reduced the essentials of the narrative to fifteen scenes. By the fall of 1920 he had the complete opera in orchestral sketch; he finished the orchestration in April 1921. Although excerpts from it were performed in 1924, the first complete performance did not occur until December 14, 1925, when the Berlin State Opera staged it. By the time the Nazis got round to banning *Wozzeck* as decadent art or *Kulturbolschewismus,* Berlin had heard it twenty-one times; it has now been performed entire (either as staged opera or as a concert work) in the cultural capitals of the Western world, and its popularity grows.

This story of an army captain's regimental soldier-servant who is driven by mistreatment and the collapse of his sanity to murder the mistress by whom he has had a child and then to commit suicide, was a full predecessor of expressionism in the drama; it is also often hysterically near incoherence, savagely and cruelly disturbed, and feverishly intense. Berg cast it in three acts of five scenes each, organizing the patterns of the mostly atonal music (not yet dominated by the twelve-tone system) through the use of rigidly formal patterns and informal usages adopted from the baroque, pre-classic, and classic past, as well as from both popular and folk music. Formally analyzed, the three acts are made up of the following movements and forms:

I: 1. suite, 2. rhapsody and hunting song, 3. military march and cradle song, 4. passacaglia (twenty-one variations on a melody), 5. *quasi rondo*

II: 1. sonata form, 2. fantaisie and fugue on three melodies, 3. largo for chamber orchestra, 4. scherzo, 5. martial rondo (the entire movement being a "symphony in five movements")

III: 1. invention (variations) on a theme, 2. invention on a tone
(pedal point), 3. invention on a rhythm, 4. invention on the
chord A♯-C♯-E♯-G♯-E♭-F♭, 5. invention on the tonality of D
minor, and a toccata-like section in persistent eighth-note pattern.

Clearly, no listener is expected to hear these movements and
forms as such: they were of importance to Berg as tools of composition. Their meaning to a listener is best absorbed without concentration on that process.

As Ernest Newman once pointed out, the idiom of *Wozzeck*
cannot be called uniform throughout. Berg composed it in wide
variants of several idioms, not only in response to the demands of
the shifting dramatic substance, but because he himself was changing during the years of its composition. The way to enjoy *Wozzeck*
(and thus to approach understanding of it through the best-situ-
ated entrance) is to pay attention to the text and absorb the characters. Despite all of its incredible technical legerdemain, and despite its long sections of atonality (which are interspersed here
and there with elaborate but semi-"tonal" treatments of recognizable tunes), the music will in no way obstruct this attention. A
good performance of Berg's *Wozzeck* is an overwhelming human
experience—from which most members of the audience who are
hearing it for the first time will probably come away bearing no
more specific memory of the music itself than they would bring
from a first hearing of *Pelléas et Mélisande*. They will, that is,
likely recall it as an atmosphere, the environment in which the
drama has its being.

Only gradually we come to realize that Berg's emulsion of late-
German chromatic harmony, atonality, rigid patterns, and peculiar song-speech is one perfect clothing for characters so manic-
depressive or actually schizophrenic, situations so compulsive, explosive, and irrational, subjects so morbid, mortal, and real. What
Berg accomplished in composing *Wozzeck* is music magnificent
for the exact purpose of being absorbed into hectic drama, for
tightening the shuddersome horrors and slashingly macabre hu-
mors of Büchner's play. To say that most of this music has small

significance when parted from the play is to tell a meaningless truth. For Berg performed his chosen task successfully: he has convinced us that the tonal utterances of instruments and singers are the inevitable speech of the characters, spontaneous emanations of the tragedy in which they are involved. In this respect, though in no other, it is very close indeed to *Pelléas et Mélisande.*

In the few compositions later than *Wozzeck,* Berg increasingly employed twelve-tone methods, though never with the rigidity of Schoenberg or Webern. The Chamber Concerto (1924), for example, is erected out of a tone-row derived from those letters in the names Schoenberg, Webern, and Berg which are also (in German) the names of musical tones. The Lyric Suite of 1926 is twelve-tone music with a difference. And in 1928 Berg began to compose his second opera to a telescoped version of two related "tragedies of sex" by Frank Wedekind: when he died in 1935 *Lulu* was complete in sketch, but he had not fully orchestrated much of the third act.[6] The whole melodic-harmonic fabric of this musico-dramatic story of "the eternal feminine manifestation of evil," the sex-crazed woman who sinks through layer after layer of degradation, is derived by astonishing manipulation from this single tone-row:

An example of the ingenuity of Berg's compositional methods is pointed out by Adolfo Salazar. By dividing the tone-row quoted above into four groups of three successive tones each and then making chords of them, we can get:

If we next make a new tone-row by reading the notes of these four chords from left to right, top notes first, middle notes second, bottom notes last, we get:

[6] Schoenberg later completed the orchestration.

And this new tone-row, derived from that of the first example on
page 313 by these methods, and then couched in waltz-time, is actually used to symbolize Lulu, the heroine-villainess of the opera!

Lulu has not been widely performed, and only Berg himself
could accurately define his intentions in this bewildering score.
But careful listening to the suite of Five Symphonic Pieces which
Berg extracted from it shows that he was in the process of evolving
a non-atonal twelve-tone texture. Some of this music *sounds* tonal
when it is not; some of it, in intermittent passages, discovers a definable tonality even in the printed score. There is, of course, no
inescapable reason why a twelve-tone theme must be treated
atonally. That Berg was indeed on the verge of producing a new
mixture of tonality and atonality seems proved by the texture of
his last and perhaps, *Wozzeck* excepted, finest work, the Concerto
for Violin and Orchestra.[7]

The Violin Concerto is predominantly atonal; it mostly follows
the twelve-tone schemes. After an introduction, apparently intended to announce the sorrowing mood, it begins with a tone-
row.[8] In this row, three successive tones form a major triad, three
other successive tones the minor triad—a fact that unquestionably
casts at least a glow of tonality over the row itself. Also, the final
four tones of the row are elements of a whole-tone scale—and not
purposelessly. For in the final movement (derived, of course, from
the same row) Berg draws attention to these four tones as a way
of introducing smoothly, practically with its original harmonies,
the chorale *"Es ist genug"* from Bach's cantata *O Ewigkeit, du
Donnerwort.* Berg had no hesitation about mixing tonality and
atonality.

[7] It is probable that if Berg had not been asked to compose a violin concerto,
and then had not conceived it as a requiem for a young friend who had died,
therefore feeling the need to complete it in six weeks, he might have finished
Lulu instead. But he himself died only a few months after completing the Concerto.

[8] The tone-row is cleverly drawn from implications of the mood-opening, which
is made up of a series of perfect fifths: these appear as alternates in the row.

Berg could concoct musical ingenuities as well as any man, and often did so. But he was first of all musical, and seldom sacrificed expressiveness (which he did not conceive inevitably as self-expression) to the tenets of a system. He triumphed over the method, rather, being powerful, individual, and talented enough to start breaking it apart and then—with the help of other elements, both borrowed and created—remaking it in the image of his own needs and desires and artistic intentions. He absorbed what was useful to him into a style and idiom entirely his own. What the rigidly doctrinaire atonalists and twelve-tone-method proponents seem not to have noticed is that Berg, surely a heretic, won nothing but praise from Schoenberg. If it is too much to suggest that Schoenberg was a voice crying in the wilderness, was he not an old man not destined to enter the promised land?

Certainly, a talented composer, rich in inherent musical feeling and intellectual acuity, can evolve living music from textures mixing twelve-tone atonality and tonal procedures. The twelve-tone usages may be the most important ingredients of such music; they may even occupy ninety-five per cent of its extension—but the essential catalyst, if they are not to remain bristlingly rebus-like, is some small ingredient of tonality, something to suggest the home from which we have been removed, even though we may never sight it clearly again. This mixture, in fact, appears to be the useful present and the future of the lessons taught by Schoenberg, Webern, Berg, and such a composer-musicologist as Egon Wellesz: the methodology of the twentieth-century Viennese school is an addition of value, an enriching adjunct, to the supply of compositional tools. But there is no more reason today than there was one hundred years ago to believe anyone, however persuasive, who says that the future of music is the exclusive possession of one region or one group of composers. No one can say by which (or by how many) of the possible routes open to it the art of music will move onward into the future.

POSTLUDE

The new kind of music especially characteristic of the first thirty years of the twentieth century is always best listened to for the daring with which it attempts—and the success with which it achieves—musical deeds never before considered or performed. But the music of the 1930's and later often disappoints when it is listened to that way. For by 1930 the reaction against experimentation *per se* and the frightfulness of shock was gathering momentum. Much of this more recent music—particularly as the symbolic, century-splitting date 1951 came near—attempts to calm down, heal, consolidate, and build. On top of the reaction called neo-classicism came another called neo-romanticism—which now seems to mean the addition of unfrightened emotional evocativeness to neo-classicism.

Since 1930, Paul Hindemith, a formidable musical talent and brain that too often had seemed to be producing academically admirable but inert modern eclecticism, has begun to make music full of warmth, vitality, and even charm. Stravinsky, in the ballet *Orpheus* and elsewhere, has composed mature pieces sovereign in their gestures of restrained expressivity. Béla Bartók, synthesizing the widest variety of spiritual and technical elements, left his own fruitful experiments behind to write a group of large-spirited pieces which has won him a very wide audience. In England Ralph Vaughan Williams, vigorous at nearly eighty, has composed his Sixth Symphony, massive and solid in its architecture—and inconceivable without the fury and daring of the 1920's. In both North America and South America, music seems to be taking welcome steps toward a coming-of-age. There have been other omens.

316

The signs, taken together, indicate consolidation, the sort of expanded handling of existing musical means which has always succeeded a romantic (and portended a classic) period. Never has a young composer had at hand half the wealth of musical tools which the novice of today can acquire from his immediate predecessors and his mature contemporaries. The nurture he needs for achieving greatness, it is said, remains scarce in the alarum-ridden world of our day. But is greatness the only aim? Perhaps it will prove to be true that the musical tendency toward a new classic balance arrives at a historical juncture wholly unfavorable to its evolution. But was the era preceding, during, and after the French Revolution really favorable in that sense to the classicism that soared to its apogee during those very decades?

Prediction is not only dangerous, but perhaps almost as silly as the strict drawing of historic parallels. Let us leave it to the soothsayers. The world of music remains incalculably rich. We can turn again to listening. For listening—with an open mind, a trained ear, and an awareness of means and methods—is itself the key to one of the enduring pleasures of living: an understanding and enjoyment of the marvelous music of the Western world.

INDEX

53931